D1600650

# CAPITALISM IN A MATURE ECONOMY

# The New Business History Series

Series editor: Geoffrey Jones, Reader in Business History, Department of Economics, University of Reading

In recent years business history has emerged as an exciting and innovative subject. A new generation of business historians has moved away from former preoccupations with commissioned histories of individual companies towards thematic, conceptual and comparative studies of the evolution of business. The pioneering studies of Alfred D. Chandler Jr on the rise of big business have inspired much of this work, but there is also a growing dialogue between business historians and their counterparts in business policy, management studies and industrial economics.

The *New Business History Series* is the successor to the former Gower Business History Series, which played an important role in the 1980s in encouraging thematic studies of such topics as the rise of multinationals, the evolution of marketing and the relationship between business and religion. The *New Business History Series* aims to build on and develop this innovative role by publishing high-quality studies in the 'new' business history.

# Capitalism in a Mature Economy

## Financial Institutions, Capital Exports and British Industry, 1870–1939

EDITED BY J. J. VAN HELTEN AND Y. CASSIS

Edward Elgar

Published by
Edward Elgar Publishing Limited
Gower House
Croft Road
Aldershot
Hants GU11 3HR
England

Gower Publishing Company
Old Post Road
Brookfield
Vermont 05036
USA

**British Library Cataloguing in Publication Data**

Capitalism in a mature economy : financial
    institutions, capital exports and British industry,
    1870–1939. – (The New business history series).
    1. Great Britain. Economic conditions, history
    I. Title    II. Series
    330.941

    ISBN 1–85278–318–4

Typeset by Speedset Ltd, Ellesmere Port
Printed in Great Britain by
Billing & Sons Ltd, Worcester

# Contents

# Tables and figures

## Tables

**Figures**

# Contributors

*John Armstrong* is senior lecturer in modern economic history at Ealing College of Higher Education. He is a member of the executive committee of the Business Archives Council and edits their journal, *Business Archives*. He has written *Business Documents* (Mansell, 1987) with Stephanie Jones and contributed chapters and articles on company promotion and aspects of transport history.

*Youssef Cassis* teaches history at the University of Geneva, Switzerland. His numerous publications on British financial history include *La City de Londres, 1870–1914* (Paris, 1987) and 'Bankers in English society in the late nineteenth century', *Economic History Review*, Vol. 38 (1985). He is currently working on a comparative study of business elites in Britain, France and Germany during the period 1880–1950.

*Michael Cowen* is a member of the Economics Department at the City of London Polytechnic. He has written numerous articles about agrarian problems in Kenya and the relationships between capital and the peasantry. He is currently working on a study of Fabian colonialism.

*Stefanie Diaper* was awarded a PhD from Nottingham University for a thesis on the history of merchant banking entitled 'The history of Kleinwort, Sons & Co in merchant banking, 1855–1961'. Between 1983 and 1986 she worked as a research fellow in the School of Management, University of Bath. She has published several articles on business and financial history and is now working on a study of the cocoa and chocolate manufacturers, J. S. Fry and Sons.

*William P. Kennedy* is a member of the Economic History Department at the London School of Economics. He is the author of *Industrial Structure, Capital Markets and the Origins of British Economic Decline* (Cambridge University Press, 1987). He is currently working on a comparative study of the financial aspects of industrial innovation in the United States, Germany and Britain in the period 1870–1914.

*Ranald C. Michie* is senior lecturer at the Department of History, University of Durham. His numerous publications on financial history include *Money, Mania and Markets: Investment, Company Formation and the Stock Exchange in Nineteenth*

*Century Scotland* (Edinburgh, 1981) and *The London and New York Stock Exchanges* (London, 1987). He is currently writing a general history of the City of London since 1850.

*Duncan M. Ross* was educated at the University of Glasgow. He has previously worked, under Professor Peter L. Payne, on the history of the North of Scotland Hydro-Electric Board and is currently attached to the Business History Unit of the London School of Economics. He is working on a PhD thesis dealing with various aspects of the relationships between the major British clearing banks and their industrial customers.

*Jean-Jacques Van Helten* is now engaged in international banking in Melbourne, Australia. He was previously a fellow of the Institute of Commonwealth Studies, University of London and a lecturer in economics and economic history at the Polytechnic of North London. He has written extensively on the mining industry and finance, and is the editor, with R. Turrell, of *The City and the Empire* (Institute of Commonwealth Studies, 1985).

# Preface

This volume of essays grew out of a conference at the London School of Economics. The authors would like to thank the companies, banks and financial institutions which opened their archives for research. The contributors would also like to thank certain individuals who have greatly assisted in the writing of these essays: Leslie Hannah, Phil Cottrell, Richard Davenport-Hines, David Kynaston, Theo Barker, Martin Daunton and Pat Thane.

A very special word of thanks is due to Geoffrey Jones, whose patience and forebearance have assisted the editors in their preparation of this collection. The editors would like to acknowledge their debt to the Business History Unit, London School of Economics, in providing them with intellectual stimulation and practical support in arranging this collection of essays. Dr Van Helten would also like to acknowledge financial support from the Economic and Social Research Council.

Jean-Jacques Van Helten<br>
Youssef Cassis

# 1 British finance: success and controversy

*Youssef Cassis*

## The problem

The financial sector is the great paradox of British business history. On the one hand, it is indisputably a success story with the banks, insurance companies and the City generally being highly profitable and competitive internationally. On the other hand, there is a widespread belief that it has contributed to Britain's economic decline, by neglecting domestic industry and diverting capital abroad.

The success was at its highest during the period 1870–1914, when the City of London was the unrivalled financial centre of the world. The bulk of world trade was financed through the medium of bills of exchange drawn on London. With over 40 per cent of the total exported capital of the world in 1913 raised on its financial markets, London was the leading centre for the issue of foreign loans and equities. The nominal value of the securities quoted on the London Stock Exchange was larger than that of the New York and Paris Stock Exchanges combined. Insurance, another British speciality, was spreading its activities all over the world. These activities, together with others such as shipping, which could also be found in centres such as Edinburgh, Glasgow, Liverpool and Manchester, became essential for the British balance of payments: invisible earnings rose from about £40 million in the mid-nineteenth century to nearly £200 million by 1900, whereas the visible trade deficit increased from £33 million to £159 million during the same period.[1]

This financial supremacy was primarily due to Britain's dominant position in the world economy: its share of world trade, for example, was at 25 per cent between 1860 and 1870, and was still at around 14 per cent in 1913 despite the emergence of its main rivals, Germany and the United States[2]; the existence of the British Empire and Britain's position at the heart of the system of international payments centred on its deficit with industrialized countries and its net surplus with India[3]; and the role of London in the smooth functioning of the international Gold Standard.[4] Yet this financial supremacy was also due in no small measure to the development of the British financial institutions. The English banking system was perfectly adjusted to the financing of world trade: the major London clearing banks, which by 1913 concentrated in their hands about two-thirds of the deposits of England and Wales, provided the necessary cash credit,[5] while the merchant banks' accepting business

1

was at the basis of world trade finance.[6] The Bank of England, despite its loss of touch with the market, had, by the beginning of the twentieth century, perfected devices to control the outflow of gold.[7] The London Stock Exchange was the cheapest in the world for dealing in highly marketable securities with the separation of the functions of broker and jobber ensuring, on the whole, a small difference between buying and selling prices.[8] The business opportunities offered in London also attracted many foreign entrepreneurs and speculators who launched new ventures and added greatly to the dynamism of the City.[9] British finance was also highly profitable, and the profits of the London major clearing banks, even though they confined themselves to traditional banking operations, were higher than those of their French and German competitors.[10] The biggest British fortunes were made in commerce and finance, not in industry, and by the late nineteenth century, there were more millionaires among merchants, bankers and shipowners than among landowners.[11] Moreover, the sizes of the fortunes made in the City of London were not matched by those made in other European financial centres, such as Paris or Berlin.[12] City men were also highly successful socially: merchants and bankers integrated earlier than industrialists into aristocratic circles and, unlike the latter, they were able to reconcile the pursuit of their professional activities with an upper-class status and had access to political power.[13]

World War I put an end to this supremacy, although the prominent international role of the City of London has continued more or less unabated to this day. The disruption of international trade and the economic depression during the inter-war period undermined many of the City's overseas activities, reinforcing its links with the domestic economy. However, the world leadership of the City was only gradually challenged by New York, and the return to Gold in 1925 was a deliberate and unsuccessful attempt to restore the City's pre-war predominance, at great cost to the economy as a whole.[14] Since World War II, the City has been able to overcome the decline of the British economy.[15] Whereas Britain's industrial capacity is today hardly more than half that of Germany, its market capitalization of stocks is nearly twice as large. Along with New York and Tokyo, London is one of the three main financial centres of the world, a development that is not attributable to Britain's predominance in the world economy but reflects the opportunities seized by the City to become the centre of new markets in the 1960s and 1970s, in particular of Eurodollars and other Eurocurrencies, and the opening of its doors to foreign banks and financial institutions that culminated in the 'Big Bang' of October 1986.

Despite this long line of successes, evaluations of the City are often highly critical. The main reason appears to be that, whatever its successes, the City has never been totally forgiven for its apparent lack of interest in domestic industry and its responsibility for the export of capital abroad. Criticism about the inadequate provision of funds to industry from the capital markets has been echoed repeatedly since the late nineteenth century and has emanated from industrial, political and academic circles. The City itself, with the assistance of outside analysts, has, of course, argued to the contrary. The debate has centred on three main themes. First, the relationships between banks and industry, in particular the absence of the provision of long-term credit to industry and the lack of a managerial role on the part

2

of the banks, especially the merchant banks. Second, the functioning of the securities market, in particular the high cost of issuing capital on the London market because of the rules of the Stock Exchange and the unscrupulousness of the company promoter. And third, the marked preference of both individual and institutional investors for foreign investment.[16] In the final analysis, the deficiencies of the capital markets have been held responsible for the relatively poor economic performance of Britain since the late nineteenth century.[17] These deficiencies have usually been set against an ideal model, the German experience of universal banking. With the acceleration of Britain's relative economic decline since World War II, at least until the 1980s, the debate has taken a more political turn to question not only the nature of City activities, but also the main options of British economic policy that have been suspected of systematically favouring the City of London to the detriment of British industry. During the period 1870–1939, there were predominantly two apparent City 'victories' in this respect: the victory of Free Trade over Protectionism in the first years of the twentieth century, and the return of sterling to the Gold Standard at its pre-war parity in 1925. This debate has led various critics to interpret British economic history largely in terms of a separation between banking and industrial capital and a domination, both at the political and social levels, of the former over the latter.[18]

This book investigates some of the most important aspects of British finance between 1870 and 1939: the capital markets; clearing banks; merchant banks; the Stock Exchange; company promotion; investment trusts; overseas investments in the form of mining finance and a commodity company. Most of the essays are based on recent archival research, and are primarily concerned with the problem of the relationships between finance and industry and present some new evidence and perspectives. This problem remains one of the most referred to, but also one of the least investigated in the debate on the decline of the British economy. It is significant that in two recent, highly valuable collections of essays on the matter,[19] the role of finance has been dealt with either very unsatisfactorily or not at all. The reader should not expect a ready answer about the alleged 'culpability' of the City in the decline of the British economy. Historical reality is far more complex, as it will be argued in the present chapter, which discusses the debate on the question, and as it will appear in the individual contributions to this volume, with their contrasting judgements.

## The banks and industry

The main criticism directed at the English clearing banks in their relationships to the domestic economy is their apparent failure to supply manufacturing industry with long-term credit, whether in the form of long-term loans or direct ownership of securities. This criticism undoubtedly corresponds to the official view held by the banking community. Felix Schuster, one of its main spokesmen in the pre-war period, declared in 1910 that 'the bank ought never to supply the trader with working capital. I think it is bad for the trader. I think the banker ought to give temporary accommodation to tide the trader over the time when he is short until the time the money comes in again, for temporary purposes only.'[20] This statement was repeated almost verbatim twenty years later by the bankers who gave evidence to the Macmillan Committee[21] and has subsequently been viewed as representing orthodox banking practice. This view of the role of banking raises two questions: first, to what extent did it correspond to the actual banking practices; and second, did these banking practices provide an adequate supply of finance to the industrial sector?

The first part of the period covered in this book, 1870–1914, seems to have been the closest to the official position. During the first half of the nineteenth century, local bankers were linked both at a personal and business level to industrialists, with permanent overdrafts and rolled-over short-term loans being equivalent to a long-term commitment in industrial finance.[22] The amalgamation movement among the banks, which accelerated in the 1880s and 1890s certainly affected banking industrial policy, although this needs to be substantiated by further empirical research. In particular, it seems likely that the general managers in London, in their endeavour to harmonize practices within their bank, decided to put an end to what they considered to be over-commitments.[23] In the same way, branch managers were submitted to a close supervision and strict conditions were imposed on their lending by the central management in London.[24] The situation changed again during the inter-war period. During the 1919–20 boom, the clearing banks abandoned much of their past conservatism and prudence and granted overdrafts, particularly to the heavy and textile industries, which with the downturn of the 1920s often had to be converted into frozen loans and nursed for the remainder of the period.[25] This new long-term involvement in industrial finance, however, appears to have been forced upon the banks by the prevailing circumstances rather than deliberately chosen as a new policy. But, as Duncan Ross's chapter clearly shows, the clearing banks adopted on the whole a positive attitude towards industry. Their support was not exclusively dictated by security motives and any advances meeting the banks' lending criteria were seldom refused, while banks were not always reluctant to play a managerial role in industry. This support, however, did not extend to the ownership of industrial securities. Banks' investments were above all a second line of reserve and, until the late nineteenth century, they were largely made up of British government funds. Some diversification took place, following the fall in Consols, from the beginning of the twentieth century to include Colonial governments' bonds and public utility companies. But industrial securities remained absent from their portfolios.[26]

If the clearing banks were reluctant to grant long-term credit to industry, on the whole they appear to have provided adequate short-term credit to their customers, whether in the form of loans, discounts or overdrafts. Here again, more detailed analysis is needed but no continuous litany of complaints about this aspect of their activities appears in the contemporary literature. The main question is therefore to assess to what extent there existed a demand for long-term credit on the part of industry. Most historical studies take banks rather than industrial companies as their starting point, thereby considering the supply of, not the demand for, capital. This approach incurs the risk of underestimating the demand for capital. Nevertheless, there appears to be little doubt that, up to 1914, there was little demand from industry, particularly from the old staple industries. Most firms remained in family hands, were jealous of their independence and financed investment from ploughed-back profits and informal sources. If outside capital was needed, the issue of preference shares or debentures at least ensured a continued family control.[27] Some doubt remains, however, concerning the emergence of the 'new industries' such as electrical engineering, chemical and automobiles. William Kennedy's chapter suggests that the capital markets were unable to channel resources productively into advanced technology enterprises. The other doubt concerns the provision of finance to small and medium-sized enterprises, also known as the 'Macmillan Gap', and it appears that there remained deficiencies in that respect during the entire period under review. Again, Duncan Ross's chapter suggests that there is no evidence of systematic discrimination by the banks when formulating their lending policies.

Another critique of the attitude of the banks towards industry concerns their lack of managerial role, particularly in comparison with their German counterparts. During the inter-war period especially, the clearing banks have been accused of not using their position as creditors to encourage a rationalization of the basic industries.[28] It is true that the banks generally did not play this role, not only because they did not want to, but also because they were not able to. They lacked expertise in industrial finance, after years of self-financing by industry and were primarily concerned with preserving their interests of creditors. But too much was probably expected from the banks in that respect. If they were unable to induce industrial re-organization, they certainly used their position as powerful creditors to discipline and reconstruct management.[29] The action of the Bank of England also represents an important example of banking intervention in industry. The formation in 1929 of the Bankers' Industrial Development Corporation, in cooperation with the major issuing houses, was an attempt to plan the rationalization of industry, whatever its motivation.[30]

Not only have the clearing banks been reproached for their lack of a managerial role, but also the merchant banks. The latter, with their vast experience of issuing foreign loans, could have been particularly well placed to use their skills for the benefit of the domestic economy in handling flotations of industrial companies. But the main reason for the merchant banks' lack of interest in domestic industry before 1914 was the size of the issues concerned, and this had nothing to do with the foreign origin of many merchant bankers.[31] The foreign issues that the merchant banks generally handled were large, often in excess of £1 million, and offered fees that were not possible to obtain with domestic issues, which averaged much less. Only in one or two cases did merchant banks involve themselves in domestic issues comparable in size to foreign ones, as for example in the well-known case of £6 million capital issued for A. Guinness Son & Co. by Baring Brothers in 1886. After World War I, with the declining opportunities for foreign issues and increasing industrial capital require-ments, merchant banks turned to domestic industry for new business opportunities. But as Stefanie Diaper's chapter shows, their adaptation to this new type of issue was not without its difficulties and, in certain cases, such as the one of Kleinwort Sons & Co., this involvement turned out to be costly in terms of capital and experience.

## The financial market

For their long-term capital requirements, British industrial companies either used internal funds or raised capital on the financial market. The main point of contention in this debate centres on the costs of placing an issue in the London market: were they too high, if not prohibitive for small and medium-sized enterprises? The mechanism of a company promotion on the London market provides a good insight to the problem, as evidenced in John Armstrong's chapter. He confirms the widely-held view that the prevailing conditions had adverse effects as far as smaller companies were concerned.

The process of raising capital was undertaken by the company promoter. The promoter was often a man of dubious repute in the City of London, with only a few exceptions, such as Henry Osborne O'Hagan.[32] Generally, a company promoter bought a company from its owners and sold it to the public, his profit resulting from the difference between the buying and selling prices, less the expenses incurred in the flotation. Hence the crucial importance of the costs of an issue. They would usually include the underwriting commission, brokerage costs, various fees paid to bankers, accountants and solicitors, whose names appeared on the prospectus, and, on many occasions, the expenses arising from measures taken to defend the new issue against speculators. For the more dubious promoters, further expenses included the bribes paid to financial journalists to comment favourably on an issue or to aristocrats, known as 'guinea pigs', to secure their presence on the board. According to the financial adviser, Henry Loewenstein, the cost of an issue on the London market in 1909 was rarely less than £20,000,[33] which can be considered either as very expensive or as very cheap depending on the size of the issue. Bearing in mind that most issues of home industrial companies were less than £250,000, this represented a transaction cost of a minimum of 8 per cent.

Another criticism against the raising of external funds through the services of the company promoter was that the promoter himself had no long-term interest in the company he floated and could therefore be tempted to seek a bigger profit by selling the company at too high a price, that is over-capitalizing it. This could compromise its future performance, affect its share price and therefore its capacity to return to the market at a later stage. This short-term view has been opposed to the long-term interest that, for example, the German banks took in the industrial companies they had promoted. Kennedy's chapter emphasizes the adverse effects of a low market quotation, particularly on the nascent British electrical industry. Because of the inability of the capital market to provide adequate information, the ratio of market capitalization to the replacement cost of physical capital (the 'q' ratio) of the British electrical firms fell from above unity to below in the 1880s. As a result, the industry was able to expand only slowly whereas the high 'q' ratio of the German electrical companies was, in Kennedy's words, 'an invitation to print money and this undoubtedly encouraged a predisposition towards aggressive expansion.'

The Stock Exchange, too, is an essential component of the financial market and has also been considered to render unsatisfactory service to domestic industry. The fact that out of 5,000 quoted securities in 1907 only 600 could be classified as home commercials and industrials[34] could certainly be viewed as indicating its rather limited contribution in this regard. In the same way, Ranald Michie points out in his chapter that, in 1913, the domestic non-government securities quoted on the Stock Exchange were equivalent to only 37 per cent of the capital stock. The London Stock Exchange did not offer as good a market for domestic as for foreign securities. The separation between the functions of broker and jobber increased rather than diminished the difference between buying and selling prices, as domestic industrial securities were rarely dealt in on the floor of the Exchange and therefore were not highly negotiable.[35] The loose regulations of the Stock Exchange with regards to new issues, in particular the possibility of dealing in shares before allotment, also encouraged speculation and added further to the cost of a new issue.[36]

The main question that arises here is, again, the extent to which domestic industry actually suffered from these deficiencies. Whatever the unscrupulousness of the company promoter or the unsatisfactory functioning of the Stock Exchange, their effects would have been of little consequence if only a handful of companies used their services. The answer is not easy because of lack of statistical data. In the case of company promotion, for example, further research is needed to quantify the proportion of foreign and domestic flotations and of industrial companies floated respectively on the London and provincial financial markets. For local sources of financing should not be underestimated.[37] In the field of company promotion the best example is probably that of David Chadwick, a Manchester accountant, who took charge in the 1860s of the conversion of some important iron and steel companies such as Bolckow Vaughan, Charles Cammel, Ebbw Vale, John Brown and Vickers. However, Chadwick acted more as a broker between the company and a circle of local wealthy investors than as a promoter in his own right.[38] This pattern of raising finance locally through a circle of personally acquainted investors, using simply the services of a solicitor rather than those of a company promoter, appears to have worked satisfactorily in the pre-1914 era. The same applies to the Stock Exchange and Ranald Michie's chapter demonstrates that, for important sectors of the economy, such as housing, self-financing was possible and viable without any recourse to the Stock Exchange. He suggests that this was largely the case for domestic industry before 1914.

The *modus operandi* of the financial markets remained basically unchanged during the inter-war period, and yet the markets channelled many more funds into domestic industry, which seems to indicate that, before 1914, the separation between finance and industry derived more from a lack of demand than from any lack of supply. This was due to the diminishing overseas business opportunities compared to increased capital demands from domestic industry. As W. A. Thomas notes: 'The mechanism was deficient, but the new market did accomplish the transformation from foreign to domestic service without the aid of the great issuing houses and before the advent of large-scale institutional investment interest.'[39] Ranald Michie points out interestingly the advantages offered by the Stock Exchange, whose role in industrial finance had by then grown considerably, by being an intermediary between short-term lenders and long-term borrowers. Banks could not lend long-term, but they could lend short-term against industrial securities representing long-term debt, and were

7

consequently in a more advantageous position than their German counterparts which, without the benefit of an active stock market, were exposed to the risks of direct investment in industry.

## The German model

Most critics of the relationship between finance and industry in Britain take for granted the superiority of the German system of universal banking. However, this German model has increasingly taken an idealized form which neglects many aspects of the realities of German banking. This section does not intend to be a reappraisal of the role of the banks in German industrialization, but simply to raise a few general questions about the received view of the relationship between finance and industry in Germany. Additionally, it seeks to encourage systematic and direct comparative research, based on banks' archives and as much as possible to provide answers to the same questions, which is the only way to achieve some progress in the present discussion.

In the first place, it should be remembered that no more research has been carried out in Germany than in Britain on this topic for the period 1870–1939; if anything probably less. There are, of course, some classic studies, in particular J. Riesser's *The German Great Banks and their Concentration* (English edition 1911), but not many historical studies based on primary sources. Banks' archives are said to have suffered damage during the war and access remains a problem both because of the banks' policy and the location of some material in East Germany.[40] Many conclusions drawn about both countries therefore do not always rest on very solid ground.

The German model is usually praised for two inter-connected virtues: the provision of long-term finance to industry as well as other services such as the issue of shares and bonds on its behalf; and, because of the risks involved, a more entrepreneurial attitude of German bankers towards industry.[41] In particular, they were prepared to take a long-term view of the prospects of an industrial company and if necessary to accept short-term loss. Because of these links, it is usually assumed that German bankers were able to exert a high degree of influence on industrial affairs through their multiple memberships of the advisory boards, an assumption which sometimes leads to the conclusion that banks 'dominated' industry. The concept of finance capital of Hilferding and Lenin basically describes the same reality.

This general picture is, of course, in sharp contrast with the British tradition. However, the amount of influence, let alone domination, exerted by German bankers over industry can easily be overestimated. Industrialists of all nations jealously cherish their independence, the more so as they grow bigger, and German industrialists are no exception. The size reached by the biggest industrial concerns in the beginning of the twentieth century, whatever the role played earlier by the banks in encouraging this growth, was the best guarantee of their independence. It gave them greater opportunities for self-financing and meant that their financial requirements had outgrown the capacities of a single bank. Banks' influence over industry seems to have reached its peak at the turn of the century, and declined thereafter. By 1905, in the mining industry where the links had been the closest, banks were actually seeking the favours of industry, not the reverse.[42]

The influence that can be exerted through a seat on the supervisory board (*Aufsichtsrat*) of a company is also limited. The respective prerogatives of the supervisory board and the executive board (*Vorstand*)[43] should not be confused with those of the directors and managers in British companies. The executive board of a German company was not only responsible for the day-to-day running of the firm, but also for its strategic decisions. It was in effect a board of executive directors, the members of the supervisory board being in a position similar to that of non-executive directors in Britain. The supervisory board held at best monthly meetings, sometimes only quarterly, which meant that the information available to its members was necessarily limited. Only the chairman of the supervisory board, very often a banker, kept in close touch with the management of the firm, but he was mainly concerned with financial matters such as a proposed amalgamation or the issue of capital, less with decisions affecting new investments.[44] It is true that in contrast, British banks were hardly represented on the boards of industrial companies before 1914.[45] However, they often appointed outside representatives on the board of industrial companies which ran into difficulties, with the task of supervising their accounts.[46] This has been little noticed and analysed so far, probably because these representatives are only detectable through internal documents, but would certainly deserve a closer analysis and a comparison with German practices.

Deficiencies in the capital markets have been held responsible for the failure of the 'new' industries to emerge in Britain in the late nineteenth century, in contrast to the prodigiously successful German chemical and electrical industries. However, it should be appreciated that the German chemical industry developed with little support from the big banks,[47] in the same way that the most successful British chemical company, Brunner Mond & Co.[48] did. The case is more convincing in the electrical industry, where the German banks played a substantial role as promoters, although the family-owned Siemens was more independent from the banks than AEG.[49] In the same way as the British capital markets have been found to be of little help to small and medium-sized industrial companies, the German banks have been criticized for favouring heavy industry at the expense of the lighter industries and more generally for neglecting small and medium-sized companies, thus slowing down German economic growth.[50]

Comparisons with inter-war German banking are rarely found in the English literature on finance and industry, perhaps understandably so, as the German model lost much of its attraction. The large industries increased their self-financing during the war and the inflation period, thus reducing the role of the banks as providers of capital and their influence on industrial policy.[51] German banks appear to have been very conservative and failed to identify entrepreneurial opportunities. Their credits for the most part went to the old industries – textiles with 11.8 per cent and the food industry with 11.2 per cent at the end of 1928, being the two biggest recipients, against 3.6 per cent for the chemical industry, 2.9 per cent for engineering and automobile construction, and 2.3 per cent for the electro-technical industry, which was less than the wood industry. Accusations of neglecting small and medium-sized enterprises were even stronger than during the pre-1914 period, and with more serious political implications, as the theme was taken up by the NSDAP.[52] The banking crisis of 1931 also cast serious doubts on the credibility of the banking system and aroused a debate in Germany about the superiority, understood in the sense of greater stability, of the English banking system.[53]

The German banking system may have better served German industry than its English counterpart did for its own country. The object of the preceding remarks has not been to answer this question. But the comparision between the two countries suggests that some of the problems related to the lending policies of the British banks may well have been due to the pace and the extent of the amalgamation movement. At the eve of World War I, a dozen banks based in London, with a network of branches covering the whole country, controlled about two-thirds of the deposits of England and Wales. The concentration process intensified after the war with the emergence of the 'Big Five', which by 1938 controlled some 90 per cent of the deposits of the country.[54] The share of the deposits of the big Berlin banks never exceeded 30 per cent until World War II.[55] There were only 41 banks left in England and Wales in 1913, the only regional banks of some significance being in Lancashire, as against 300 regional banks and 1,221 local private banks in Germany in 1900; there remained some 60 provincial banks and 1100 private banks in 1929, but their number decreased considerably during the Nazi period, falling to 491 in 1942.[56] An important difference between the two countries may therefore have been at the local and regional levels, including saving banks and cooperative banks in the more recent period. The British and German big banks appear to have been at times equally conservative, and tended to favour large industrial companies at the expense of the small and medium-sized ones. This domination of the British banking scene by the 'Big Five' has no doubt contributed to their lack of entrepreneurial impetus, as they have increasingly been seen after World War II as offering a very conservative product and forming a cartel controlling vast sums of interest-free money and protected from foreign takeover by the Bank of England.[57]

### British investment at home and abroad

The third area of contention in the debate over the City and the British economy concerns overseas investments, in particular the huge outflow of capital from Britain between 1870 and 1914. This issue has been investigated and debated more than almost any other aspect of British finance in the period covered by this book, yet it remains a controversial and open question. The only area of general agreement appears to centre on the geographical (temperate regions of new settlement) and sectorial (transport, public utilities) distributions of British overseas capital investment as well as the type of securities involved (fixed interest).[58] The total amount of capital exported which had, with some variations, been estimated at around £4 billion, has recently been considered by D. C. M. Platt as being probably too high.[59]

It has also recently been suggested that the proportion of direct investment to portfolio investment was much higher than it has generally been suspected.[60] Finally, there has been so far no conclusive answer to the central question of the effects – negative or positive – of capital exports on the British economy.[61]

The causes of capital export are a particular bone of contention. One possible explanation is that the rate of return on foreign investments was higher than on domestic ones. M. Edelstein's calculations show that, on average and over the whole period 1870–1914, and on all types of securities (equity, preference, debenture) taken together, the return on foreign securities was 5.72 per cent and on domestic securities 4.60 per cent.[62] Investors appear therefore to have made a rational choice after balancing risks and expected returns. There were, however, during this era, important variations between periods of home or overseas dominance and between types of securities. Thus, as indicated in Kennedy's chapter, if returns on foreign governments' bonds or on foreign railways debentures were higher than on their domestic counterparts, home industrial equities, in particular in the new industries such as motor vehicles, had a significantly higher yield than the much favoured foreign fixed-interest securities. Thus Kennedy asserts that investment was not drawn overseas by the promise of exceptionally high returns, but that deficiencies in the capital markets were responsible for the neglect of home industrials by British investors.[63]

Neoclassical theory argues that if overseas investments returned a higher yield, then such investments had a net benefit on the economy with funds allocated rationally and efficiently, otherwise returns on home investments would have been further reduced.[64] At the same time, others have argued that the long-term effects of capital exports were a slower economic growth and an increased dependence on exports from the old industries. Kennedy's chapter suggests that the combination of large investment flows overseas with an inability or unwillingness to commit substantial resources to newly emerging technologies retarded economic growth. The capital markets contributed to this development because they performed their tasks very poorly. Kennedy stresses the fact that investors were unable to identify and evaluate all investment opportunities as much of the information available was expensive to obtain and of poor quality. Thus, London offered the best opportunities for buying and selling foreign securities, but investors should have been able to take greater advantage of these opportunities and use them to complement the higher risks home industrial investment in order to achieve much better diversified portfolios.

The rationality of investors has been questioned, in particular with regards to the information available to them before making a choice. There is no doubt that information flows centred on the advice of a stockbroker, the financial press and, more generally, the mood of the stock market, must have played a decisive role.[65] The mining manias of the 1880s and 1890s are a good illustration of these influences. They also show that British investors were not only attracted to safe investments, but also to more risky ones. Van Helten's chapter indicates that overall – there were, of course, exceptions – speculation in mines did not generate huge profits, certainly far smaller than those expected during the speculative booms. But Van Helten also clearly points out that these frenzies and manias were an integral feature of the operations of the Victorian securities market. He provides a detailed account of the conditions prevailing in the mining market, which should in no way be considered as a marginal case, as around 8 per cent of total British overseas investment in the half-century before 1914 went into agriculture and extractive industries, while the surge of mining investments reached £20 million per annum in the mid-1890s.

It has been suggested that the absence of an investment bank type was a serious weakness in the English banking system. Attempts in this direction were made in the 1860s, following the model of the French Crédit Mobilier of the Pereire brothers, notably with the General Credit and Finance Company of London. However, the Crédit Mobilier type of bank never caught on in England, as the banking system was already well developed by the time it appeared. It is, however, worth noting that despite the collapse of the Crédit Mobilier in 1867 and the withdrawal of the French commercial banks from any involvement in industry in the 1880s, a specific type of investment bank did emerge in France, known as the 'banque d'affaires', whose function was to take a controlling interest in a variety of companies and whose best-known representative was the Banque de Paris et des Pays-Bas, established in 1872. In England, too, a new type of financial institution appeared in the 1860s in the form of the investment trusts, whose function was to diversify investments without, however, seeking to exert any control over the companies in which they invested. As Cassis's chapter shows, they responded to a need for long-term investment at the time, but they did not fill any gap in the entrepreneurial role of the English financial institutions, nor did they open new investment opportunities. Instead, they simply reproduced the general pattern of investing abroad. Although they were never a major player in the securities market, their growth in the 1880s can be viewed either as an example of adequate and successful financial innovation, or as a failure by the English banking system to adapt to the financial requirements of the second industrial revolution.

There was, however, a more dynamic face to British investment. With the re-evaluation of direct overseas investment – some estimates put it as high as 40 per cent of total British capital export in 1913[66] – greater attention has been paid to the firms operating such transfers. In the pre-1914 era, with the modern multinational enterprise still in its infancy, the bulk of direct investments appears to have taken the form of what Mira Wilkins calls the 'free-standing company', to describe companies registered in Britain but operating abroad.[67] In the case of the City of London, Stanley Chapman has recently drawn attention to the evolution of merchant firms into a type of financial company which he defines as an 'investment group'.[68] They were partnerships based in London which controlled, solely or jointly, various companies that took charge of their multiple overseas interests, whether in manufacturing industry, mining, plantation or in shipping, banking and insurance. The emergence of the British-based international mining groups, analysed in the last part of Van Helten's chapter, marked the passage from the era of mining share mania to that of a relative price stability with a stronger control by the major mining finance houses and a rationalization of the industry under the guidance of mining engineers. Michael Cowen's case study of the Forestal Company raises two further questions in this direction: first, that of the nationality of a company operating in several countries; and second, the fact that there were many instances of finance capital – in the sense given to the word by Rudolf Hilferding, that is the fusion of banking and industrial capital – in the City of London, although not in the case of companies operating in Britain, but of companies operating overseas. This characteristic has also been observed about France. French big banks were no more involved in industrial finance than their English counterparts, but in some cases their expansion abroad took the form of joint ventures with large industrial companies.[69]

## The political and social dimensions

At the economic level examined so far, the criticism directed at the British financial system for its inability to provide adequate finance to industry does not appear to be entirely justified. Is the question of the 'responsibility of the City' a case where economic explanations are not sufficient and must be complemented by social and political ones? For there exists another level of criticism, which considers that the very success of the City has been achieved at the expense of industry and consequently to the detriment of the general welfare of the country. The main argument supporting this view is that British economic policy has been primarily concerned with the prosperity of the City, penalizing industry when conflicts of interest arise. This argument is not discussed as such in any of the chapters of this book, but will be briefly commented upon here.

During the period covered by this book, two fundamental options of British economic policy are usually seen as best illustrating the predominance of the City over industrial interests: the victory of Free Trade over Protectionism in the first years of the twentieth century, and the return of the pound to Gold at its pre-war parity in 1925.

The defeat of the Tariff Reform movement launched by Joseph Chamberlain in 1903[70] is usually seen as a victory of commercial and financial over industrial interests, the former prospering under a free trade regime, the latter needing protection against foreign competition. Although schematic, this description reflects the central point of the thesis. It can be questioned, however, whether it really was a victory of the City, in the sense that the City – if one can consider it here as a single unit – clearly knew where its interest lay and fought for it. The best answer should be found in the position taken by the leading City men on the issue. This still has not been done systematically,[71] on the basis of a wide enquiry, as the free trade point of view of the City is usually taken for granted, and certainly deserves further analysis. It has, however, been suggested that even the banking community, which is the most significant grouping from our point of view, was not unanimously in favour of free trade.[72] For example, the articles published by the *Bankers' Magazine* on this issue in 1903 and 1904 were leaning in favour of imperial preference. Two conferences were given at the Institute of Bankers during the first year of the campaign, each expressing one point of view: Felix Schuster defended free trade, Inglis Palgrave protectionism. The tariff reform movement found supporters among leading bankers. Whether clearing bankers, for example Richard Martin, chairman of Martins Bank, who doubted that the imposition of a few low duties could threaten the position of London as the financial centre of the world and whose bank became bankers to the Tariff Reform League; or merchant bankers, like the Gibbs or the Hambros, who adhered to the League, or like the Rothschilds or Ernest Cassel, who from the beginning were seduced by Chamberlain's plan. There are other examples. Of course, there was a majority of City men among the Unionist Free Traders,[73] and these isolated cases should not lead to any conclusion that the City was protectionist. They indicate, however, that the City was divided on the issue, as there were divisions not only within industry as a whole – cotton was in favour of free trade, iron and steel of protectionism – but within most industrial branches.[74] Tariff Reform was a question of general policy that divided the country, but not necessarily on sectoral interest lines.

The return to Gold in 1925 is a much better documented question from the point of view of the opposition of interests between City and industry.[75] It is generally accepted that the decision was a mistake, in the sense that it overestimated the possibility of reducing prices, did not foresee the possibility that competitors such as France and Belgium would return to Gold at a lower parity, and that it prolonged the depression and was responsible for the high level of unemployment prevailing in Britain throughout the 1920s. Some authors, however, have argued that the industries most affected were the old industries which faced structural problems and would not have fared any better with a lower currency.[76] It has also been argued that the decision was an attempt to restore the pre-war position of the City by re-establishing the conditions which, it was believed, were the reasons of its pre-eminence, namely the international Gold Standard and the free convertibility of the pound, whatever the consequences of such measures on industry and employment.[77] However, although Keynes had argued against the return to Gold at the pre-war parity and warned about its consequences,[78] industrialists, on the whole, favoured the decision, as they were fearful of managed money and wanted a resumption of capital outflows and the stimulus they gave to exports, and had in any case no alternative policy.[79] It is therefore debatable whether the decision was taken solely in order to favour the City, or in order to re-establish a golden age when not only the City, but also industry, prospered.

Nevertheless, there is little doubt that the return to Gold was more advantageous to the City than to industry, as was the continuation of the free trade regime, and that on the whole, the ideas held in political circles about what was beneficial for the country, including the vision of its role as a great power, were closer to the interests of the City. In addition, British politicians and senior civil servants turned to City men rather than industrialists for advice[80] and City opinion was highly respected, not only in political but also in industrial circles. Why was that the case? There have been global explanations of the weaknesses of industry in terms of an incomplete bourgeois revolution in Britain because of its historically premature character, with the consequence that the bourgeoisie remained ideologically dominated by the landed aristocracy.[81] This is not the place to discuss them.[82] More directly in connection with the financial sector, the thesis of the 'City–Bank–Treasury' nexus,

14

linked by a common interest of preserving the established order or restoring it and opposing any attempt of self-assertion by industry which would have led to a modernization of the country – from Joseph Chamberlain to Harold Wilson – has recently enjoyed a certain vogue.[83] Despite a few insights, its schematic and over-simplistic character docs not fit the complexities of historical reality, as can be readily seen from the brief discussion of the Tariff Reform and return to Gold controversies.

However, the privileged position of commerce and finance within the British economic elite, both in terms of wealth and social status, has been clearly demonstrated. In particular, it has been argued that, in the late nineteenth century, City merchants and bankers were not only closer to landowners, senior politicians and civil servants than industrialists, but that a more complete merger took place between landed and City aristocracies resulting in the formation of a renewed elite which added the financial power of the City of London to the prestige of the old aristocracy.[84] This view, however, has recently been challenged on the grounds that the 'non-aristocratic' group of merchant bankers was the more significant economic feature of the City of London, and the debate remains open.[85] But it is worth noting that German bankers, whatever their influence on, or 'control of', industry, never enjoyed the social prestige of the Ruhr industrialists; the latter themselves, apart from a few exceptions such as Krupp, were not fully integrated into the upper classes before 1914.[86] In any case, one should be cautious about the conclusions to be drawn from the high social status of bankers in English society. The vision of a government systematically standing behind financial and commercial interests, whether at home or abroad, is certainly erroneous. Rather, this social integration can explain the identity of views between political and banking circles, and it reinforced the recognition of financial interests as superior interests on which depended the prosperity of the whole country. This has remained the case after World War II.

## Conclusion

Most of the questions related to British finance between 1870 and 1939 are still relevant today. German banks and, increasingly, Japanese banks, are held up as models of the overall advantages to their respective economies of the long-term links between finance and industry in sharp contrast to the short-term profit-maximizing view prevailing in the British system. The big institutional investors like the pension funds are criticized for their passive, non-entrepreneurial attitude. Recently, the costs of takeover bids and leveraged buy-outs and the widespread criticism that they attract are curiously reminiscent of the opposition generated by the company promoter in the 1890s. Throughout this period, the role of the merchant banks has remained that of an intermediary. Monetarism has been seen as harmful to industry and beneficial to the commercial sector, and more than ever the upper classes in Britain are symbolized by City magnates, with the effect that the City is much more attractive, and better remunerated, to the most promising graduates than industry.

It would be tempting to see in some of the long-term continuities a confirmation of the City's malign contribution to the British economic performance. However, the book's overview of some of the main aspects of British finance between 1870 and 1914 shows that this would be too facile: for despite serious imperfections, British finance appears, on the basis of the current state of research, to have been able to respond well to the capital requirements of domestic industry. This, however, should not be considered as the last word on the matter, and further historical research remains indispensable for a more precise evaluation of the quality of the services offered by the financial sector in Britain. The most fruitful area of investigation should prove to be direct comparisons with other countries,[87] both at the national and local levels, globally as well as by industrial branches. It might then be possible to locate adequately the working of the capital markets in the constellation of the causes of the British economic decline – causes which also include the size and structure of the firm, education, social structures, attitudes and so on. It remains true, however, that the weight of the financial sector at the social and political levels is heavier than in any other comparable country. This also deserves further investigation in a comparative perspective. Finance has enjoyed a privileged position in Britain in the sense that it has benefited from successive attempts by the ruling elite to maintain Britain as a great power. Thus during the inter-war period and after the Second World War the strength of the pound has been seen as a major symbol of this status. And in today's Britain, the world role of the City certainly enhances Britain's international economic status. 'I would rather see finance less proud and industry more content,' said Churchill in 1925, on the eve of deciding whether to return to Gold. Over sixty years later these words still have resonance.

## Notes

I should like to thank the contributors to this volume for their useful comments on an earlier draft of this chapter. In particular, exchanges of views with Jean-Jacques Van Helten, as well as his suggestions and corrections have proved most helpful. I have also benefited from conversations with Geoffrey Jones, David Kynaston and Martin Daunton.

1. B. R. Mitchell and P. Deane, *Abstract of British Historical Statistics* (Cambridge, 1962), p. 334.
2. S. Kuznets, *Modern Economic Growth* (New Haven and London, 1966), pp. 306–7.
3. See S. B. Saul, *Studies in British Overseas Trade, 1870–1914* (Liverpool, 1960).
4. See B. Eichengreen (ed.), *The Gold Standard in Theory and History* (New York and London, 1985); I. M. Drummond, *The Gold Standard and the International Monetary System 1900–39* (London, 1987); M. de Cecco, *Money and Empire* (Oxford, 1974); J.-J. Van Helten, 'Empire and high finance: South Africa and the International Gold Standard, 1890–1914', *Journal of African History, Vol. 23* (1982).
5. See J. Sykes, *The Amalgamation Movement in English Banking* (London, 1926), F. Capie and G. Rodrik-Bali, 'Concentration in British banking',

*Business History*, Vol. XXIV (1982); C. A. E. Goodhart, *The Business of Banking, 1891–1914* (London, 1972); M. Collins, *Money and Banking in the UK: A History* (London, 1988).

6. See S. D. Chapman, *The Rise of Merchant Banking* (London, 1984).
7. R. S. Sayers, *Bank of England Operations 1890–1914* (London, 1936); Idem, *The Bank of England, 1891–1944*, 3 vols (Cambridge, 1976).
8. D. Kynaston, 'The London Stock Exchange, 1870–1914: an institutional history', (Unpublished PhD thesis, London University, 1983), pp. 236–62.
9. S. D. Chapman, 'The international houses: the continental contribution to British commerce, 1800–1860', *Journal of European Economic History*, Vol. VI (1977); idem, *Rise of Merchant Banking*, op. cit.; C. Jones, *International Business in the Nineteenth Century: The Rise and Fall of an International Bourgeoisie* (Brighton, 1987).
10. Y. Cassis, 'Profits and profitability in English banking, 1870–1914', *Revue Internationale d'Histoire de la Banque*, forthcoming.
11. W. D. Rubinstein, 'Wealth, elites and the class structure of modern Britain', *Past and Present*, Vol. 76 (1977); idem, *Men of Property* (London, 1981).
12. See R. Martin, *Jahrbuch des Vermögens und Einkomens der Millionäre in Preussen*, 2nd edn, 2 vols (Berlin, 1913); D. L. Augustine-Perez, 'Very wealthy businessmen in Imperial Germany', *Journal of Social History*, 22 (1988); W. E. Mosse, *Jews in the German Economy* (Oxford, 1987); A. Daumard, *Les Fortunes Françaises au XIXe siècle* (Paris, 1973); C. Charle, *Les élites de la République, 1880–1900* (Paris, 1987); W. D. Rubinstein (ed.), *Wealth and the Wealthy in the Modern World* (London, 1980).
13. Y. Cassis, *Les Banquiers de la City à l'époque édouardienne, 1890–1914* (Geneva, 1984); idem, 'Bankers in English society in the late nineteenth century', *Economic History Review*, 2nd series, Vol. XXXVIII (1985); J. Harris and P. Thane, 'British and European bankers 1880–1914: an aristocratic bourgeoisie?', in P. Thane, G. Crossick and R. Floud (eds), *The Power of the Past: Essays for Eric Hobsbawm* (Cambridge, 1984); M. Lisle-Williams, 'Merchant banking dynasties in the English class structure: ownership, solidarity and kinship in the City of London, 1850–1960', and idem, 'Beyond the market: the survival of family capitalism in the English merchant banks', *British Journal of Sociology*, Vol. XXXV (1984).
14. See D. E. Moggridge, *British Monetary Policy 1924–1931* (Cambridge, 1972); S. Pollard (ed.), *The Gold Standard and Employment Policy between the Wars* (London, 1970).
15. See, for example, H. McRae and F. Cairncross, *Capital City. London as a Financial Centre*, 2nd edn (London, 1984); J. Coakley and L. Harris, *The City of Capital: London Role as a Financial Centre* (Oxford, 1983); M. Reid, *All Change in the City: The Revolution in Britain's Financial Sector* (London, 1988).
16. The literature is vast on the subject. See in particular P. L. Cottrell, *Industrial Finance 1830–1914. The Finance and Organization of English Manufacturing Industry* (London, 1980); idem, *British Overseas Investment in the Nineteenth*

*Century* (London, 1975); W. A. Thomas, *The Finance of British Industry, 1918–1976* (London, 1978); F. Lavington, *The English Capital Market* (London, 1921); A. Cairncross, *Home and Foreign Investment, 1870–1913* (Cambridge, 1953); M. Edelstein, *Overseas Investment in the Age of High Imperialism: the United Kingdom, 1850–1914* (London, 1982); S. Pollard, 'Capital exports, 1870–1914: harmful or beneficial', *Economic History Review*, 2nd series, Vol. XXXVIII (1985).

17.  W. P. Kennedy, 'Institutional response to economic growth: capital markets in Britain to 1914', in L. Hannah (ed.), *Management Strategy and Business Development* (London, 1976); Idem, *Industrial Structure, Capital Markets and the Origins of British Economic Decline* (Cambridge, 1987); and Chapter 2 in this volume.

18.  See in particular P. Anderson, 'The Figures of descent', *New Left Review*, Vol. 161 (1987), F. Longstreth, 'The City, industry and the state', in C. Crouch (ed.), *State and Economy in Contemporary Capitalism* (London, 1979); G. Ingham, *Capitalism Divided? The City and Industry in British Social Development* (London, 1984).

19.  B. Elbaum and W. Lazonick, *The Decline of the British Economy* (Oxford, 1986); idem, *Oxford Review of Economic Policy*, Vol. 4 (1988), 'Long-run economic performance in the UK'.

20.  National Monetary Commission, *Interviews on the Banking and Currency Systems of England, France, Germany, Switzerland and Italy* (Washington, 1910), pp. 47–8.

21.  Committee on Finance and Industry (Macmillan Committee): Report and Minutes of Evidence, 1931 (Cmnd 3897), passim.

22.  Cottrell, *Industrial Finance*, pp. 200–36.

23.  J. Leighton-Boyce, *Smiths the Bankers, 1658–1958* (London, 1958), pp. 289, 301; Cottrell, *Industrial Finance*, pp. 236–9.

24.  Cassis, *Les Banquiers*, pp. 146–51; Cottrell, *Industrial Finance*, pp. 237–8.

25.  S. Tolliday, *Business, Banking and Politics. The Case of British Steel, 1918–1939* (Cambridge, Mass., 1987), pp. 177–8; J. H. Bamberg, 'The government, the banks and the Lancashire cotton industries, 1919–1939', (Unpublished PhD Thesis, University of Cambridge, 1984), pp. 20–30.

26.  Goodhart, *The Business of Banking*, pp. 127–32.

27.  Cairncross, *Home and Foreign Investment*; Cottrell, *Industrial Finance*; Lavington, *English Capital*; R. C. Michie, *Money, Mania and Markets: Investment, Company Formation and the Stock Exchange in Nineteenth Century Scotland* (Edinburgh, 1981); and Chapter 5 this volume.

28.  M. H. Best and J. Humphries, 'The City and industrial decline', in Elbaum and Lazonick, *The Decline of the British Economy*.

29.  Tolliday, *Business, Banking and Politics*, pp. 269–77.

30.  Sayers, *Bank of England* (1976), pp. 314–30; H. Clay, *Lord Norman* (London, 1957), pp. 318–59; Tolliday, *Business, Banking and Politics*, Bamberg, 'Government, banks and the Lancashire cotton industries'.

31.  This explanation has been suggested by Chapman in *Rise of Merchant Banking*,

pp. 98–9, however, by the late nineteenth century, most leading merchant banks of foreign origin had been completely anglicized and in any case a foreign firm would never overlook a lucrative business opportunity in Britain if this were to arise.

32. See his autobiography, *Leaves from my Life*, 2 vols (London, 1929).
33. H. Lowenfeld, *All about Investment* (London, 1909), pp. 174–5.
34. L. Hannah, *The Rise of the Corporate Economy* (London, 1976), p. 21.
35. Kynaston, 'Stock Exchange', pp. 236–62.
36. *Ibid.* pp. 270–85.
37. W. Thomas, *The Provincial Stock Exchanges* (London, 1973); Michie, *Money, Mania and Markets*.
38. Cottrell, *Industrial Finance*, pp. 113–40.
39. Thomas, *Finance of Industry*, p. 34.
40. M. Pohl, *Konzentration im deutschen Bankwesen, 1848–1980* (Frankfurt/Main, 1982), pp. 13–16.
41. Riesser, *Great German Banks*; J. Kocka, 'Entrepreneurs and managers in German industrialization', in *Cambridge Economic History of Europe*, Vol. VII, part 1 (Cambridge, 1978), pp. 565–70; W. Feldenkirchen, 'The banks and the steel industry in the Ruhr, 1873–1914', *German Yearbook in Business History* (1981); R. Rettig, *Das Investitions- und Finanzierungsverhalten deutscher Grossunternehmen 1880–1911* (Diss., Münster, 1978); K. E. Born, *International Banking in the Nineteenth and Twentieth Centuries* (Leamington Spa, 1983).
42. Kocka, 'Entrepreneurs and managers', p. 570.
43. See N. Horn, 'Aktienrechtliche Unternehmensorganisation in der Hochindustrialisierung (1860–1920). Deutschland, England, Frankreich und die USA im Vergleich', in N. Horn and J. Kocka (eds.), *Recht und Entwicklung der Grossunternehmen im 19. und frühen 20. Jahrhundert* (Göttingen, 1979), pp. 123–89.
44. See O. Jeidels, *Das Verhältnis der deutschen Grossbanken zur Industrie* (Munich, 1913); H. Pogge von Strandmann, *Unternehmenspolitik und Unternehmensführung. Der Dialog zwischen Aufsichtsrat und Vorstand bei Mannesmann 1900 bis 1919* (Düsseldorf, 1978); Mosse, *Jews in the German Economy*.
45. Y. Cassis, 'Management and strategy in the English joint stock banks, 1890–1914', *Business History*, Vol. XXVII (1985).
46. Cassis, *Les Banquiers*, pp. 176–7; D. Ross, Chapter 3 this volume.
47. See J. J. Beer, *The Emergence of the German Dye Industry* (Urbana, Illinois, 1959); L. F. Haber, *The Chemical Industry during the Nineteenth Century* (Oxford, 1958).
48. W. J. Reader, *Imperial Chemical Industries: A History*, 2 vols (London, 1970, 1975).
49. Kocka, 'Entrepreneurs and managers', p. 569.
50. H. M. Neuberger and H. H. Stokes, 'German banks and German growth, 1883–1913: an empirical view', *Journal of Economic History*, Vol. XXXIV

(1974), and the response by R. Fremdling and R. Tilly, 'German banks, German growth and econometric history', *Journal of Economic History,* Vol. XXXVI (1976).

51. G. D. Feldman, 'Bankers and banking in Germany after the First World War', unpublished paper for the conference on 'Finance and financiers in Europe, 19th–20th Centuries', Geneva, October 1989.

52. H. James, *The German Slump. Politics and Economics 1924–1936* (Oxford, 1986), pp. 128–46.

53. K. E. Born, *Die deutsche Bankenkrise 1931* (Munich, 1967), pp. 155 et seq.; quoted by H. James, *The Reichsbank and Public Finance in Germany 1924–1933. A Study of the Politics of Economics during the Great Depression* (Frankfurt/Main, 1985), pp. 208–9.

54. T. Balogh, *Studies in Financial Organization* (Cambridge, 1947), pp. 14–15, 114–18.

55. Deutsche Bundesbank, *Deutsches Geld- und Bankwesen in Zahlen 1876–1975* (Frankfurt, 1976).

56. Ibid.; see also Born, *International Banking.*

57. I am grateful to Geoffrey Jones for drawing my attention to this last point.

58. M. Simon, 'The pattern of new British portfolio investment, 1865–1914', in A. R. Hall, *The Export of Capital from Britain 1870–1914* (London, 1968); L. Davis and R. A. Huttenback, 'The export of British finance', *Journal of Imperial and Commonwealth History,* Vol. XIII (1985).

59. D. C. M. Platt, *Britain's Investment Overseas on the Eve of the First World War* (London, 1986).

60. P. Svedberg, 'The Portfolio – Direct Composition of Private Investment in 1914 Revisited', *Economic Journal,* Vol. LXXXVIII (1978).

61. Pollard, 'Capital exports'.

62. Edelstein, *Overseas Investment,* pp. 111–40.

63. In addition to Chapter 2 in this volume, see Kennedy, 'Institutional Response', *Industrial Structure,* 'Foreign investment, trade and growth in the United Kingdom, 1870–1913', *Exploration in Economic History,* Vol. 11 (1973–4).

64. See, for example, D. N. McCloskey, *Enterprise and Trade in Victorian Britain* (London, 1981).

65. See D. Kynaston, *The Financial Times. A Centenary History* (London, 1988); and idem, 'Stock Exchange', pp. 317–41.

66. Svedberg, 'Portfolio–Direct Composition'; J. H. Dunning, 'Changes in the level and structure of international production: the last one hundred years', in M. Casson (ed.), *The Growth of International Business* (London, 1983).

67. M. Wilkins, 'The free-standing company, 1870–1914: an important type of British foreign direct investment', *Economic History Review,* 2nd series, Vol. XLI (1988).

68. S. D. Chapman, 'British-based investment groups before 1914', *Economic History Review,* 2nd series, Vol. XXXVIII (1985); and the ensuing discussion, R. V. Turrell and J. J. Van Helten, 'The investment group: the missing link in British overseas economic expansion before 1914?'; and S. D. Chapman, 'A

reply: investment groups in India and South Africa', *Economic History Review*, 2nd series, Vol. XL (1987).

69.  J. Thobie, *La France impériale* (Paris, 1982); J. Bouvier and R. Girault, *L'impérialisme à la française* (Paris, 1986).

70.  See on this question P. J. Cain, 'Political economy in Edwardian England: the Tariff Reform controversy', in A. O'Day (ed.), *The Edwardian Age. Conflict and Stability* (London, 1979); B. Semmel, *Imperialism and Social Reform, 1895–1914* (London, 1960), E. Halévy, *Les Impérialistes au pouvoir 1895–1905* (Paris, 1926), A. Sykes, *Tariff Reform in British Politics 1903–1913* (Oxford, 1979).

71.  Some general indication, however, can be gathered from a memorandum sent to Chamberlain in 1903; see W. Mock, *Imperiale Herrschaft und Nationales Interesse: 'Constructive Imperialism' oder Freihandel in Grossbritanien vor dem Ersten Weltkrieg* (Stuttgart, 1982), Appendix IV (memorandum by H. A. Gwynne, December 1903), pp. 393–97.

72.  Cassis, *Les Banquiers,* pp. 357–64.

73.  R. A. Rempel, *Unionists Divided. Arthur Balfour, Joseph Chamberlain and the Unionist Free Traders* (Newton Abbot, 1972), chapter 6.

74.  A. J. Marrison, 'Businessmen, industries and Tariff Reform in Great Britain, 1903–1930', *Business History,* Vol. XXV (1983).

75.  See on this question Moggridge, *Monetary Policy,* Pollard (ed.), *Gold Standard*; S. Howson, *Domestic Monetary Management in Britain 1919–1938* (Cambridge, 1975); F. C. Castigliola, 'Anglo-American financial rivalry in the 1920s', *Journal of Economic History,* Vol. 37 (1977); L. S. Presnell, '1925: the burden of sterling', *Economic History Review,* 2nd series, Vol. XXXI (1978), N. H. Dimsdale, 'British monetary policy 1920–1938', *Oxford Economic Papers,* Vol. 33 (1981), Clay, *Lord Norman*; Sayers, *Bank of England.*

76.  R. S. Sayers, 'The return to Gold, 1925', in Pollard, *Gold Standard.*

77.  S. Pollard, 'Introduction', to his *Gold Standard*; Longstreth, 'The City'.

78.  J. M. Keynes, 'The economic consequences of Mr Churchill', in *Essays in Persuasion* (London, 1931), which was written immediately after the return to Gold.

79.  C. P. Kindleberger, *A Financial History of Western Europe* (London, 1984), p. 337.

80.  S. Checkland, 'The mind of the City, 1870–1914', *Oxford Economic Papers,* New series, 9 (1957).

81.  P. Anderson, 'Origins of the present crisis', *New Left Review,* 23 (1964), and idem, 'Figures of descent'.

82.  For a recent criticism of this approach, see M. Daunton, ' "Gentlemanly capitalism" and British industry 1820–1914', *Past and Present,* Vol. 122 (1989).

83.  Ingham, *Capitalism Divided*; S. Newton and D. Porter, *Modernization Frustrated. The Politics of Industrial Decline in Britain since 1900* (London, 1988).

84.  Cassis, 'Bankers in English society'; see also Harris and Thane, 'British and

European bankers'; Lisle-Williams, 'Merchant banking dynasties', idem, 'Beyond the market'.

85. S. D. Chapman, 'Aristocracy and meritocracy in merchant banking', *British Journal of Sociology*, Vol. XXXVII (1986); Y. Cassis, 'Merchant bankers and City aristocracy'; and S. D. Chapman, 'Reply to Youssef Cassis', both in *British Journal of Sociology*, Vol. XXXIX (1988).

86. For a comparison between top businessmen in Britain, France and Germany see Y. Cassis, 'Wirtschaftselite und Bürgertum. England, Frankreich und Deutschland um 1900', in J. Kocka (ed.), *Bürgertum im 19. Jahrhundert. Deutschland im europäischen Vergleich,* 3 vols (Munich, 1988), Vol. 2.

87. For the contemporary period, see for example the comparative analysis of Colin Mayer, 'New Issues in corporate finance', Inaugural lecture, City University Business School, London (May 1987).

# 2 Capital markets and industrial structure in the Victorian economy

*William P. Kennedy*

## Introduction

The operations of Victorian capital markets constitute a convenient vantage-point for those concerned to understand Britain's economic performance since 1870, for it was in the decades before World War I that the most crucial features of the twentieth-century British economy were firmly established. Two aspects of the Victorian economy, both closely linked to capital markets, particularly merit attention. First is the unprecedented British transfer of resources overseas. Although reservations have been raised about the accuracy of the conventional estimates of British foreign investment and its attendant return flow of earnings,[1] it is nevertheless conceded that British foreign portfolio investment flows in the half-century before 1914 were uniquely large; were growing over the period; and made up a substantial fraction of total British investment in those years. Edelstein has estimated that, on average, foreign portfolio investment claimed at least one-third of all British investment after 1870, actually becoming larger than total domestic investment briefly in the early 1870s, more persistently in the late 1880s and early 1890s, and finally continuously from 1905 to the outbreak of World War I.[2]

The other aspect of the Victorian economy that has persistently attracted historical attention is the slow-down in economic growth, which became progressively more evident as the nineteenth century drew to a close. Recent work by R. C. O. Matthews and his collaborators has established the outlines of this slow-down clearly. They show that despite sustained rates of factor input growth, the rate of output growth gradually weakened from the mid-nineteenth century onwards.[3] The increasing difficulty Victorian Britain experienced in sustaining technological advance culminated in an actual productivity decline in the period 1899–1913, an unprecedented event in an advanced industrial economy during peacetime. While such a pervasive occurrence as an economy-wide productivity retardation may not itself be obviously linked to capital market operations, a notable feature of the retardation serves to support the connection: 'new' industries (such as automobiles and electrical engineering) and greatly rejuvenated old ones (such as chemicals and telecommunications) closely linked to the technological advances of the period and prominent in other advanced economies were in Britain either absent entirely or operating on a much smaller scale. The stunted development of these crucial industries was closely linked to a series of stock exchange fiascos, in which early eager enthusiasms were methodically exploited by market manipulators whose cynical but successful rush for immediate gains weakened the affected industries sufficiently seriously to impair subsequent investment in them.[4]

It is obvious, then, that resources adequate to bring about substantial changes in the structure of the domestic economy were going overseas in the form of portfolio investment. Given the extent of the technological changes of the period and the importance of newly emerging technologies in maintaining the high income levels enjoyed by the advanced economies, it seems clear that these resources did not go overseas because there were no potentially profitable uses for them at home. The average rate of return on all domestic property gross of depreciation was never for any substantial time less than 10 per cent for the entire period 1870–1913, while the average private rate of return on the private reproducible capital stock exclusive of dwellings – the domestic investments most directly comparable with foreign projects – was consistently over 11 per cent (gross of depreciation).[5] The relevant lower bound estimate net of depreciation – deliberately calculated on only a slightly

Table 2.1   Aggregate British foreign portfolio investments and average yields in selected activities, 1907–1908

| Activity | Amount | Estimated share of British aggregate foreign portfolio investment as of end, December 1907 | Yield |
|---|---|---|---|
| | £m | % | % |
| Banks | 54.1 | 2.00 | 13.6 |
| Canals & docks | 6.0 | 0.22 | 19.9 |
| Mines | 230.4 | 8.55 | 11.1 |
| Nitrate extraction | 10.9 | 0.40 | 15.0 |
| American railways | 600.0 | 22.27 | 4.5 |
| All other overseas railways | 599.0 | 22.23 | 4.3 |
| Colonial governments | 531.6 | 19.73 | 3.6 |
| Foreign governments | 167.0 | 6.19 | 4.8 |

Source:
George Paish, 'Great Britain's capital investment in other lands', *Journal of the Royal Statistical Society*, Vol. 72, (1909), pp. 475–6.

modified gross capital stock basis (deducting only the current year's depreciation from the gross capital stock estimate) in order to bias the result downwards – was approximately 8.1 per cent. Total property income net of depreciation from the total net capital stock yielded approximately 10.75 per cent.[6] Although perhaps 11 per cent of all British foreign portfolio investments earned a rate of return as great as that earned on the average of domestic investment, that is over 10 per cent (and this 11 per cent of the British overseas portfolio stock accounted, on Paish's reckoning, for fully 25 per cent of recorded British property income from abroad in the years 1907–8), the great bulk of British foreign portfolio investment, concentrated in the issues of governments, municipalities and railways, earned far less (see Table 2.1). A similar picture of British foreign portfolio investment as generally unspectacular has also emerged from recent work by Davis and Huttenback.[7] Moreover, indications of trading volume in London – such as coverage in the financial press and relative numbers of specialist jobbers – suggest that the assets conventionally believed to be most important did in fact dominate wealth-holders' interests and that therefore the conventional estimates of the yield on foreign portfolio investments still remain the most plausible ones.

Of course, these estimates of average yields are useful only as guides to the marginal rates which determined investment decisions. However, two factors suggest that the average yields serve as plausible, if conservative, indicators of the relevant marginal yields. First, the sheer size, wealth and diversity of the British economy offered enough scope to ensure sustained demand for high levels of capital formation, especially in activities where strong productivity advances acted to lower costs and prices or where product innovation created new markets. Secondly, the rapid growth of manufactured goods imported into Britain and of foreign direct investment in British industry can only be explained by the widespread perception of high but uncaptured returns to domestic British industrial capital formation. It therefore appears that while a sub-set of foreign investments – such as the proverbial gold mine – could, at best, on average compete reasonably favourably with the best domestic opportunities in terms of expected yields,[8] the great bulk of the foreign assets British investors purchased could not. Hence portfolio investment was not drawn overseas by the promise of inordinately large returns. The most that can be claimed is that, for example, overseas railways tended to pay better by the late nineteenth century than did domestic railways and that overseas government and municipal bonds tended to pay better than domestic ones. But the yields both on overseas railways and on overseas government and municipal bonds were on average clearly dominated by the yields on British domestic industrial investments. For example, between 1905 and 1913, the yield on financial investment in the fledgling British motor industry was over three times the financial yield on a representative sample of British foreign investments.[9] Given the rapid expansion of the British motor industry during this period, it is reasonable to assume that the internal rate of return on the physical capital employed in the industry was at least comparable to the financial yield. Overseas investment in railroads and government bonds was attractive only for the diversification it offered, not for its modest yields.

The combination of large investment flows overseas with an inability or unwillingness to commit substantial resources to newly-emerging technologies at home can readily be seen to have retarded economic growth and to have contributed to freezing the industrial structure of the domestic British economy into an increasingly obsolescent – and hence vulnerable – pattern.[10] In retrospect, this pattern can be clearly seen to be disadvantageous. One must ask, then, whether Victorian capital markets were incidental to this process, passive conduits through which resources directed by other forces flowed, or whether the operations of the capital markets themselves contributed directly to this outcome.[11]

**Capital markets and the fostering of competition**

In assessing the role of capital markets, it may be useful to begin by asking what ideally one would expect from capital markets and to see how closely Victorian Britain's capital market institutions approached this ideal. It is important to stress at the outset that it is assumed individual decision-makers are generally rational, that whatever eccentricities may mark individuals, as a group they will not consistently make mistakes that can reasonably be anticipated and avoided. Individuals, however, cannot determine unilaterally the institutional environment within which they exercise this rationality, leaving open the possibility that environments may exist in which individually rational decisions do not yield a Pareto efficient outcome for the economy as a whole. (That is, there may exist substantial unexploited opportunities to make most people better off without making anyone worse off, but there exists no social mechanism by which these opportunities can be realized).

The tasks of capital markets broadly construed may be considered to fall into three categories:
1.  the identification and evaluation of all investment opportunities;
2.  the widespread availability of this information at low cost;
3.  the provision of channels through which judgements based on such widely available information can be exercised in order both to increase resources devoted to successful activities and to withhold, withdraw or alter the management of resources devoted to unsuccessful activities.

If all three tasks are carried out well, prices are determined in such a way that the marginal, risk-adjusted rates of return for all savers and producers is identical (although taxes may prevent the full realization of this possibility). Conversely, if some or all of the tasks are not carried out adequately, large, persistent differences in risk-adjusted rates of return will exist and consequently resources will not be optimally allocated.[12]

The adequacy of the accomplishment of these tasks in Victorian Britain may usefully be gauged by considering two aspects of Victorian economic behaviour: the competitive pressures maintained on firms in technologically progressive areas of the economy and the degree of diversification wealth-holders could readily achieve. The first aspect involves a consideration of the linkages between real and financial activity to determine how effectively the signals generated in financial markets are translated

26

into the allocation of tangible resources. The second aspect concerns the efficiency with which wealth-holders are able to share the risks of capital formation and thereby to determine the values attached to risky assets. While these are not the only aspects that could be considered, because they are of fundamental importance and would be included in any wider study, they serve as a useful point of departure.[13]

The competitive pressures placed by financial markets on firms in technologically advanced areas is a fruitful way to consider the linkages between real and financial activity. The theoretical nature of these linkages has been considered by James Tobin.[14] Tobin has argued that when the market capitalization of the financial assets of a firm exceeds the replacement cost of the capital of that firm, a financial signal has been generated indicating, in competitive circumstances, that the firm should expand its capital stock (including human resources), a process that should continue until the market capitalization of the firm just equals the total replacement cost of the firm's capital stock.[15] Obviously, in efficient markets a firm whose market capitalization exceeds the replacement cost of its physical capital – the ratio of market capitalization to the replacement cost of physical capital is called the 'q' ratio and hence capitalization in excess of replacement costs implies a 'q' ratio greater than unity – would face no financial constraint in expanding its stock of physical capital since it could, as long as its 'q' ratio were greater than unity, sell financial assets for more than the cost of additions to its stock of physical capital. In normal circumstances as more and more of a firm's financial assets are sold, the price of those assets will fall, eventually bringing about equality between market capitalization and the total replacement cost of the firm's capital stock, even as the capital stock itself is increasing.[16] If the firm possessed adequate funds internally, it would enhance its market capitalization most by using those funds to expand its capital stock and thereby earnings per share. The increased capital stock would eventually encounter decreasing returns which in turn would depress net earnings per share, once again bringing market capitalization into equality with replacement costs.

Analogous arguments may be made in terms not just of firms but of entire industries. In situations where the market capitalization of assets engaged in a particular activity or industry is systematically greater than the replacement costs of those assets, a clear signal for entry into the industry is generated. Conversely, a 'q' ratio less than unity indicates that financial markets value a firm less than the replacement costs of its capital, implying that the firm should be wound up or restructured, either by a hostile takeover bid by an alternative management group that believes it could make better use of the firm's assets than the existing management or by the firm selling off all or part of its capital stock and distributing the proceeds to shareholders. An exodus of firms should occur in industries where the 'q' ratios of individual firms tend to be less than unity.

Highly concentrated industries provide a revealing vantage-point to study this process. If the linkage between financial markets and real investment activity is sufficiently weak, the present market value of the discounted flow of the profits of a firm enjoying monopolistic market power will be fully reflected in the firm's share price, causing the expected yield on the financial asset, given its risk characteristics, to equal the (risk-adjusted) return currently available through the Stock Exchange.

27

The super-normal monopoly profits, however, were reaped by those who possessed the shares when the market valuation embedding the expectation of monopolistic profits was first made, not those who bought the shares subsequently. The important point, however, is that a 'q' ratio greater than unity will not in this case induce real investment. For real investment to take place, new entry into the industry is needed. A profit-maximizing firm enjoying monopolistic profits will only increase investment when demand shifts outward, even if that means that the valuation of financial assets will remain greater than the replacement value of the capital stock, because, when facing a fixed demand curve, the marginal revenue obtained through increased output following investment is less than the marginal cost of that expansion. Such inhibitions, however, will not apply to new entrants to the industry. In markets with adequate information flows, new entrants will be able to observe the high market valuations of earnings arising from a given ensemble of capital goods (including research and development capacity). Unless there are unusually formidable barriers to entry that make the acquisition of the ensemble of capital goods of potential newcomers prohibitively expensive, they will find entry profitable even if the monopolist does not. In this case, a high 'q' ratio will induce real investment and monopoly profits will be eventually competed away, to the benefit of the economy at large, if not the monopolist.

New entry or the effective threat of new entry in monopolistic industries has been shown in a recent paper by Akerlof and Yellin to have implications beyond the familiar welfare benefits that arise from reducing the gap between marginal costs and output prices.[17] Akerlof and Yellin show that the failure by a monopolist to adopt every feasible cost saving innovation will result in only minor losses to the monopolist but very much larger costs to the wider economy. (See Figure 2.1). This may be demonstrated by the following example.

Suppose the initial price the monopolist charges is $P_o$, generating sales of $Q_o$ units of output. The monopolist's costs are assumed for simplicity to be constant per unit of output, causing average cost to be equal everywhere to marginal cost, denoted by $MC_o = AC_o$ in Figure 2.1. The monopolist's revenues are $P_o Q_o$ (represented by the rectangle $P_o A\ Q_o O$ in Figure 2.1), which are equal to total costs $Q_o$. ($MC_o$) (represented by the rectangle $HEQ_o O$) plus super-normal profits $Q_o$. ($P_o - MC_o$) (represented by the rectangle $HEAP_o$). Consumer's surplus beyond total cost is the area under the demand curve above $P_o$ (represented by the triangle $GP_o A$). Now assume the monopolist discovers a cost saving possibility which lowers costs from $MC_o$ to $MC_1$. Consider first the case of a completely rational monopolist who seeks always to extract the full benefit of his market position. When marginal cost falls from $MC_o$ to $MC_1$, marginal revenue must also fall by the same amount in order to preserve the equality between marginal revenue and marginal cost necessary for profit-maximization. The required fall in marginal revenue is achieved by reducing prices and raising output. The fully rational monopolists' revenues are now $P_1 Q_1$, with profits equal to $(P_1 - MC_1).Q_1$, which may be expressed usefully as follows:

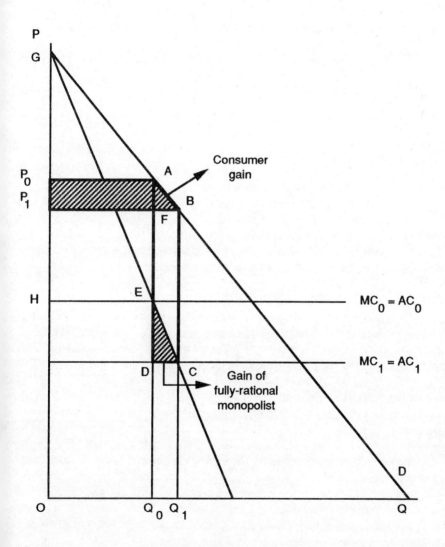

Figure 2.1   Costs, profits and consumers' surplus in a monopolistic industry.

(1)  $(P_1 - MC_1).Q_1 = (P_0 - MC_0).Q_0 + (MC_0 - MC_1).Q_0 + (MC_0 - MC_1).(Q_1 - Q_0) . (\frac{1}{2})$.

The increase in the level of profits is equal to the sum of the last two terms in Equation (1), that is, the extent of the cost reduction times the initial level of output plus a small amount determined by half the product of the cost reduction and the change in output (represented by the shaded triangle EDC in Figure 2.1). The first term, of course, is just the original level of profits. Clearly, the decrease is advantageous to the monopolist. It is, however, also advantageous (although less so) to consumers. Consumers gain an amount equal to $P_1P_0AB$. Total consumer gain, C, is given in Equation (2):

(2)  $C = (P_0 - P_1)Q_0 + (P_0 - P_1) . (Q_1 - Q_0) . (\frac{1}{2})$.

Since the equations shown in Figure 2.1 relating price, P, to output, Q – the demand schedule – and marginal revenue, MR, to output are as follows:

(3)  $P = a - bQ$
(4)  $MR = a - 2bQ$,

it can be shown[18] that

(5)  $(MC_0 - MC_1) = 2 (P_0 - P_1)$.

Hence the monopolists' gains are exactly twice those of consumers. The main point is that *both* the producers and consumers gain and that consumers' gains are proportional to the monopolist's (albeit smaller).

Now consider the case of a near-rational monopolist who through indolence and inertia fails to exploit fully the benefits of a successful reduction in costs by leaving price and output unchanged. The near-rational monopolist's profits, are:

(6)  $\pi_{N-R} = (P_0 - MC_0) Q_0 + (MC_0 - MC_1) Q_0$.

Comparison of Equation (6) with Equation (1) shows that in conditions of substantial market power, where the gap between price and marginal cost is great, the near-rational monopolist's profits are nearly as great as the rational monopolist's. The near-rational monopolist pays only a small price for his indolence and inertia. The price is only of second-order magnitude, equal to $(MC_0 - MC_1).(Q_1 - Q_0).(\frac{1}{2})$, compared to the first-order magnitude of $(MC_0 - MC_1).Q_0$.[19] However, the small cost to the monopolist of only near-rational rather than full-rational behaviour may be contrasted to the loss that befalls consumers. Consumers gain *no* advantage whatsoever from the near-rational monopolist's ability to lower costs. For them, prices and output remain unchanged as the near-rational monopolist's costs fall. Only when prices fall in response to cost changes do consumers reap any benefits. The consumers' benefits, however, are very large relative to the marginal gain of the full-rational monopolist over his near-rational counterpart. The economy-wide costs of lethargic innovation in monopolistic industries are therefore many times – the exact multiple increases with the inverse of the elasticity of demand facing the industry – the direct costs to the monopolist. These economy-wide costs will be amplified to the extent that the monopolistic firm supplies producers goods to the rest of the economy. The more significant is the industry in an input–output sense (the greater the number of rows in an input–output table the industry appears in as a supplier) the more widely distributed are the costs to the economy as a whole of optimizing errors by producers with market power, even if the errors appear small to the individual monopolist. Hence the ability of the financial system to force the physical and human capital stock of a firm, particularly a firm providing intermediate inputs to many sectors of the economy, into a size such as to yield equality between the replacement costs of its inputs and the market value of its outstanding financial issues is of crucial importance.

The implications of this analysis might be examined by considering two examples, electrical engineering and chemical manufacture. The early days of the British electrical engineering industry saw a great flurry of new issues on the London Stock Exchange. Quite clearly in London in 1882, the financial instruments issued by a firm purporting to exploit the recent advances in the generation and use of electricity were worth more than the ensemble of capital goods the putative firm proposed to employ. As is well known, however, this enthusiasm was short-lived. Virtually all the firms floated on the Exchange in 1882 were defunct within five years, many before 1882 was out.[20] Little was left for liquidators to distribute to creditors and irate shareholders. The legacy, of course, was that the credit of electrical engineering firms was gravely tarnished and that the industry was able to expand only slowly as firms engaged in related activities, mainly mechanical engineering, gradually took up electrical manufacture. Ultimately, the industry in Britain came to be dominated by subsidiaries of foreign firms that had secured their foundation elsewhere before turning to the British home market.[21] The failure can clearly be attributed to an inability of potential shareholders to become, and stay, well informed about the plans and prospects of the firms whose shares were available, combined with the absence of an effective channel through which control over managers could be exercised. Moreover, since potential shareholders had so little reliable information, it was difficult if not impossible for company outsiders to distinguish viable firms from fraudulent ones. It is not surprising, then, that such a chaotic market would function badly, with viable firms obtaining too low a market valuation and fraudulent ones too high,[22] leaving all those with an enduring (rather than opportunistic) interest in the industry dissatisfied. Consequently, after a disastrous start, electrical engineering in Britain developed – by international standards – badly, with only limited recourse to external financing, and much of that only extended to foreign firms able to offer good collateral.[23] By placing a discount on financial instruments issued by domestic electrical engineering firms, British capital markets discouraged capital formation in this crucial industry.

This process might usefully be contrasted with Germany, where rivalry between the established firm of Siemens and Emil Rathenau's upstart AEG produced two of the world's largest electrical engineering firms by 1914.[24] When the new opportunities in electrical engineering opened up in the 1880s, the established, family-controlled firm of Siemens was in a favourable position. Its previous concentration on telegraphy ensured some familiarity with the new technology and provided a useful basis for subsequent diversification. Siemens proceeded to exploit this situation with all the caution and deliberation attributed to closely held British family firms. However, unlike in Britain, Siemens' position in Germany was threatened by a new entrant. Emil Rathenau was able to persuade influential Berlin bankers of the promise of electricity and received their support for expansion both by internal growth, aided by stock flotations, and by merger, often engineered with bank help. As Rathenau's firm rapidly grew larger, it offered increasingly threatening competition to Siemens. Eventually Siemens was forced to seek, with banking support, merger opportunities and generally to expand more rapidly and with more risk than it clearly would have chosen to have done had it not been prodded by persistent competitive pressure. In this case, family pride dictated a stout (and expensive, if ultimately profitable) defence of family interests and traditions. German banks in this episode can be seen as playing an important informational role in screening technically complex proposals and lending their reputations and resources to approved ventures in whose operations they also exercised some control, particularly at those crucial junctures where difficulties were encountered. In this manner the financial instruments issued by German electrical engineering firms were valued highly relative to their input costs; their high 'q' ratio was like an invitation to print money and this undoubtedly encouraged a predisposition towards aggressive expansion. Moreover, the rivalry between Siemens and AEG made these two firms highly conscious of marginal advantages and this acted to mitigate the consequences of their considerable market power. The purchasers of German electrical goods at least had the benefit of any profit-enhancing innovation either of the two firms could devise and, as Akerlof and Yellin have argued, this benefit was large relative to the marginal benefits to the firms of exploiting the full extent of their market power.

The other illustration offered in this paper is drawn from the chemical industry where the patterns of British external finance once again yielded an unfavourable outcome. In Britain in 1890, the bulk of the assets in the industry were devoted to the manufacture of alkali, used for making soap and many other products. In 1891, all the major manufacturers of alkali employing the Leblanc process merged, to form United Alkali, an entity which they hoped would wield considerable market power. This endeavour had Stock Exchange support despite rumblings of unease in the financial press and ultimately netted approximately £1.3 million from a trusting public. Combined with approximately £7.2 million in vendors' shares, United Alkali was briefly the largest chemical firm in the world. The firm was, however, fatally wedded to an obsolete technology and it gradually sank into insignificance, its experiences serving to add a further discount to the value of 'high-tech' financial instruments issued in London.

United Alkali was eased into profitless marginality by its symbiotic relationship with Brunner, Mond who also made alkali, but with the Solvay process. Brunner and Mond, despite considerable effort, were unable to solve their external financing requirements through formal intermediaries and institutions, finally obtaining limited support in the traditional manner through personal contacts, in this case £5000 from a boyhood friend of John Brunner. Once established, however, Brunner, Mond was highly profitable. The firm's pricing policy consisted of setting a price just above United Alkali's costs, yielding derisory profits to United Alkali Ltd but large and increasing profits to Brunner, Mond as it was able to reduce its operating costs. Price decreases for consumers, however, were dictated until well into the twentieth century by United Alkali's ability, not Brunner, Mond's, to cut costs. In this manner, both British consumers who purchased soap directly and British textile manufacturers who used soap as an input in preparing their products for sale were harmed, first because prices fell only as fast as United Alkali, and not the more advanced Brunner, Mond could force them down profitably, and secondly because Brunner, Mond itself was not under any external compulsion to minimize its own costs. For example, William Reader has stressed the difference between the intense and successful search by the Solvays and their German allies for a means of incorporating the manufacture of chlorine into their alkali product-cycle and the relaxed indifference to this problem displayed by Brunner, Mond until the eve of World War I.[25]

These illustrations, drawn from two of the industries prominent in the 'Second Industrial Revolution', portray Britain's capital markets in an unfavourable light. They suggest that the inability of capital markets to channel resources productively into technologically advanced enterprises slowed the development in Britain both of important industries and of related services such as education, a process that cumulatively contributed substantially to the productivity slow-down charted by Matthews *et al.* The absence of effective competitive pressure in these industries further retarded the dissemination of the benefits of the limited technological advance that did occur, serving to hold down the growth of real incomes. This process in turn acted to encourage foreign investment. First, the retardation of real income growth of itself made Britain a less attractive place to invest and the rest of the world more attractive, especially since the retardation arose from an inability of British firms to absorb beneficially resources in precisely those industries that exhibited such an enormous appetite for productive investment in other advanced countries. Of course, once this process had got under way, prospective British producers in technologically advanced areas had to be increasingly wary of well-established foreign firms that might compete with them through exports or through direct investment in their home market. Secondly, the dismal experience of early new issues in technologically advanced areas may reasonably be believed to have blighted the prospects of subsequent issues from the same or similar industries, although the precise dimensions of this blight remain to be discovered. To the extent it did occur, it meant that British firms wishing to expand operated without the licence to print money which relatively high 'q' ratios appear to have conferred upon their German counterparts. If some classes of British financial assets laboured under depressed market valuations, other issues, many if not most foreign, were correspondingly more attractive. Footloose entrepreneurs would not fail to notice the difference.

The other facet of this process, equally frustrating for ambitious would-be entrepreneurs wishing to exercise their talents in Britain, was that by 1900 established British firms like Brunner, Mond were able to protect their favoured positions in a manner unavailable to comparable German firms like Siemens, which

33

faced rivals who, provided they could attract bank support, were able to encroach upon even well-established market positions. While German firms certainly exercised market power, they could do so only from a position of fundamental strength. If that strength were not well maintained, aggressive interlopers such as Emil Rathenau would move in decisively. Rathenau's would-be British counterparts had much less powerful institutional support to draw upon to help fulfil their ambitions.

## Capital markets and the fostering of diversification

Because investment is inherently risky, opportunities for diversification are one of the most vital services capital markets can offer. Diversification is the only systematic way to manage exposure to risk. Through diversification it is, in principle, possible to construct a portfolio that exhibits less risk than any component asset contained in the portfolio, while enjoying an expected yield for the portfolio as a whole that is greater than the lowest yield of any component asset. Efficient portfolios possess the desirable property that for any level of risk borne, expected yields are maximized. Conversely, in efficient portfolios, the least risk possible is accepted in order to obtain any given expected yield. Only in efficient portfolios is it necessarily true that the pursuit of higher yields must entail acceptance of greater risks. In all other portfolios it is possible either to obtain higher yields without increasing exposure to risk or to maintain yields while decreasing risks.

The theory of the efficient pricing of risky assets holds that the equilibrium expected yield of an asset is equal to the sum of the equilibrium expected yield on the least risky combination of assets available plus the market price of risk multiplied by a measure of the riskiness of a given asset (see Equation 7).

$$(7) \quad E_{jm} = E^* + \frac{Cov(R_j, R_m)\,(E_m - E^*)}{6m^2}$$

where $E_{jm}$  = equilibrium expected yield on the $j^{th}$ asset in the market portfolio;

$E^*$  = equilibrium expected yield on the riskless (or least risky) asset or combination of assets;

$E_m$  = equilibrium expected yield on the market portfolio;

$6m^2$  = variance of the yield on the market (that is, the most highly diversified) portfolio;

$Cov(R_j, R_m)$ = covariance of yield on the $j^{th}$ asset and the market portfolio.

The ratio

$$\frac{E_m - E^*}{6_m^2}$$

is often referred to as 'the market price of risk' and the term

$$\left[ \frac{\text{Cov}\,(R_j, R_m)}{6_m{}^2} \right]$$

often called '$\beta_0$', is the degree of risk in efficient equilibrium which attaches to a specific asset j.

Notice that in Equation (7) the risk of the $j^{\text{th}}$ asset is determined entirely by the degree to which the yield of the $j^{\text{th}}$ asset moves in sympathy with the yield on the market portfolio, which may be conveniently thought of as the yield of a representative group of assets.[26] The specific risk of the asset – most importantly the extent to which its own yield is expected to fluctuate over time – is irrelevant (except in so far as its fluctuations coincide with the market as a whole), because specific risk can be entirely avoided by efficient diversification. Only that degree of risk which is common to all assets – called systematic risk – cannot be avoided and ultimately it is this systematic risk alone which determines the value of assets in efficiently diversified portfolios. In an efficient portfolio, a relatively low price (high yield) is attached to any asset whose pay-out moves closely (say rising 10 per cent as the market pay-out as a whole rises 10 per cent and falling 5 per cent when the market as a whole falls 5 per cent) with the pay-out of the market portfolio because such an asset offers little opportunity for diversification from market-wide risks. Those assets whose yields are magnified by market movements – for example, rising 30 per cent when the market as a whole rises by 10 per cent and falling 15 per cent when the market as a whole falls by 5 per cent – are valued even less because the holder of them increases his exposure to overall market risk and must be correspondingly compensated by higher yields (which means the purchase price of the asset must be lower).

Conversely, assets whose yields are expected to exhibit only a small degree of covariance with the market portfolio will command a much smaller yield, one close to the risk-free rate, because they are relatively free from market-wide risks, and hence warrant a proportionately higher price. If, unusually, $\beta_j$ were negative, indicating that the $j^{\text{th}}$ asset was expected to achieve a high pay-off when the market as a whole fell, the price of asset j (for any given expected value of pay-out) would rise further to produce an expected yield *less* than E*, the risk-free rate. This follows because, in the exceptional case of an asset whose pattern of return is negatively correlated with a return of the market as a whole, the addition of such a negatively correlated asset to an efficiently diversified portfolio sharply reduces the riskiness of the entire portfolio. This reduction in risk provides any risk-averse wealth-holder with valuable, and hence costly, insurance against unfavourable outcomes. In this manner the prices of risky assets are efficiently determined. If capital markets perform their functions poorly, for example, through high transactions costs, or through the expensive provision of poor quality information, or through excessive vulnerability to fraud and manipulation, then the prices attached to risky assets will deviate from the optimal values dictated by inherent risks that cannot be avoided by diversification.[27]

It is possible to obtain some insight into the extent to which capital market imperfections affect the value of an asset relative to its value in an efficient portfolio.

First, Equation (7) is transformed to facilitate analysis. The transformed version is shown in Equation (8):

(8)   $R_j = \alpha_j + B_j R_m + e_j$

where $R_j$      = total realized return on the $j^{th}$ asset;

$\alpha_j$      = $E^* - B_j E^*$, where $E^*$ is the equilibrium expected yield on the riskless (or least risky) asset or combination of assets;

$B_j$      = $\left[ \dfrac{\text{Cov }(R_j, R_m)}{6_m{}^2} \right]$ : $B_j$ is generally calculated from historical data, thus embodying the assumption that the future will be like the past;

$R_m$      = total realized return on the market portfolio;

$e_j$      = random error term, independent of the market (i.e. Cov $(R_m, e_j) = 0$).

Equation (8) is in the form of a regression, whereby $R_j$ is regressed on $R_m$. This procedure ensures that the covariance between $R_m$ and $e_j$ is zero. The interpretation of the first two terms is similar to the interpretation of Equation (7). The random error term measures the diversifiable risk of asset j. In an efficient portfolio, the expected value of $e_j$ will be zero and return will be determined only by a pure (risk-free) time discount, $E^*$, equal for all assets, and a fixed price of risks,

$$\left[ \frac{R_m - E^*}{6_m{}^2} \right]$$

paid in proportion (measured by $B_j$) to the extent the pay-out of the $j^{th}$ asset coincides with the pay-out pattern of the market as a whole. Calculating the variance of $R_j$ from Equation (8) yields an operational measure of asset j's riskiness. The expected variance of asset j's return is given in Equation (9):

(9)   $E(6_j{}^2) = B_j{}^2 E(6_m{}^2) + E(6^2)e_j))$

where $E(6_j{}^2)$      = expected variance of returns on the $j^{th}$ asset (the measure of asset j's riskiness);

$E(6_m{}^2)$      = expected variance of returns on the market portfolio;

$B_j$      = $\left[ \dfrac{\text{Cov }(R_j, R_m)}{6_m{}^2} \right]$;

the regression procedure imposes the assumption $E(B_j) = B_j$

$E(6^2(e_j))$      = expected variance of $e_j$, the random error associated with the returns of asset j.

Because the only sources of expected variance in Equation (8) are $R_m$ and $e_j$ ($B_j$ being treated as a constant – [see note 28]) and because the calculation of $B_j$ ensures zero covariance between $R_m$ and $e_j$, Equation (9) has only two terms. Hence we see from Equation (9) that the variance of returns on the $j^{th}$ asset consists only of two parts: (1) the (systematic) variance due to the variance of returns on the market portfolio multiplied by the relationship between $R_j$ and $R_m$ (that is, by $B_j{}^2$); and (2) the (unsystematic) expected variance due to the specific variance of the returns on asset j.[28] Systematic variance remains after all opportunities for diversification have been exploited; efficient diversification will eliminate the expected variance of $6^2(e_j)$.

By assigning plausible values to $B_j$, $6_m^2$ and $6^2(e_j)$, Equation (9) can be used to evaluate the costs of inefficient diversification in a variety of circumstances. In particular, as we shall see below, Equation (9) can be used to assess the consequences of the Victorian portfolio behaviour that is revealed in a systematic examination of probate inventories, the most promising source of evidence on wealth-holding patterns. Three numerical examples will help establish the magnitude of the gap (or discount) between the value of a given asset (or assets) in an efficiently diversified portfolio and the value of the same asset (or assets) in an inefficiently diversified one.

Consider a portfolio P consisting of four assets.[29] In the first of the three examples, let $B_j = B_p = 1.00$, indicating that on average portfolio P, which we are treating here as if it were just a single asset, tracks the market as a whole closely. For concreteness, let $E(6_m^2)$ be set equal to the standard deviation of the returns on a broadly based stock market index; employing the FT–Actuaries All Share Index for recent years yields $E(6_m^2) = (0.19)^2 = 0.036$. Finally, let the specific risk for the illustrative portfolio of four assets be drawn from the *Risk Management Service* of the London Business School. The four assets selected for the example were all equities of small firms and hence they usefully illustrate the magnitude of the specific risks associated with hazardous ventures. As a group, their specific risk was $E(6^2(e_p)) = 0.077$. Appropriately substituting these values for $B_p$, $E(6_m^2)$ and $E(6^2(e_p))$ into Equation (9) yields:

(10)  $\begin{aligned}E(6_p^2) &= B_p^2 E(6_m^2) + E(6^2(e_p)) \\ &= (1.00)^2 (0.190)^2 + 0.077 \\ &= (1.00)(0.036) + 0.077 \\ &= 0.113.\end{aligned}$

Now let us find an efficient portfolio, $\hat{P}$, such that its expected variance, $E(6_p^2)$, also equals 0.113. Recall that efficient portfolios are ones in which all expected unsystematic risk has been eliminated and that all the remaining risk arises, on average, only from the effect of market fluctuations as a whole on a given portfolio. Hence to obtain an expected portfolio variance $E(6_p^2)$ for an efficient portfolio equal to the expected portfolio variance for an portfolio (which also includes some unsystematic (diversifiable) risk), it is necessary to accept greater expected systematic risk in the efficient portfolio than in the inefficient one. Solving Equation (11) yields this greater value of $B_p$:

(11)  $\begin{aligned}E(6_p^2) &= B_p^2 E(6_m^2) + E(6^2(e_p))) \\ 0.113 &= B_p^2(0.19)^2 + 0.0, \text{ since } E(6^2(e_p)) = 0 \text{ by the assumption of efficient} \\ &\quad\text{diversification;} \\ B_p^2 &= \frac{0.113}{0.036}; \\ B_p^2 &= 3.139; \\ B_p &= 1.772.\end{aligned}$

This solution, $B_p = 1.772$, gives us the systematic risk an efficient portfolio must possess in order to have the same overall riskiness as the illustrative four-asset portfolio with $B_p = 1.00$ and additional unsystematic risk of 0.077. To complete the example, we now calculate the equilibrium yield of the illustrative four assets as a group within an *efficient* portfolio and then compare the equilibrium yields in the two efficient portfolios, one where the riskiness was determined by $B_p = 1.772$, equal to the overall riskiness of the inefficient illustrative portfolio (that is, both systematic and unsystematic risk), and the other where the riskiness was determined only by $B_p = 1.000$, the systematic risk assumed for the illustrative four-asset portfolio of this example. In Equation (12) we obtain the equilibrium (percentage) returns required by wealth-holders to accept an efficient portfolio with the same overall riskiness as the inefficient portfolio:

(12)  $E(R_p) = (1-B_p)E^* + B_pE(R_m)$;

where $E(R_p)$ = the equilibrium expected return on portfolio $_p$;

$B_p)$ = 1.772 (from Equation (11));

$E^*$ = equilibrium expected yield on the riskless (or least risky) asset or combination of assets; for the period 1870–1913, $E^*$ may be set equal to the real annual yield on Consols, or 0.02;

$E(R_m)$ = 0.08, a conservative approximation of the annual yield on the market portfolio in the period 1870–1913;

Hence:

$E(R_p)$ = (1.000–1.772) (0.02) + (1.772) (0.08)

= −0.015 + 0.142;

= 0.127.

Next, in Equation (13), we calculate the yield required to hold the illustrative four assets in an efficient portfolio, $_E$, in which all systematic risk has been eliminated, but still assuming $B_E = 1.00$:

(13)  $E(R_E) = (1-B_E)E^* + B_EE(R_m)$

where $E(R_E)$ = the equilibrium expected returns on an efficient portfolio with $B_E = 1.00$;

$E^*$ = 0.02; $E(R_m)$ = 0.08 as before.

Hence:

$E(R_E)$ = (1.00 − 1.00) (0.02) + (1.00) (0.08)

= 0.00 + 0.080

= 0.080;

$\dfrac{0.080}{0.127}$ = 0.630.

Comparing Equation (12) with Equation (13), it is easily seen that the efficient portfolio with the greater systematic risk earns the higher rate of return. Equation (13) shows the lower return necessary to compensate only for the systematic risk assumed to arise from holding the four specified assets in an efficient portfolio. The presence in Equation (10) of diversifiable risk of $6^2(e_p) = 0.077$, in addition to systematic risk of 0.036, was equivalent to higher systematic risk of 0.113, produced by a $B_j$ of 1.772 rather than 1.000. It is now a simple matter, at least for equities, to convert the return relatives into price relatives:[30] the price relative is equal to the inverse of the return relative. Thus the warranted price of the portfolio yielding an expected return of 12.7 per cent is only 63.0 per cent = 0.080/0.127 of that of the portfolio yielding 8.0 per cent. The cost of inefficient diversification, assuming intrinsic B = 1 000 for the four illustrative assets and unsystematic risk of $6^?(e_p)$ = 0.077, was a discount of 37 per cent over the value of the same four assets in an efficient portfolio (which by definition would contain no unsystematic risk).

It now remains to consider the discount for inefficient diversification when the B assumed for the four illustrative assets is: (1) greater than unity; and (2) less than unity, while holding asset-specific (diversifiable) risk constant at 0.077, a reasonable level for individual risky assets. In the first case, let $B_p$ = 2.000; in the second, $B_p$ = 0.500. The other parameters [$E(6_m^2)$ = 0.036; $E(R_m)$ = 0.08; $E^*$ = 0.02] remain unchanged. In the first case:

$$E(6_p^2) = (B_p^2)E(6_m^2) + E(6^2(e_p));$$
$$= (2.00)^2(0.19)^2 + 0.077;$$
$$= (4.00)\ (0.036) + 0.077;$$
$$= 0.221.$$

$$0.221 = B_p^2\ (0.036) + 0.00;$$
$$B_p^2 = \frac{0.221}{0.036} = 6.139;$$

$$B_p = 2.480.$$
$$R_p = (1.000 - 2.480)\ (0.02) + 2.480\ (0.08);$$
$$= -0.030 + 0.198;$$
$$= 0.168.$$

$$E(R_E) = (1.00 - 2.00)\ (0.02) + 2.00\ (0.08);$$
$$= -0.020 + 0.160;$$
$$= 0.140$$

$$\frac{0.140}{0.168} = 0.833.$$

Thus, for $B_p$ = 2.000, denoting intrinsically riskier assets due to a greater degree of systematic (undiversifiable) risk caused by the (assumed) greater responsiveness of the four assets' yields to the realized yield of the market as a whole, the discount caused by inefficient diversification is 16.7 per cent (= 1.000 − 0.833), less than half that imposed when $B_p$ = 1.00.

In the second case, $B_p$ = 0.500:

$$E(6_p^2) = (B_p^2)E(6_m^2) + E(6^2(e_p));$$
$$= (0.50)^2\ (0.19)^2 + 0.077;$$
$$= (0.25)\ (0.036) + 0.077;$$

$$E(6_p^2) = 0.086.$$
$$0.086 = B_p^2\ (0.036) + 0.00$$
$$B_p^2 = \frac{0.086}{0.036} = 2.389;$$

$$B_p^2 = 1.542;$$
$$E(R_p) = (1.00 - 0.50)\ (0.02) + 1.542\ (0.08);$$

$$\begin{aligned} &= 0.010 + 0.123; \\ &= 0.133. \end{aligned}$$

$$\begin{aligned} E(R_E) &= (1.00 - 0.50)\,(0.02) + 0.500\,(0.08); \\ &= 0.010 + 0.040; \\ &= 0.050. \end{aligned}$$

$$\frac{0.050}{0.133} = 0.376.$$

For $B_p = 0.500$, denoting intrinsically less risky assets due to a smaller degree of systematic (undiversifiable) risk caused by the (assumed) weaker responsiveness of the four assets' yields to the realised yield of the market as a whole, the discount caused by inefficient diversification is 62.4 per cent ($= 1.000 - 0.376$), nearly 69 per cent

$$\left[ = \frac{0.624 - 0.370}{0.370} \right]$$

more than the discount imposed when $B_p = 1.000$.

These two examples indicate that the discount imposed on the value of assets by inefficient diversification decreases as the inherent riskiness (the systematic risk) of the asset increases whereas the discount rises (that is the cost of specific risk increases) as the systematic risk decreases. Together, all these examples illustrate the significance of diversification but indicate that the cost of inefficiency will affect different assets differently, uniformly rising as systematic risk falls. This occurs because as systematic risk falls, specific (avoidable) risk becomes a larger proportion of total risk.

These results are important because an examination of a sample of 475 Scottish probate inventories strongly suggests that British capital markets offered poor facilities for diversification.[31] The probate inventories, far from exhibiting the homogeneity predicted by the theory of efficient diversification, showed instead extensive segmentation along lines of wealth, occupation and location. The inventories exhibit very considerable willingness to take risks, especially among Glasgow industrialists, but, due to inefficient diversification, the risks were greater and the rewards less than might reasonably have been expected. Moreover, the pattern of risk-taking that does appear conforms to the pattern of discounts shown above in the three examples. Risk-taking in mining ventures, the pay-off to which would depend closely upon the overall level of economic activity, occurred more frequently than in technologically advanced areas like electrical engineering or chemical manufacture where the application of innovations proceeded at a more uniform rate,[32] possibly because so many of the products of those two industries in the late Victorian period made possible such cost savings in other sectors of the economy that demand for them was sustained even during recessions, thereby reducing the tendency for the prosperity of these two crucial industries to depend upon the buoyancy of the economy as a whole.

The high degree of covariance between the profitability of mining ventures and overall British economic activity would tend to make the systematic risk of mining a relatively large proportion of the industry's total risk, causing the 'stand-alone' price of participation in risky mining ventures to be relatively close to the price commanded by the same assets in efficient portfolios. The situation would be quite different in activities characterized by low beta values, for in those cases systematic risk would be only a small proportion of total risk and hence the 'stand-alone' price of participation in those activities would diverge widely from the price commanded by the same assets in an efficient portfolio.[33] Such a pattern of relationships between systematic risks and total risks would help explain the pattern of risky assets found in the probate inventories, where a willingness to take substantial risks was so much more clearly shown in the case of mining than in technologically progressive activities such as electrical engineering or chemical manufacture. It should be noted, however, that other factors, particularly the nature of personal contacts, the time horizon over which pay-offs were realized – manufacturing activities would generally require a longer time to register large gains – and technical complexity were also likely to have been important. In general then, the pattern of asset-holding found in British portfolios shows that despite the growing integration of British capital markets that Michie has recently discussed,[34] the costs of holding well-diversified portfolios were still too great to make them commonplace.

Evidence drawn from the asset yield data-base compiled by Michael Edelstein also indicates that the opportunities offered in London for the convenient buying and selling of foreign securities were badly exploited.[35] Assuming a limited form of foresight, in that wealth-holders of the period formed expectations of yield and risk in conformity with the rankings of actual outcomes (that is wealth-holders needed to rank assets by yield and risk, not predict what the level of yields and risks would actually be), efficient portfolios contained large proportions of domestic securities issued by technologically advanced industries operating at home combined with selected foreign assets. Foreign assets did indeed appear to offer valuable opportunities for diversification, but these opportunities were hardly ever seized. The efficient portfolios were ones almost never observed in reality. Domestic investors in advanced technology areas benefited little from enhanced diversification opportunities, very possibly because badly distorted financial markets did not allow them to sell shares in their operations to their fellow citizens at acceptable prices while those who invested heavily overseas did so in activities they also invested in liberally at home (e.g. railroads and government issues). Thus *rentiers* and large landowners, wealth-holders who apparently had few business commitments themselves, were generally the heaviest foreign investors. In all, relative to an optimal structure of prices, British asset prices appear to have been distorted in such a way that discouraged innovation and technological advance.

**Conclusion**

In conclusion then, it is argued that British capital markets performed their trinity of tasks poorly. The marked segmentation of wealth-holding patterns strongly suggests

41

that investors were unable to identify and evaluate all investment opportunities; at best, they appear only to have been aware of subsets of the possibilities, and the subsets known varied from group to group. It is a reasonable inference then that much of the information available in British capital markets was expensive to obtain and of low quality, creating sharp informational differentials among classes of assets and among groups of wealth-holders, differentials that led to sub-optimal choices relative to the choices that would have been made with more complete information of uniform costliness. Finally, the channels available to wealth-holders to monitor the managers of their investments and respond appropriately varied markedly across classes of assets but arguably were weakest and least effective in areas of new technology, where established links were least developed and thus most vulnerable to abuse. Certainly, as John Armstrong's paper in this volume makes clear, company promoters did not constitute a reliable channel through which shareholders could monitor their investments and exercise informed control over them. In any event, research in this area of shareholder information and control is sparse relative to its importance. In part, this may be because the theoretical importance of the matter has only recently been fully appreciated, but also because of the uncritical acceptance by historians of a model of financial intermediation in which it is assumed that the function of intermediaries is only to assist initiatives taken by either ultimate borrowers or lenders. The central nature of the intermediation process suggests, however, that the process itself is a fertile area for the practice of entrepreneurial initiative and that the inability of the British system of financial intermediation to give scope to economically beneficial initiatives was a serious weakness. All these considerations together induce the belief that capital markets were not submissive, compliant instruments lulled into somnolence through lack of stimulus and which were in any event responding to stronger forces while producing the strange pattern of Victorian resource allocation, but instead actively contributed to it.

### Appendix: A preliminary consideration of the macroeconomic implications of D. C. M. Platt's revised estimates of the level of British foreign investment in the nineteenth century.

Using the conventional estimates of British foreign investment combined with unpublished estimates of British gross domestic fixed capital formation prepared by Charles Feinstein – the latter series being consistently higher than the published version – Michael Edelstein shows Britain, relative to other advanced countries of the period, to have possessed an investment rate (the total national savings rate) that is well towards the lowest levels recorded for any advanced industrial country during the late nineteenth century. (See Table 2.2). Only Sweden exhibits a lower rate and even this may change as the Swedish national income statistics are revised in the same manner as Feinstein has revised the UK statistics. The main factor in the upward revisions proposed by Feinstein is an adjustment for small amounts of investment that were important in the aggregate but which too easily escaped detection. If comparable adjustments are justified for the other countries, then Britain's position

*Table 2.2    Gross national saving as a proportion of GNP in selected countries (1890/ 1910)*

| Countries | GNS/GNP | |
|---|---|---|
| | % | % |
| United States[a] | 21.7 | (21.5) |
| Germany[b] | 18.0 | (12.8) |
| Sweden[c] | 10.9 | |
| France[d] | 20.1 | |
| United Kingdom | 14.2 | |

*Notes:*
a. First figure: Gross Domestic Fixed Capital Formation (GDFCF).
   Second figure: GDFCF less net foreign investment (approximate).
b. 1First figure: Conservative estimate of GNS/GNP based on conversion of the ratio Net Domestic Fixed Capital Formation (NDFCF)/Net National Product (NNP) to the ratio GDFCF/GNP. Using British data for both gross and net domestic fixed capital formation taken from Feinstein, *National Income*, Tables 1, 3 and applying the same conversion ratio to the German NDFCF/NNP ratio yields a GDFCF/ GNP ratio for Germany of nearly 36 per cent. The figure 18.0 per cent was half that produced by the unaltered conversion ratio and is believed to be conservative.
   Second figure: NDFCF/NNP.
c. GDFCF only.
d. GDFCF only. Due to foreign investment, GNS was substantially higher.
*Source:*
Edelstein, *Overseas Investment*, Table 9.1 and, for the UK, Table 2.3.

at the bottom of the savings league will become more pronounced. What is important in this context is that before making allowance for Professor Platt's downward revision of British foreign investment, Britain appears to have invested relatively little. (See Table 2.2).

Platt's proposed revision reinforces this impression. If the conventional estimates of British foreign investment in the period 1860–1914 are uniformly reduced by 25 per cent, then, assuming GNP estimates to remain unchanged, the average British ratio of savings to GNP falls from the 14.2 per cent shown in Table 2.2 to a mere 13.0 per cent. The decrease will be somewhat less (but still significant) if GNP is revised downward, as it must be to preserve consistency in the national income accounts, but such a downward revision will only serve to make Britain's faltering growth performance appear even more feeble than it does on the basis of the conventional published estimates. The net macroeconomic consequence of Platt's revision is to propose a very troubled Victorian economy saving even less than has been widely believed, but allocating a larger share of the revised investment totals at home. The productivity collapse observed by Matthews *et al.* will thus appear even more pronounced in the revised figures than in the old.

*Table 2.3  Net foreign investment, gross national product, gross national accumulation, 1861–1913*

|  | (1)<br>NFI/Y | (2)<br>GNA/Y | (3)<br>NFI(P)/Y | (4)<br>GNA(P)/Y |
|---|---|---|---|---|
| 1861–70 | 0.037 | 0.129 | 0.028 | 0.120 |
| 1871–80 | 0.041 | 0.152 | 0.031 | 0.142 |
| 1881–90 | 0.055 | 0.141 | 0.041 | 0.127 |
| 1891–1900 | 0.030 | 0.132 | 0.022 | 0.124 |
| 1901–1910 | 0.047 | 0.142 | 0.035 | 0.130 |
| 1911–1913 | 0.087 | 0.170 | 0.065 | 0.140 |

NFI       = Net Foreign Investment
Y          = Gross National Product
GNA      = Gross National Accumulation
NFI(P)    = Net Foreign Investment (Platt's basis)
GNA(P)   = Gross National Accumulation (Platt's basis)
*Sources:*
Column (1) = Edelstein *Overseas Investment* Table 2.3 and Appendix 1 (for 1911/1913); Column (2) = Edelstein Table 2.3 and Appendix 1 (for 1911/1913); Column (3) = Column (1) × 0.75; Column (4) = Column (2) + Column (3) − Column (1).


Another aspect of Professor Platt's revisions concern the stability of Victorian national accumulation. The first two columns of Table 2.3 show the conventional estimates; the last two the picture if Platt's revisions are accepted.

Because the conventional estimates of British national accumulation show foreign investment tending to rise when domestic investment fell, thus imparting a stability to total accumulation, one might expect that acceptance of Platt's revisions would entail acceptance of a picture of Victorian investment at once more volatile and smaller than commonly believed, especially, in those increasingly frequent periods when British foreign investment was running at relatively high levels, since it would be during these periods when Platt's revisions would have the greatest impact. This is not, however, what emerges from Table 2.3; although the estimates of GNA are indeed smaller, column (4) exhibits virtually the same variance as column (2). This equality is due in part to the use of Feinstein's preliminary unpublished estimates of gross domestic fixed capital formation rather than his published series. Use of the earlier, published series would indeed cause column (4) to show greater variance, because foreign investment, which had by far the greater volatility, would then be a larger component of GNA. Another reason is that the decadal averages shown in Table 2.3 are too highly aggregated to offer a useful measure and that use of annual data processed by regression analysis would constitute the appropriate test.

# Notes

1. See C. H. Feinstein, *National Income, Expenditure and Output of the United Kingdom, 1855–1965* (Cambridge: Cambridge University Press, 1972), pp. 156–7, and D. C. M. Platt, 'British portfolio investment overseas before 1870. some doubts', *Economic History Review*, Vol. 33 (February 1980), pp. 1–16; *Foreign Finance in Continental Europe and the USA 1815–1870: Quantities, Origins, Functions and Distribution* (London: Allen & Unwin, 1984); *Britain's Investment Overseas on the Eve of the First World War* (London: Macmillan, 1986). A preliminary examination of the macroeconomic consequences of Professor Platt's revisions to the British national income accounts is presented in the Appendix, pp. 42–4.
2. M. Edelstein, *Overseas Investment in the Age of High Imperialism: The United Kingdom, 1850–1914* (New York: Columbia University Press, 1982), pp. 24–5. Edelstein's evidence relates to portfolio investment alone (*Overseas Investment*, pp. 18–19). Estimates of the volume and profitability of British direct investment are much less securely documented than are the portfolio estimates and hence vary more widely among the authors who venture an opinion on the subject. For the argument of this chapter, an estimate of the value of the stock of British direct investment in 1914 of £750,000,000 (versus the £500,000,000 estimated by Paish in 1909) is assumed, with an estimated average yield at least that of domestic British investment, at least for those investments in North America, Australasia and Europe. That substantial direct British foreign investment occurred in the decades before 1914 is not surprising and, to the extent it was undertaken by profitable and experienced enterprises, may be interpreted as a sign of economic vitality. The real puzzle lies in the huge volume of lower-yielding foreign portfolio investment and it is this less productive investment which is the focus of this chapter.
3. R. C. O. Matthews, C. H. Feinstein, and J. C. Odling-Smee, *British Economic Growth, 1856–1973* (Oxford: Clarendon Press, 1982), pp. 497–507.
4. William P. Kennedy, *Industrial Structure, Capital Markets, and the Origins of British Economic Decline* (Cambridge: Cambridge University Press, 1987), pp. 134–44.
5. This figure may be compared with the value of 15.9 per cent reported in the *Bank of England Quarterly Bulletin*, 26 (September 1986), p. 391, Table A, as the return on capital employed (historical cost basis) by a changing sample of the 1500 largest companies in the UK from the period 1970–85 (inclusive). The data reported here exclude oil companies, which had a higher rate of return throughout the period. The use of historical cost accounts in a period of rapid inflation approximates the rate of return gross of depreciation.
6. For details of this calculation, see Kennedy, *Industrial Structure*, pp. 187–8, Table E6.
7. Lance E. Davis and Robert A. Huttenback, 'The political economy of British imperialism: measures of benefit and support', *Journal of Economic History*, Vol. 42 (March 1982), pp. 120–5, have calculated the financial rates of return

on equity for a substantial number of British domestic, foreign and colonial ventures. They conclude (p. 122) that 'over the years it appears that foreign returns were if anything, slightly less than domestic' while being 'certainly much more variable'. They note (p. 124) that Empire returns 'were much above domestic in the decades of the 1860s and 1870s (there were relatively few firms), then fell substantially below domestic, recovering only in the years after 1905.' More recently, Davis and Huttenback, *Mammon and the Pursuit of Empire: The Political Economy of British Imperialism, 1860–1912* (Cambridge: Cambridge University Press 1986), pp. 91–6, 104–10, have confirmed these findings, noting again the contrast between the general (but not unbroken) vitality of the domestic economy and the fading yields earned by overseas investment, particularly in the Empire after 1880.

8.  While foreign mines at best compared reasonably well with good domestic investments in terms of average realized yield, they performed far worse in terms of the variance of realized yield. For an impressionistic discussion of the evidence, see Ranald C. Michie, 'Options, concessions, syndicates, and the provision of venture capital, 1880–1913', *Business History*, Vol. XXIII (July 1981), pp. 157. The inherent riskiness of foreign mines, of course, made them less attractive to risk-averse investors than domestic investments *with a similar expected yield*.

9.  Wayne Lewchuk, 'The return to capital in the British motor vehicle industry, 1896–1939', *Business History*, Vol. XXVIII (March 1986), p. 15, Table 3. Lewchuk makes clear that investment in the British motor industry before 1914 was hazardous, with especially high failure rates among the larger early firms. However, for all but the most risk-averse investor, the yields were high enough to compensate for the risk (an unweighted index of total return on the ordinary shares of all British public motor companies over the period 1905–13 outperformed a broad index of British foreign investments in the same period by a factor of three to one), especially if the investor held the shares of as many different firms as possible, with equal amounts invested in each firm, since before 1914 smaller firms tended to out-perform larger ones; see Lewchuk, 'Return', pp. 10–11, 16.

10. For an interesting account of one dimension of this vulnerability, see Corelli Barnett, *The Audit of War* (London: Macmillan 1986). It might be noted that, by not considering the long-term growth and productivity performance of the British economy, Barnett fails both to appreciate Britain's economic performance during World War II – which by comparison with Britain's performance relative to Germany's in the previous sixty years was reasonably good – and to comprehend the full seriousness of the late Victorian collapse of productivity growth.

11. Although the emphasis here is on the capital markets which allocated physical investment, the close link between these markets and the educational system, the main means by which human capital was created, should also be noted. Most importantly, the choices students will make among the educational system's offerings will depend upon their perceptions of subsequent career

opportunities as well as their assessments of their own capabilities and preferences. Hence any failure of capital markets to support the expansion of technologically progressive industries will be compounded by a related failure to promote scientific and technological education. A trap is thus created whereby technological activities once thwarted appear to continue to be unattractive to investors because of the lack of trained manpower while students are discouraged from technological areas because of the paucity of obvious job opportunities there, neither students nor investors being fully aware of their mutual dependence and lacking any means of beneficially coordinating their decisions. See Robert R. Locke, *The End of the Practical Man: Entrepreneurship and Higher Education in Germany, France and Great Britain, 1880–1940* (London: JAI Press, 1984), especially Chapters 1 and 2.

12. No general statement can be made about the impact of taxes upon an economy where substantial non tax-induced distortions exist, but the odds favour an outcome where taxation exacerbates rather than reduces the distortions.

13. Other aspects would include: (1) an attempt to measure the equality of expected risk-adjusted rates of return across activities; (2) the level and stability of the flow of resources to various activities capable of sustaining high rates of return, many of which would be closely related to technological progress; (3) the level of innovation, particularly in technologically advanced areas; (4) the rate of diffusion of innovations, again particularly in technologically advanced activities.

14. James Tobin, 'A general equilibrium approach to monetary theory', *Journal of Money, Banking and Credit,* Vol. 1 (February 1969), pp. 15–29.

15. In this context, it is important to note that a firm's capital stock is considered to include human resources, particularly the capacity to hire, retain and utilize highly qualified people. An example of the importance of this capacity may be drawn from the early history of electrical engineering. In his efforts to develop a workable incandescent lamp, Thomas Edison spent more than $50,000 over fifteen months on personnel and laboratory apparatus alone before the first successful prototypes emerged in 1878–9. Because he was able to spend so lavishly on personnel and equipment – having taken considerable care to establish and nurture good contacts on Wall Street – Edison was able to develop simultaneously with the incandescent lamp bulb the other components – the generators, switches, meters and so on – needed to support a complete lighting system. This system-wide approach made Edison one of the early leaders in a field that attracted many inventive minds all over the world. For further details see T. P. Hughes, *Networks of Power: Electrification in Western Society, 1880–1930* (Baltimore: Johns Hopkins University Press, 1983), pp. 24–42.

16. This adjustment will be accelerated the steeper is the upward sloping supply curve of the capital goods industry.

17. George A. Akerlof and Janet L. Yellin, 'Can small deviations from rationality make significant differences to economic equilibria?', *American Economic Review,* Vol. 75 (September 1985), pp. 708–20.

18. For details, see any reasonable microeconomics textbook such as Hal R. Varian, *Macroeconomic Analysis* (New York: W. W. Norton, 2nd edition, 1984), especially Chapter 2, pp. 80–1.

19. Only in nearly competitive situations where the 'monopolist' faces a highly but not infinitely elastic demand curve and is correspondingly highly exposed to market discipline will the difference in output $(Q_1 - Q_0)$ be large relative to $Q_0$. Hence only in these circumstances will the 'monopolist' necessarily be concerned to exploit all his advantages. In the competitive limit, all, even the most marginal, advantages must be exploited to avoid elimination from the industry.

20. I. C. R. Byatt, *The British Electrical Industry, 1875–1914* (Oxford: Clarendon Press, 1979), pp. 17–21. Leslie Hannah, *Electricity Before Nationalisation: A Study of the Development of the Electricity Supply Industry in Britain to 1948* (London: Macmillan, 1979), pp. 6–7.

21. I. C. R. Byatt, 'The British electrical industry, 1875–1914', (unpublished PhD thesis, Oxford University, 1962), pp. 360–70; I. C. R. Byatt, 'Electrical products', in Derek H. Aldcroft, *Development of British Industry and Foreign Competition, 1875–1914* (London: Allen & Unwin, 1968), pp. 255–8.

22. George A. Akerlof, 'The market for lemons: quality uncertainty and the market mechanism', *Quarterly Journal of Economics,* Vol. 90 (August 1970), pp. 488–500; William P. Kennedy, 'Notes on economic efficiency in historical perspective: the case of Britain, 1870–1914', in Paul H. Uselding (ed.), *Research in Economic History: A Research Annual, Vol. 9* (London: JAI Press, 1984), pp. 118–21.

23. Philip L. Cottrell, *Industrial Finance, 1830–1914: The Finance and Organization of English Manufacturing Industry* (London: Methuen, 1980), pp. 232–4.

24. Jürgen Kocka, 'Entrepreneurs and managers in German industrialization', in Peter Mathias and M. M. Postan (eds), *Cambridge Economic History of Europe,* Vol. VII, Part I: *The Industrial Economies: Capital, Labour, and Enterprise* (Cambridge: Cambridge University Press, 1978), pp. 558–63. Georg Siemens, trans. A. F. Rodger, *History of the House of Siemens,* Vol. I: *The Era of Free Enterprise* (Freiburg and Munich: Karl Alber, 1957), pp. 150–67.

25. William H. Reader, *Imperial Chemical Industries: A History,* Vol. I: *The Forerunners, 1870–1926* (Oxford: Clarendon Press, 1970), pp. 103–23. Reader's book was the main source used for the account of the early history of Brunner, Mond and United Alkali. For the flotation of United Alkali, see also Cottrell, *Industrial Finance,* p. 172.

26. Strictly speaking, $R_m$ should refer to the yield of a portfolio of all marketable assets, the weight of each asset determined by the ratio of the total value of each type of asset (i.e. its price per unit times the number of units outstanding) to the total value of all assets added together. For example, if the equities of a given company made up 0.001 per cent of the value of the total market portfolio, the yield of those equities would have a weight of 0.00001 in determining the yield of the market portfolio.

27. For a thorough discussion of the costs of inefficient diversification, see Haim Levy, 'Equilibrium in an imperfect market: a constraint on the number of securities in the portfolio', *American Economic Review,* Vol. 68 (September 1978), pp. 643–58. It should be noted that, as Levy's article makes clear, inefficient diversification has not been confined to Victorian Britain but is a pervasive problem. However, the structure of Victorian financial inter-mediation, bereft of individuals or institutions systematically spanning a wide range of activities through equity stakes, suggest that wealth-holding in Victorian Britain was particularly prone to inefficient diversification just at the time when increasing capital requirements and competitive pressures com-bined to increase sharply the costs of this deficiency.

28. Because ordinary least squares regression ensures that the estimated co-efficients are the best linear unbiased estimates of the true but unknown coefficients that can be obtained from the available data, the expected value of $B_j$ may be treated as a constant. The actual value of $B_j$, drawn from sample data of one sort or another, will of course deviate from the expected value because of sample error. While explicit recognition of the intrinsic variance of $B_j$ would serve to increase the expected variance of efficient portfolios, it would increase, through the addition of further terms, the expected variance of inefficient portfolios even more. Thus, the analysis of the costs of inefficient diversification given here may be considered a lower bound to the true costs.

29. Ideally the illustration would use historical data. However, although the data are available, it has not yet been collected and presented in a usable form. Therefore the examples use data extracted from the London Business School's Risk Measurement Service issue for July/September 1982. See Janette Rutterford, *Introduction to Stock Exchange Investment* (London: Macmillan, 1983), pp. 238–43, for details. Also note that had a single security rather than a portfolio of four been used in the illustration, the asset specific risk would have been greater, thus making the price discounts due to inefficient diversification even greater than they are in the examples given in the text.

30. This follows from the argument that the equilibrium price of an equity instrument is equal to the expected present discounted value of the stream of dividends it yields, as in the following equation:

$$P_{oj} = \left[ \frac{D_{ij}}{(1+R_{jm})} \right] + \left[ \frac{D_{2j}}{(1+R_{jm})^2} \right] \ldots + \left[ \frac{D_{n}+P_{nj}}{(1+R_{jm})^n} \right]$$

where $P_{0j}$ = equilibrium price of asset j at time t=0;
$\quad\quad$ $D_{ij}$ = dividend on asset j paid at time i, i=1, . . .n;
$\quad\quad$ $P_{nj}$ = price of equity at time n
$\quad\quad$ $R_{jm}$ = equilibrium expected yield on asset j; equal to $E_{jm}$ in text
$\quad\quad\quad\quad$ Equation (7).
For simplicity assume that dividend payments remain unchanged forever (i.e. $D_{ij} = D_{ij} = \ldots = D_{nj}D_j$), a conservative assumption that particularly

undervalues assets likely to support increased dividends. Then, letting n become arbitrarily large:

$$P_{oj} = \left[ \frac{D_j}{R_{jm}} \right]$$

Normalizing all assets for their dividend such that $D_j = D_i$ for all assets i and j, prices (per unit of dividend) will vary only by the inverse of their equilibrium yield,

$$\left[ \frac{1}{R_{jm}} \right]$$

31. For a discussion of the probate inventory data and their interpretation, see William P. Kennedy and Rachel Britton, 'Portfolioverhalten und Wirtschaftliche Entwicklung im späten 19. Jahrhundert: Ein Vergleich zwischen Grossbritannien und Deutschland. Hypothesen unde Spekulationen', in Richard Tilly (ed.), *Beiträge zur Quantitativen Vergleichenden Unternehmensgeschichte* (Stuttgart: Klett-Cotta, 1985), pp. 59–74.

32. This claim abstracts from the consequences of large shifts of investment between domestic and foreign destinations. See Kennedy, *Industrial Structure,* Chapter 6, for a discussion of how large-scale shifts between foreign and domestic investment increased the riskiness of technologically progressive investments in the domestic Victorian economy. For evidence of the counter-cyclical nature of technologically progressive investments, see G. Mensch, *Stalemate in Technology: Innovations Overcome the Depression* (Cambridge, Mass.: Harvard University Press, 1979). Mensch's evidence is discussed in Solomos Solomou, *Phases of Economic Growth, 1850–1973: Kondratieff Waves and Kuznets Swings* (Cambridge: Cambridge University Press, 1987), pp. 89–100, who is not inclined to attach much weight to it. But note that Solomou, *Phases,* pp. 99–100, is cautious in dismissing Christopher Freeman's notion that innovations might cluster in a counter-cyclical Schumpeterian 'swarming effect'.

33. Although these results were derived using the Capital Asset Pricing Model (CAPM) which relies upon a number of strong assumptions, there are grounds for believing that the results are nevertheless broadly robust. First, the CAPM results can be shown to hold when most of the assumptions upon which the model depends for its relatively easy derivation are relaxed. Secondly, the CAPM can be shown to be a special case of a more general theory, the Arbitrage Pricing Theory (APT), which is the most clearly articulated alternative model to the CAPM. Finally, testing of the APT shows that the covariance of the yield of an asset (or group of assets) to the market portfolio yield is the dominant factor in determining risk (and the price of risk) although in the APT, unlike the CAPM, other factors (which factor analysis cannot identify but only detect) are also important. For these reasons, it is reasonable

to expect that while a more satisfactory model than the CAPM will yield somewhat different results, the CAPM offers a useful approximation. Indeed, so far only powerful and subtle statistical tests have uncovered any difference at all. Hence a margin of error of less than 25 per cent in the estimates of the cost of risk would appear to be well within the capabilities of the CAPM. See T. E. Copeland and J. F. Weston, *Financial Theory and Corporate Policy* (Reading, Mass.: Addison-Wesley, 2nd edition, 1983), Chapter 7, for further discussion.

34. Ranald C. Michie, 'The London Stock Exchange and the British securities market, 1850–1914', *Economic History Review,* XXXVIII (February 1985), pp. 61–82; and Idem, 'The London and New York Stock Exchanges, 1850–1914', *Journal of Economic History,* Vol. 46 (March 1986), pp. 171–81. See also *The London and New York Stock Exchanges* (London 1987).

35. The data are found in Michael Edelstein, 'The rate of return on UK home and foreign investment, 1870–1913' (unpublished PhD thesis, University of Pennsylvania), Appendices III and IV, pp. 275–300. The data are analysed in William P. Kennedy, 'Portfolio behaviour and economic development in the late nineteenth century – observations on Great Britain and Germany: hypotheses and conjectures', in Joel Mokyr (ed.), *The Vital One: Essays in Honor of Jonathan R. T. Hughes* (Greenwich, Conn.: JAI Press, forthcoming).

# 3 The clearing banks and industry – new perspectives on the inter-war years

*Duncan M. Ross*[1]

## Introduction

The banking system in Britain has long been considered to be at best indifferent to the needs of industry for capital; and the provision of industrial finance has equally been considered to be outwith the bounds of normal banking practice. W. A. Thomas, writing a textbook on the financing of British industry, felt it necessary to justify the inclusion of two chapters on the contribution of the banking system, one dealing with the years either side of the 1939–45 war, fearing that this may have been over generous. He argued that from a strictly banking viewpoint it is not a major function of the banking system to provide funds either short term or long term for industry '. . . there is no duty on the banking system to provide finance for industry'.[2]

Most work on the relationship between the clearing banks and industry in the inter-war years centres either on the role of the Bank of England and its offshoots in trying to effect rationalization in the staple industries, primarily steel and cotton,[3] or on specific cases which by their nature are exceptional in some way.[4] This chapter is an attempt to gauge the extent to which we can unquestioningly accept the idea, on which much of the previous work is based, that there was some kind of institutional separation between the banking system and industry in this period. By taking the methodology a little further, and looking at the lending patterns and the relationships established by two of the major English banks, Midland and Lloyds, across a range of industrial customers, it is hoped that a more representative picture of the banks' attitudes towards this kind of business will emerge.

The first section traces the historical development of the banking system and industry in Britain, and considers the close, almost symbiotic nature of the relationship between the two sectors for much of the nineteenth century. The second section then outlines the various arguments presented to the (Macmillan) Committee on Finance and Industry in 1929–30. This evidence is of great importance since it represents the authentic voice of the main proponents, both bankers and industrialists, in the debate. The third section contains the bulk of the empirical evidence, gleaned from various archival sources, in support of a new perspective on the nature of the nexus which existed between these two sectors of the economy. While not absolving the banking system totally from criticism, the argument will be made that much more time and effort was devoted to supporting and assisting industrial customers than has hitherto been appreciated.

## The nineteenth century experience

It is generally accepted that throughout much of the nineteenth century, while there were a number of factors dictating the duration, scale and nature of lending, there can be little doubt that a close relationship existed between banks and businesses in the same locality.[5] This relationship was rooted in the mutual benefit to be gained from a prosperous local economy, and was often nurtured by very close ties of family, friendship and interlocking directorships. In many cases bankers and industrialists would even be the same people. The advances involved were often small-scale or short-term, but could in practice be easily converted into long-term loans as confidence grew and a good working relationship was established between the two parties. Ollerenshaw, in his work on Irish banking in the nineteenth century, makes great play of the discretionary element in the policies of the Belfast banks in this period.[6]

The close and supportive relationship established in the nineteenth century, however, has been seen as containing the seeds of its own destruction.[7] Too close an identification with many local firms, and consequent over-lending in times of expansion, led directly, under this analysis, to the spate of bank failures which culminated in the collapse of the City of Glasgow Bank in 1878. Having had their fingers burnt playing with the fire of industrial lending, and not immune to the prevailing wind of concentration blowing throughout the economy in this period, the banks chose to recoil from this business and seek the consoling company of other banks in a flurry of amalgamations. Indeed, the number of joint-stock banks fell from 109 in 1886 to 38 in 1914,[8] and by 1917, two-thirds of the resources of the banking system in England and Wales were concentrated in the five major clearing banks – Lloyds, Barclays, Midland, National Provincial and Westminster.[9] In Scotland, the 'Big Seven' (Bank of Scotland, Commercial Bank of Scotland, National Bank of Scotland, Royal Bank of Scotland, Union Bank of Scotland, Clydesdale Bank and the British Linen Bank) remained, perhaps due to the kind of competitive cartel in which they operated, presided over by the General Managers' Committee. Affiliation and a measure of amalgamation was to come to this system in the 1920s.[10] This argument continues that, increasingly attracted by the relatively safe profits to be made in foreign transactions at the end of the nineteenth century, and having lost much of their commitment to the local economies from which they had developed, these large banks began to pay less attention to their industrial business.

## The bankers' views

The separation of the banking system from industry was a key issue in the testimony of the representatives of the major banks before the Committee on Finance and Industry (Macmillan Committee). The Macmillan Committee was set up in November 1929 'to enquire into banking, finance and credit . . . and to make recommendations calculated to enable these agencies to promote the development of trade and commerce and the employment of labour'. Implicit in this minute of appointment and central to much of the report was the realization that the financial system had an important role to play in determining the level of prosperity in the economy at any particular time. Sir James Lithgow, Vice-President of the Federation of British Industry, writing to a member of the FBI Committee on Finance and Industry set up to consider evidence to Macmillan, argued that 'there is, to my mind, far too great a tendency both for labour and industry to seek to put the blame on some third party, the popular scapegoat at the moment being the bankers'.[11] In the bleak economic conditions of 1930–31, with the financial system being pilloried as a contributory factor in the depression, the Macmillan Committee saw its main task as considering the extent to which the various financial institutions could be held responsible, and how they might aid recovery.[12]

Given that this was the case, the public utterances of the bankers before the Committee were extremely defensive, perhaps even aggressively so. One of the most remarkable things about their evidence was its consistency. The bankers argued that there were three main characteristics in their dealings with industrial customers. First, it was not their place to formulate policies for dealing with the problems of British industry; second, all creditworthy borrowers would be accommodated; and third, bank finance was provided for the purposes of working capital only, and not for investment in capital assets.

They felt that it would have been an extremely dangerous development if the banks, either individually or collectively, began to form industrial policies for dealing with their customers, rather than considering the circumstances of each case individually. That way lay the path of intervention in affairs external to their proper sphere of business. Goodenough, the Chairman of Barclays, felt that an industrial policy on the part of the banks would be undesirable because

> it would militate against the liquidity of the banks and that would in its turn militate against our large foreign earnings, and that in turn would militate against our balancing our imports and exports, and we should find ourselves very soon unable to pay our way.[13]

Particular antipathy was reserved for the idea that the banks should become actively involved in promoting mergers or schemes of rationalization. In these remarks can be seen the dislike which the clearing bankers had for the Bankers Industrial Development Company (BIDC), and the Securities Management Trust (SMT), bodies which had been created precisely with these functions in mind, and which the banks felt had been foisted on them.[14] They also countered the argument that the biggest failure of the banking system in these years was its inability or unwillingness to use the power it held by virtue of many firms' indebtedness to force large-scale mergers and rationalization in the staple industries. The *Economist* in January 1930 criticized the banks for exercising extreme caution when using their influence to promote reorganization,[15] while Hewit, the most vociferous member of the FBI industry and finance committee, lambasted the banks for not taking a more direct and active role in this direction.[16]

J. W. Beaumont-Pease, the Chairman of Lloyds, argued that taking the intitiative in promoting industrial mergers or greater integration was 'not one of the functions of our English joint-stock banks',[17] while John Rae, Director and Chief General Manager of the Westminster, entirely rejected the idea of banks assuming responsibility for the running of industry in any way.[18] Reginald McKenna, a former Chancellor, now Chairman of the Midland and a member of the Macmillan Committee, made the point while interviewing Sir James Lithgow (the shipbuilder, but representing the FBI at the Committee) that Lithgow would not refuse an order for a ship on the grounds of there being too many ships in existence, and continued: 'It is our business to provide our clients with credit when they ask for it, just as I suggest that it is your business to build the ship that the shipowner orders from you.'[19]

The second strand of the argument presented by the bankers to the Committee was that a request for an advance was seldom refused, provided that the applicant met the bank's criteria of security and creditworthiness. Bank financing of industry almost exclusively took the form of an overdraft/open credit account, by which an amount of money was made available to the business.[20] The entire accommodation could be utilized, or none of it. The limits were set according to the needs of the business, and its ability to repay. In Scotland, this service was known as a cash credit, a form of provision legally unknown in England, although in fact the two systems operated along very similar lines.[21]

This overdraft service, the banks maintained, was open to all who applied for it, and who could meet their requirements regarding repayment. Beaumont-Pease attested to the fact that he could not remember the case of a meritorious advance being refused,[22] while W. H. N. Goschen, Chairman of the National Provincial, felt that his bank had always been able to provide funds for "any well-managed concern that offers reasonable possibilities of profit".[23] It must be remembered, however, that issues such as what constituted a meritorious advance or a well-managed concern were essentially value-judgements and certainly varied from bank to bank. The chairman of the north-east regional board of Lloyds in the 1930s, later a Deputy Chairman of the bank itself, remembered that body being in despair about requests for finance from several people whom they had supported being turned down by the main Board. Barclays, he felt, were much more adventurous and consequently gained considerable business from Lloyds.[24]

The third major line of argument presented by the bankers was that bank overdrafts were a service provided to businesses for the purposes of working capital only. They disliked providing funds for capital investment or speculative activities;

'The sort of applications that we should most favourably consider would be those from our trading customers who want temporary accommodation in connection with their ordinary in and out business – not applications for capital expenditure but just temporary advances that in the course of a few weeks or possibly a few months would liquidate themselves'.[25]

This, obviously, is the purist argument regarding the role of the banks in providing industrial finance, and is a response to the criticisms that had been formed of the banks becoming too heavily involved in many firms, and so protecting inefficient and unprofitable concerns from bankruptcy. The Balfour Committee, for instance, had noted that 'the more dangerous temptation to the banks in present circumstances is to do too much rather than too little to keep weak concerns in being'.[26]

The National Chamber of Trade, in its submission to the Macmillan Committee, had argued that the essential point to be made when considering bank loans to industry was that 'the highest standards of wise and conservative finance must be maintained'.[27] Implicit in these observations was the fear that 'the highest standards of wise and conservative finance' had not been maintained in the period after the war. Balogh noted that the sharp expansion in bank advances recorded after World War I was a result of credit policies that were 'not conservative. Many advances were granted which should never have been permitted'.[28]

The post-war boom of 1919–20 certainly saw a substantial increase in bank lending. Advances of all banks rose from £580 million in 1919 (38.4 per cent of deposits) to £832 million (48.4 per cent of deposits) in 1920.[29] Tolliday has shown that the high profits to be gained in the steel industry in these years overcame traditional banking caution, and many overdrafts were granted without much in the way of systematic credit analysis on the part of the banks. The downturn of the 1920s meant that many of these overdrafts were soon converted into frozen loans which then had to be nursed through the 1920s and 1930s.[30]

Bamberg's work on the cotton industry has illustrated a very similar pattern.[31] In 1919–20, many spinning mills were purchased at highly inflated prices with money borrowed from the banks. This was to be repaid from the proceeds of a re-flotation of the company, or from future profits if this proved insufficient to cover the entire amount of the loan. When the boom broke in the second half of 1920, some of the banks were caught with substantial advances made to companies that could not be re-floated at a value anywhere near the levels at which they had been bought. Additionally, the fall in profits meant that repayment of the debts from that source was no longer an option. The only hope the banks had of regaining their capital was to nurse the companies through the inter-war years, pending an upturn in trading conditions. Progressively, the indebtedness of the cotton-spinning industry became concentrated in the banking system which served it.[32] By the mid-1920s it was clear that the problems of the cotton industry and its bankers had become inextricably linked. The Bank of England was forced to intervene, 'partly to help the cotton industry, partly to keep the question away from politics, but more especially to relieve certain of the banks from a dangerous position'.[33]

The way in which this nursing of an overdraft could become a frozen loan was put to Frederick Hyde, Managing Director of the Midland, by Lord Macmillan,

'Do you find yourselves insensibly passing the line between a bank's legitimate business and the position . . . of being investors? You may embark first of all on a course of business with a customer which is pure banking business. You are tiding him between when he is manufacturing his goods and the time when he gets his money in, but depression overtakes that business and you find the customer is not able, when the due date arrives, to meet his obligations. You are sympathetic; you give him a renewal and increase the figure. May not that process result in the course of time, by this insensible addition, in your waking up one morning and finding that you have passed from being his banker to being to all intents and purposes a participator in his business? – Yes'.[34]

In fact, the major banks were quite deeply involved in the affairs of a number of businesses. The Midland was a major creditor of the Lancashire cotton industry,[35] Lloyds was mostly involved in the coal industry of the north-east coast of England and the south Wales steel industry,[36] while the National Provincial was deeply concerned with iron and steel and the Yorkshire woollen trade.[37] Hewit, a member of the Calico Printers Association, told the FBI committee that the District Bank of Manchester had

'advanced money in all directions to the mills; they put one man on to the work and in a few years that man knew more than the mill owners and told them where to buy their cotton etc.; and worked the whole thing on overdrafts.'[38]

Goschen felt that many large concerns in the iron and steel industry were 'very much in the hands of the banks . . . the banks are able to put them in liquidation if necessary'.[39] The adverse effects of such a move in creating further unemployment were, however, seen as outweighing the financial risks taken by continuing to support these concerns.

One of the most explicit statements of this is contained in Lloyds' (whom we have already seen was considered even by its own management to be a conservative bank) involvement with the Rover company. Extending their overdraft limit to £220,000 in June 1932, the bank stated that 'In extending this accommodation given to the Company [Lloyds are] taking considerable risk out of regard for shareholders, suppliers, distributors, work-people, and all others interested in the Company.'[40] We can see therefore that while the banks professed not to deal with their industrial customers on anything other than a narrowly defined sound and profitable basis, in fact this position, by the time of the Macmillan Committee, had been considerably eroded. Ill-advised loans in the brief inflationary boom of 1919–20 came home to roost in the succeeding decade, and it appears that the banks were not as immune or as cold-hearted in their approach to forcing businesses into liquidation as the implications of a policy of non-involvement in business would surely have dictated.

Holmes and Green, in their history of the Midland Bank, have hinted at an explanation to this paradox between the story which the bankers would have liked everyone to believe, and the actual situation as grudgingly conceded by Hyde to Lord Macmillan. They argue that public pronouncements by the banks on their levels of support for industrial customers would first have been a breach of confidentiality, and second would have released information to competitors on interest rates, securities and the asset and market position of each customer.[41] Additionally, as

Bamberg has shown for the cotton industry, it was possible for the competitive position of the banks to dictate against them forcing any firm into liquidation. To do so would have meant a loss of confidence on the part of its less indebted customers, who would have fled to its competitors leaving the bank with a greater concentration of high-risk accounts.[42]

It seems then, that the banks were open to criticism no matter how they conducted their industrial business. Too little involvement and they were lambasted for not using their position of influence to effect rationalization in the staple industries. On the other hand, if the banks became too greatly involved in the affairs of the firms with which they dealt, criticism focused on the risky, non-conservative nature of such business, and stressed that it was not the role of the banks to undertake this type of lending. It must be borne in mind, however, that the one example of active lending to which the detractors of the banks were able to point, the post-war boom, was indeed a period of which the banks had every right to be embarrassed.

## Lending patterns – some evidence

C. W. Munn, in his work on the Clydesdale, has shown how a history of an individual bank can include a number of illustrations of the working of the relationship between a bank and its industrial and commercial customers.[43] His evidence, taken from a wide variety of the bank's customers across a number of industries, shows not so much a bank shy of contact with this kind of business, but one keen in fact to attract industrial clients. The building, engineering, automobile, textile, shipbuilding and service and retail sectors were all sought out and materially aided by the generous provision of overdraft and loan facilities by the bank. It is possible that the Clydesdale, a bank situated in the industrial heartland of Scotland, will be in many senses untypical of the entire British system. Table 3.1, however, is an attempt to take this kind of empirical methodology a stage further, by presenting some observations on the working of a number of industrial accounts in Midland and Lloyds banks in the 1930s. By looking at the industrial lending activities of two banks across a range of firms and sectors, it is possible to make better informed comments and come to more representative conclusions on the role of the banks in providing finance for their industrial customers, as well as on the importance of bank provision to these customers, than has hitherto been possible. The data were extracted from a number of sources in Midland and Lloyds archives,[44] and for reasons of customer confidentiality, the individual companies must remain anonymous.

There are a number of general comments which should be made regarding the data in Table 3.1. It does not purport to be a representative sample of British industry in the inter-war years. In terms of sampling theory, indeed, it is almost entirely worthless. However, it should be stressed that extracting the data from the archives of the two banks involved a considerable amount of cross-referencing of records, guess-work and sheer luck. A larger and more representative cross-section of British industry was simply impossible to create. The table is offered, therefore, on the

Table 3.1  Some observations on bank relationships with industrial customers Midland and Lloyds Banks, 1930s

| Industries | Total firms in sample (1) | Renewal a formality (2) | Security problems (3) | Unsecured overdraft (4) | Refused increase (5) | Demand reduction (6) | Bad debt provision (7) | Liquidation (8) | Merger/supervision (9) | Finance reconstruction (10) | Capital expenditure (11) | Not categorized (12) |
|---|---|---|---|---|---|---|---|---|---|---|---|---|
| Cotton spinning | 9 | | 2 | | 1 | | 1 | 3 | | 2 | | |
| Worsted spinning | 1 | | | | 1 | | 1 | | 1 | | | |
| Woollen manufacture | 2 | | 1 | | 1 | 1 | | | | | | |
| Jute manufacture | 1 | 1 | | | | | | | | | | |
| Textile merchants | 1 | | 1 | | | | | | | 1 | | |
| Textile machine manufacture | 1 | | | | | | | | | 1 | | 1 |
| Coal mining | 2 | 1 | | 1 | | 1 | | | | | | |
| Iron and steel | 6 | 1 | 3 | 1 | 2 | 2 | | | 1 | 2 | | |
| Heavy engineering | 5 | | | 2 | | | | | 3 | | | |
| Shipbuilding | 2 | 1 | 2 | | 1 | | | | | | | |
| Aircraft manufacture | 4 | | 2 | 2 | 1 | | | | 1 | | | |
| Motor manufacture | 1 | 2 | 1 | 1 | 1 | | | | 1 | | | 2 |
| Metal manufacture | 1 | | | 1 | 1 | | | | | | 1 | |
| Light engineering | 3 | | | 1 | 1 | 1 | | | 1 | | | |
| Leather merchants | 1 | | | | | 1 | | | | | | |
| Rubber | 2 | | | 1 | 1 | | | | 1 | | 1 | |
| Chemicals | 4 | 2 | 2 | 1 | 1 | | | | 1 | | | |
| Cable manufacture | 1 | | 1 | 1 | 2 | | | 1 | 1 | | | |
| Electrical engineering | 7 | 3 | 1 | 1 | 2 | | | 1 | 1 | 1 | | |
| Paper manufacture | 2 | 1 | 1 | | 1 | | | | | 1 | | 1 |
| Shipping | 6 | 1 | | 1 | | | | | 3 | 1 | | 2 |
| Garage | 1 | 1 | | | | | | | | | 1 | |
| Builder | 2 | | | | | | | | | | 1 | |
| Total | 66 | 14 | 17 | 14 | 17 | 6 | 2 | 4 | 15 | 8 | 4 | 6 |

Observations

Source: See text.

historian's premise that some information from which we can draw (guarded) conclusions is better than no information whatsoever.

The presence of a company in the sample is a reflection purely of the availability of records relating to it and as it is essentially an exercise in straightjacketing elements that may change over time, there are a number of inconsistencies and repetitions in the table. One firm is present in both coal mining and iron and steel, and several are represented in more than one column. There is quite a close relationship, for example, between those firms that experience trouble finding sufficient security to underpin their overdrafts, and those refused an increase in their limit, or of whom a reduction in their indebtedness was demanded. Similarly, the presence of one characteristic may have precluded the operation of another. In many cases, an inability to provide security, or an unsatisfactory profit and loss account or capital position meant that renewal of an overdraft was much more than a formality and involved protracted negotiations. Meanwhile, the bank often continued to provide support in the form of substantial accommodation. There are a number of reasons why six firms are not categorized and appear only in columns (1) and (12). Mostly they are present in the records in negotiations regarding interest or discount rates. The fact that these were negotiable is of considerable interest in itself.

Despite its shortcomings, the table does provide some interesting general insights into the operations of two banks across a range of different industries and on the nature of overdraft accommodation. It will be possible later to illustrate these with some individual case-study material.

We can see that the banks in question did not strictly adhere to the policies which they professed to the Macmillan Committee. Columns 9 and 10 indicate that the banks took a close interest in the running of many firms, as well as financing a number of mergers and capital reconstructions. The type of involvement indicated by categorizing a company as coming under the supervision of their bank is varied. In most cases, it represents a situation where the bank insisted on the production of periodic (weekly, monthly) figures if the company were working fairly consistently at the limits of their overdraft, or were pressing to have those limits raised. In some cases, however, the supervision took the form of daily interviews and very close involvement with the company over a short period. Such a 'hands-on' approach is obviously at odds with the banker-preferred image of distance between the two groups.

Column 2 indicates that many firms were able to have their overdraft facility renewed with very little difficulty. This would usually be at intervals of three, six or twelve months, and was a purely formal arrangement. In many cases this simple renewal was repeated throughout the decade.

Column 3 is an indication that the security provided by a firm was often an important factor in determining whether an overdraft could be granted, and if so, the extent of such provision. The types of security considered acceptable to the banks were many and varied, ranging from insurance policies on directors' lives, personal or joint and several guarantees, to a mortgage and charge on assets, or a freehold on premises. Promissory notes, debentures, government stocks and equity in the borrower or parent company were all cited as acceptable backing for an overdraft. There is some evidence that the amount of security required was dependent on the length of time for which the company in question had been a customer of the bank, how satisfactory the balance sheet position was, or the state of the profit and loss account. If these were satisfactory, there were in fact many occasions when the bank would offer unsecured overdrafts or loans, and column 4 is an indication of this. While the phenomenon is perhaps surprising, given the bankers' protestations on the need for creditworthiness and security, the extent of this kind of accommodation is certainly so. In addition to these companies operating overdrafts without any security, there are also many cases of indebtedness being only partially secured.

Many of these points can be illustrated by reference to individual companies contained in the table. The case of one cotton spinning firm banking with the Midland is particularly illuminating. The result of a previous combination, but not full merger, between a prosperous company and a loss-making one, the combined company was by August 1930 suffering under the heavy burden of the latter's debentures.[45] The company had a limit of £650,000 on their account, against which the bank held first debentures of £1 million, charged against assets. The bank insisted on a reduced combined limit on the accounts of £620,000, of which the loss-making company had not to account for more than £450,000. They also asked for economies of at least £20,000 per year in the running of the firm.

Sir William McLintock, a noted cotton industry entrepreneur and merger promoter, was called in by the directors to assess the company's prospects, and on 15 December he presented a plan for reconstruction which included a complete merger of the two companies.[46] After an analysis of the balance sheet of the combined company and of the merger proposals, the bank felt that the company would experience serious liquidity problems and the proposal was impracticable.[47] They submitted a counter-proposal, the main characteristic of which was greater protection for the bank; in the following two months negotiations continued regarding a reconstruction of the company. The bank for its part was insistent that their advances be fully secured and refused to raise the overdraft limit to £700,000.

On 10 February 1931, the issue appears to have been settled, with the bank agreeing to continue the limit of £600,000 for one year, the security to be a first charge on the prosperous company's, and 4/7th of the combined assets of both companies.[48] Prospects for the company obviously improved, for in December 1934, carrying a limit of £532,000, they asked for an increase of £15,000. The bank agreed, noting that they were busy and that the future looked good.[49]

There are two major points to emerge from this. In the first place, it is interesting that the bank, instead of simply disagreeing with the proposed merger, felt it necessary to put forward an alternative proposal of their own. Second, it is clear that the bank saw the security of their advance as being of paramount importance in any reconstruction of the company. A similar priority was to be found in the case of a textile machinery manufacturer. This company had an overdraft limit at the Midland of £120,000 in June 1931, in support of which the bank held a mortgage and charge over all assets.[50] They had been making profits and were proposing to enter an amalgamation scheme mooted by Sir Gilbert Garnsey. The scheme provided that each of the companies involved were to transfer such of their assets as were to be taken over by the combined company, which was to be the trading company. They would then receive ordinary shares in a subsidiary company in payment for their fixed assets and preference shares for the liquid assets. These shares were then to be exchanged, one for one, in the holding company.

The bank, however, felt that if this scheme were to be carried through, they would have great difficulty in realizing their assets. In addition, they did not regard shares in the combine as suitable security. They therefore would not agree to the scheme, but offered to continue their advance to the company for a further six months at a reduced level of £100,000. This was then to be further reduced by the proceeds of the uncalled capital, which the bank insisted was to be called in immediately.[51] The company argued that the bank's conditions would result in liquidation, and early in 1932 in fact joined the Textile Machinery Merger Ltd., in which the bank had to accept shares as security.[52] The bank considered them to be less than wholly satisfactory as security for the loan and quickly set about trying to sell them.[53]

An example from Lloyds of a Manchester firm of textile importers and exporters serves to illustrate the involvement of that bank in supporting one of its customers through a re-organization. This company was experiencing difficulties at the end of 1932 in effecting a re-organization of their capital, and throughout 1933 had to ask the bank to grant continued extensions to their overdraft.[54] In June of that year, at a meeting of the creditors of the company, it was revealed that the liabilities of the company, at £50,500 (£5,500 to the bank, £10,000 to trade creditors and £35,000 on loan account to the proprietor), were well in excess of the assets, which stood at £16,000.[55] The company made an offer to the creditors of twelve to thirteen shillings in the pound for the assignment of the respective claims, failing which the proprietor would rank as an ordinary creditor, and the dividend would be reduced to five or six shillings.[56] The latter course was adopted, and the bank, while pressing for payment of its dividends, continued to provide substantial overdraft facilities.[57] The company was forced to write off loan capital to the extent of £40,000 in its reconstruction, and the bank insisted on the production of half-yearly balance sheets. In February 1936 the company went into voluntary liquidation, and a new one of the same name was formed, the bank agreeing to carry loan facilities forward to the new company. They refused however to release the owner of the company from his personal guarantee.[58]

What we can see very strongly in these cases of bank involvement and support throughout a merger or capital reconstruction is the managerial function and the close supervision which in many cases the banks were drawn into. One of the most startling examples of this was the Midland's involvement in a worsted spinning firm. This company was carrying an overdraft of around £250,000 in the first two years of the 1930s, and while the bank continually pressed for a reduction, none was forthcoming.[59] A doubtful debt provision of £40,000 had been made, and a balance sheet dated 31 October 1932 showed liabilities of £304,000 and assets of £168,400. The bank considered the security it held (debentures and the joint and several guarantee of the directors) to be approximately £9,000 short of the amount outstanding.[60] They also thought that the company directors were paying themselves too much and insisted on a reduction of their remuneration to a maximum of £1,000 per annum each and required them to appoint an accountant to supervise the banking account 'and all cheques would have to be initialled by our supervisor'.[61] These measures allowed the company to remain solvent, although eighteen months later the bank granted a further overdraft, noting that 'we must keep up pressure to get this down'.[62]

In all these examples it appears that the sole motive of the bank in becoming involved in the affairs of their customers was to protect their original loan or to improve the nature of their security. As noted above, however, security was not the only driving force behind the banks and many loans and overdrafts were granted without security. One example of this is a Newcastle engineering company which banked with Lloyds in this period. In November 1931, this company was granted an overdraft of £50,000 for 12 months on absolutely no security,[63] while later in the same decade their overdraft limit was consistently well in excess of the security offered to the bank.

Even in those cases where the bank was reasonably satisfied with the working of an account, and where the security and profit and loss position was satisfactory, the Midland felt within its rights to suggest that improvements could be made in the financial position of the company. Considering one such account of an iron and steel company, the bank felt that although the security was adequate, and the loan was not in any serious danger, that 'it is evident . . . that more capital is needed to relieve the bank overdraft'.[64] This firm provides another example of the bank tiding the company through a period of some difficulty. The company was unable to issue any new capital at the time requested by the bank, and although they refused to raise the overdraft limit, it stood at £200,000 for the first two years of the 1930s, a situation with which the bank was not unduly unhappy.[65]

Such supportiveness could not be relied on by every firm, regardless of financial situation or profitability, whether that be actual or potential. If a bank saw no mitigating factors, it was not slow to insist on liquidation. This was the situation with a number of cotton firms. One such firm had, in February 1935, an overdraft of £115,000 on which the Midland had made a doubtful provision of £45,873. The firm had been experiencing bad trading results for a number of years, and the bank, after examining the balance sheet and finding the assets : liabilities position to be unsatisfactory, 'Agreed that we would tell the company we were not prepared to continue our loan. They must either sell the mill or the company must go into liquidation'.[66] The mill was eventually sold for scrap after being refused by the Lancashire Cotton Corporation.

Despite the fact that most of the firms that had bank support withdrawn were in the cotton industry (75 per cent of those in the table), there appears to have been no policy formulation either in favour of or against any particular industry. These decisions were based on the merits of each individual case, and while the general state of an industry may have had some role in determining the quality of security offered (e.g. cotton spindles being valued at fairly low prices for much of the 1930s), on the whole there is no evidence to support a hypothesis of systematic policy bias. It has been noted above that a number of cotton firms were supported through a capital reconstruction by their bank. The Management Committee of Midland, surveying the account of one iron and steel company in June 1932 concluded that 'We have to be satisfied that there is a prospect of them carrying on the business without loss, otherwise it would be better to seriously consider winding up the company'.[67]

This can be further illustrated by references to Lloyds' involvement in a company involved in one of the growth industries of this period, electronics. Having had a steadily increasing overdraft throughout the 1930s it stood, by July 1938, in excess of £25,000.[68] The bank considered this to be excessive and insisted on a reduction.[69] The company, unable to meet the demands of the bank to pay off the debt, asked it to appoint a receiver. This was done, and the company was taken over by new management, sold and the debts repaid.[70]

Another of the main planks of the evidence to the Macmillan Committee was that the banks were unhappy about providing finance for capital expenditure. A good example of this attitude can be found in Midland's dealings with a London-based manufacturer of motor lorries. This company, which already had an overdraft limit of £100,000, applied in April 1930 for a further advance of £40,000.[71] Despite the fact that the firm's profits had recently improved, and the bank had no fears for the security of the advance, they considered that 'as the whole of the advance is for capital purposes we suggest that our present limit is a generous one'.[72]

It can be seen from the table, however, that a number of firms in the sample did, in fact, receive funding for capital purposes. One example of this can be found in the rubber manufacturing company which borrowed up to £20,000 in September 1937 to purchase property for the extension of their business. This was done in advance of an issue of equity. The company felt that further borrowing would be necessary to finance the purchase of plant in the following year. The company, considered to be doing well, was given the money without any security.[73]

This contradiction is one of the fundamental points to be made when considering the evidence on the role of the banks in providing finance for their industrial customers in the inter-war years. Pragmatism and consideration of each case on its merits characterized the attitude of the banks. There appears to be no evidence of any consistent policy of non-involvement, and equally no consistent policy of involvement and support regardless of the financial situation of the individual firm. This holds true, from the evidence presented, across industries and, as far as can be discerned from the available data, across firms of different sizes. There is no evidence that the banks systematically discriminated against smaller firms. This is, in fact, contrary to what we might expect to find. The major legacy of the Macmillan Report was after all the discovery that small and medium-sized firms often experienced considerable difficulty in raising finance. The Bolton Committee in 1971 stated that 'the lack of knowledge and understanding within the small firm sector of the financial services available and of the costs and benefits attached to them', and the subsequent shortage of outside capital was 'an eternal problem'.[74] It is possible that there is a bias in the sample of firms since it encompasses only those with established overdrafts and that have, therefore, passed the threshold of familiarity with their banker.

There is indeed much evidence from the 1930s to support the argument that the banks failed not only in the provision of finance for small firms, but also in the supply of venture capital for new enterprises. These years saw the emergence of various alternative forms of financial institution in the market, which must bring into question the nature of the product offered by the banking system. When Charter-house Industrial Development Company was established in 1934, the estimate of applications for loans in the first week of business reached as high as 9,000.[75] Credit for Industry, set up by the United Dominions Trust, and Leadenhall Securities were also formed at this time in an attempt to fill the gap left by the banks. On the official side, the Special Areas Reconstruction Association and a special fund administered by the Treasury were designed to aid the financing of firms in the depressed industrial regions. Additional to this was the work of the Nuffield Trust, a fund of £2 million privately donated by Lord Nuffield to help relieve unemployment in the distressed areas.[76] To some extent insurance companies also moved into supporting small business in this decade.[77]

That these forms of finance appeared in the 1930s can to some extent be interpreted as a failure on the part of the banks to meet the needs of industry. In many cases, however, the extremely speculative nature of many of the requests for finance ensured that they were turned down. Of the 9,000 applications to the Charterhouse Organization, only about a dozen were considered worth investigating in any detail.[78] To obtain money from any of these alternative institutions, borrowers had to be able to show good prospects, considerable security and/or a good profit record.

They did not, any more than the banks, function as providers of venture capital. If specialist institutions created largely for this very purpose felt nervous about providing capital to many new businesses, then the banks, with a high proportion of short-term deposits, should not be criticized too severely for adopting a similar risk-averse position.

## Conclusion

The evidence presented in this chapter indicates that the banks were considerably more involved in supporting their industrial customers than they have hitherto been given credit for. This is not, however, to argue that the banking system met all needs for finance from the industrial sector. The emergence of a number of competitors, as well as the official attempts to plug various holes, and continued pressure from the Bank of England, Board of Trade and the Treasury leading to the creation of the Industrial and Commercial Finance Corporation in 1945, show this not to be the case.

Tolliday has argued that the biggest indictment of the banking system in this period is its failure to develop an institutional framework to deal with the indebtedness situation in the steel and other industries.[79] No less important, however, was the very real support, both financial and qualitative, provided across a broad range of industries by the clearing banks.

Cameron and Patrick in 1969 defined three ways in which the financial and industrial sectors in an economy could interact;[80]

(1) the case in which inadequate finance restricts or hinders industrial or commercial development;
(2) the case in which the financial system is purely permissive and accommodates all credit worthy borrowers;

(3) the case in which the financial institutions either actively promote new investment opportunities or encourage applicants for finance to come forward, provide them with advice and extra services, etc.

If we are to measure the two banks included in this survey against their rubric, it is clear that the second of the three types of relationship most nearly fits the evidence presented here. The banks, however, may well have been more permissive than active, but they were certainly not passive. They did take a role, contrary to the statements of the leading bankers to the Macmillan Committee, in shaping and encouraging mergers. Where it suited their purpose, a policy to deal with a particular problem was formulated and pursued.

Errors of judgement were certainly made, and the salutary experience of the post-war boom remained a harsh reminder that they could not provide uncritical support to high-risk borrowers. Nevertheless, they were involved in industrial finance, and they did take their responsibilities in that sphere seriously.

## Notes

1. The author would like to record his thanks to Dr Geoffrey Jones and Dr Youssef Cassis for their helpful comments and assistance in the preparation of this paper.
2. W. A. Thomas, *The Finance of British Industry 1918–1976* (London, 1978), p. 53.
3. See S. W. Tolliday, *Business, Banking and Politics, the Case of British Steel, 1918–1939* (Cambridge, Mass., 1987); J. H. Bamberg, *The Government, the Banks and the Lancashire Cotton Industries, 1918–1939* (Unpublished PhD thesis, University of Cambridge, 1984); M. H. Best and J. Humphries, 'The City and industrial decline', in B. Elbaum and W. Lazonick, *The Decline of the British Economy* (Oxford, 1986), pp. 223–39; R. S. Sayers *The Bank of England 1891–1944* (Cambridge, 1976).
4. E.g. Edwin Green and Michael Moss, *A Business of National Importance. The Royal Mail Shipping Group, 1902–1937* (London, 1982); John Hume and Michael S. Moss, *Beardmore: The History of a Scottish Industrial Giant* (London, 1979); J. Foreman-Peck 'Exit, voice and loyalty as responses to decline: the Rover Company in the inter-war years', in *Business History*, Vol. XXXIII No. 2 (July 1981), pp. 191–207; R. Church, *Kenricks in Hardware. A Family Business* (Newton-Abbott, 1969).
5. See P. L. Cottrell, *Industrial Finance, 1830–1914: The Finance and Organization of English Manufacturing Industry* (London, 1980); C. W. Munn, *The Scottish Provincial Banking Companies 1747–1864* (Edinburgh, 1981); R. S. Sayers, *Lloyds Bank in the History of English Banking* (Oxford, 1957); R. Cameron, 'England 1750–1844', in R. Cameron and H. T. Patrick, *Banking in the Early Stages of Industrialisation* (Oxford, 1967), pp. 15–59; P. Ollerenshaw, *Banking in Nineteenth Century Ireland* (Manchester, 1987).

6.  Ollerenshaw, *Irish Banking,* pp. 94–101, 193.
7.  W. P. Kennedy, 'Institutional response to economic growth: capital markets in Britain to 1914', in L. Hannah (ed.), *Management Strategy and Business Development* (London, 1976), pp. 151–83; M. H. Best and J. Humphries, 'City and industrial decline'.
8.  S. G. Checkland, *Scottish Banking. A History, 1695–1973* (Glasgow, 1975), p. 532.
9.  P. L. Cottrell, *Finance of British Industry,* pp. 194–8; C. A. E. Goodhart, *The Business of Banking 1891–1914* (London, 1972).
10. Checkland, *Scottish Banking,* pp. 576–81.
11. Sir J. Lithgow to Walker, 5 March 1930, FBI Finance and Industry Committee – Correspondence, Minutes and Related Papers – Modern Records Centre (MRC) CBI Predecessors Archive MSS 200/F/3/E1/3/7.
12. Committee on Finance and Industry (henceforth cited as Macmillan Committee), *Report,* para. 7 (HMSO, 1931, Cmnd 3897).
13. F. C. Goodenough, evidence to the Macmillan Committee, 13 December 1929, QQ583–6.
14. The SMT and the BIDC were set up in 1929 and 1930 respectively, under the patronage of the Bank of England. The SMT consisted of a group of businessmen convened to investigate proposed schemes of rationalization in British industry, and to make recommendations pertaining to such rationalization. The BIDC was created to assist in providing finance for these schemes, its capital supplied by its shareholders, the banks. These two institutions were mostly involved in the steel and cotton industries. For a fuller analysis of their operation see Bamberg, *Lancashire Cotton Industries*; and also 'The rationalization of the British cotton industry in the inter-war years', in *Textile History,* Vol. 19, No. 1 (Spring 1988), pp. 83–103; Tolliday, *Business, Banking and Politics*; and also 'Steel and rationalization policies, 1918–1950', in Elbaum and Lazonick, *Decline of the British Economy,* pp. 82–108.
15. *The Economist,* 18 January 1930.
16. Notes of meeting of industry and finance committee, 19 June 1930. MRC MSS 200/F/3/E1/3/7.
17. J. W. Beaumont-Pease, Evidence to the Macmillan Committee, 13 February 1930, Q2203.
18. John Rae, Evidence to the Macmillan Committee, 14 February 1930, Q2396. See also W. H. N. Goschen, Chairman, National Provincial, 7 February 1930, Q1818.
19. Sir James Lithgow, representing the Federation of British Industries, Evidence to the Macmillan Committee, 18 July 1930, Q8488.
20. Although the use of Bills of Exchange was still offered by the banks to mostly their large or long-established customers, as a popular means of obtaining credit it had been dying since before World War I. This is lamented by Goodenough in his evidence to the Macmillan Committee, 13 December 1929, Q517.

21. J. Rae, evidence to the Macmillan Committee, 14 February 1930, Q2408.
22. J. W. Beaumont-Pease, evidence to the Macmillan Committee, 13 February 1930, Q212.
23. W. H. N. Goschen, evidence to the Macmillan Committee, 7 February 1930, Q1842. See also F. C. Goodenough, 13 December 1929, Q606.
24. Report of an interview, Lloyds Bank Archives (LBA), Winton Files.
25. F. Hyde, evidence to the Macmillan Committee, 9 January 1930, Q889; see also Beaumont-Pease, 13 February 1930, Q2119.
26. *Final Report of the Committee on Industry and Trade* (Balfour Committee), p. 52. 1928/29, Cmnd 3282.
27. Statement of Evidence Submitted by the National Chamber of Trade to the Macmillan Committee, 28 May 1930, para. 5.
28. T. Balogh, *Studies in Financial Organization* (Cambridge, 1947), p. 77.
29. *Bank Advances During and After the Last War,* Midland Bank Archives (MBA), Intelligence Files, 8 October 1940.
30. Tolliday, 'Steel and Rationalisation Policies', p. 94.
31. Bamberg, *Lancashire Cotton Industries,* pp. 20–30.
32. The Lancashire banks had resisted amalgamation with the Big Five clearing banks before World War I by forming defensive mergers among themselves. By 1920, there emerged five Lancashire banks providing a competitive and specialized service for the local industries. These were the banks which had been involved in the re-flotation boom. Their risk was not evenly diversified. See Bamberg, *Lancashire Cotton Industries,* pp. 20–1.
33. Sayers *Bank of England*, p. 319.
34. F. Hyde, Evidence to the Macmillan Committee, 9 January 1930, Q981.
35. Bamberg, *Lancashire Cotton Industries* (1984), Appendix 1:3, p. 33.
36. J. W. Beaumont-Pease evidence to the Macmillan Committee, 13 February 1930, Q2018. J. R. Winton, *Lloyds Bank 1918–1969* (Oxford, 1984), chapter 4, outlines the effects of the depression on Lloyds.
37. W. H. N. Goschen, evidence to the Macmillan Committee, 7 February 1930, QQ1809–10.
38. Notes of the meeting of industry and finance committee, 19 June 1930, MRC MSS 200/F/3/E1/3/7.
39. W. H. N. Goschen, evidence to the Macmillan Committee, 7 February 1930, Q1821.
40. Quoted in Foreman-Peck, 'Exit, Voice and Loyalty,' p. 202.
41. A. R. Holmes and Edwin Green, *Midland. 150 Years of Banking Business* (London, 1986), pp. 179–80.
42. Bamberg, *Lancashire Cotton Industries*, p. 26; see also Hewit in the meeting of the FBI industry and finance committee, 9 June 1930. MRC MSS 200/F/3/E1/3/7.
43. C. W. Munn, *Clydesdale Bank The First Hundred & Fifty Years* (Glasgow, 1988), Chapter 4.
44. In Lloyds' case the sources were: the main Board Minutes, vols 36–49 (Lloyds Bank Archives (henceforth cited as LBA) vols. 905–18), branch managers

personal memoranda books from King Street, Manchester (LBA PM Books 16, 19), and from Aston Road, Birmingham (LBA PM Books 3276, 3277), and Minutes of the Newcastle Regional Board. For Midland the sources were the Minutes of the Management Committee (Midland Bank Archives (henceforth cited as MBA) Management Committee Minutes, vols 7–26), and the Inquiry into the Decline of Advances 1931–6 (MBA Intelligence Section Files, *Inquiry into the Decline of Advances 1931–1936,* 11 December 1936).

45.  MBA Management Committee Minutes, 9 August 1930, Vol. 8.
46.  Ibid., 15 December 1930.
47.  Ibid., 16 December 1930.
48.  Ibid., Vol. 9, 10 February 1931.
49.  Ibid., Vol. 16, 6 December 1934.
50.  Ibid., Vol. 9, 22 June 1931.
51.  Ibid., 22 June 1931.
52.  Ibid. Vol. 11, 24 March 1932.
53.  Ibid.
54.  LBA PM Book No. 16, King Street, Manchester, 19 December 1932, 24 February 1933, 8 April 1933, 13 June 1933.
55.  Ibid., 29 June 1933.
56.  Ibid.
57.  Ibid., 14 August 1933.
58.  Ibid., 15 February 1936.
59.  MBA Management Committee Minutes, Vol. 7, 22 May 1930; Vol. 12, 27 August 1932.
60.  Ibid., 4 February 1933.
61.  Ibid.
62.  Ibid., 7 June 1934.
63.  LBA Newcastle Area Board Minute Book, 2 November 1931.
64.  MBA Management Committee Minutes, Vol. 7, 11 March 1930.
65.  Ibid., Vol. 8, 2 December 1930, Vol. 11, 12 May 1932.
66.  Ibid., Vol. 17, 19 February 1935.
67.  Ibid., Vol. 9, 3 March 1931.
68.  LBA PM Book 3277, 22 July 1938.
69.  Ibid., 18 August 1938.
70.  Ibid., 5 April 1939, 8 April 1939, 4 July 1939.
71.  MBA Management Committee Minutes, 25 April 1930.
72.  Ibid.
73.  LBA PM Book 19, 8 September 1937.
74.  *Report of the Committee of Inquiry into Small Firms* (1971–72, Cmnd 4811), para. 12.1.
75.  L. Dennet, *The Charterhouse Group 1927–1979. A History* (London, 1979), p. 40.
76.  C. E. Heim, 'Inter-war responses to regional decline', in Elbaum and Lazonick, *Decline of the British Economy,* pp. 240–65.
77.  Public Record Office T[reasury] 230/72. Memorandum by Board of Trade to Committee on Post-War Employment, Annex II, Finance for Industry.

78. Dennet, *Charterhouse*, p. 40.
79. Tolliday, *Steel and Rationalisation Policies, Business, Banking and Politics*.
80. Cameron and Patrick, *Banking in the Early Stages*, p. 2.

# 4 The Sperling Combine and the shipbuilding industry. Merchant banking and industrial finance in the 1920s

*Stefanie Diaper*

## Introduction

The Sperling Combine was formed by a group of industrialists and City of London bankers, who attempted to rationalize part of the British shipbuilding industry in the years just after World War I. Their activities were part of a growing trend in the British economy at the time, as leading businessmen tried to create larger, more efficient companies that would be able to meet international competition on an equal footing. The Sperling Combine was unusual, however, in involving bankers, and particularly traditionally overseas-oriented merchant bankers, in the business of industrial finance and re-organization. The members of the Combine embarked upon their project in the buoyant economic climate of the post-war boom, but their expectation of profit from the venture declined sharply as the British shipbuilding industry moved into depression in the 1920s, along with much of Britain's heavy industry. The shipbuilding industry was thus a hard school for merchant bankers to learn about industrial finance during the inter-war period.

## Merchant banks and the domestic industry

The subject of industrial finance and the role that the banks should play in the provision of finance for industry has been a perennial topic for discussion among industrialists, bankers and politicians, and the discussion has intensified as Britain's manufacturing industry has lost its earlier world lead. Some have attributed the couuuntry's relative economic decline over the last century, at least in part, to the nature and activities of the British banking system. The joint-stock banks have hindered industrial development by their reluctance to lend long-term to industry, the argument runs,[1] while the merchant banks have traditionally found their outlets abroad and have had little interest in the domestic economy. 'The banks have failed the nation by their failure to invest in industry,' has been a clarion cry resounding through a succession of government reports and inquiries since the end of the nineteenth century, surfacing most prominently in the Macmillan and Radcliffe Reports, and in the conclusions of the recent Wilson Committee on the workings of the financial institutions.[2] The charge is a serious one, but it has never been fully developed. The British banks undoubtedly played a smaller role in financing domestic industry in the years before World War I than their counterparts in some other countries, most notably Germany, but that in itself does not prove that Britain's economic growth would have been faster if they had followed the German example. Before that could be established we would require, among other things, proof of unfulfilled demand for industrial investment in the British economy and some estimate of the extent of the opportunities thus neglected.

Whatever the consequences for the British economy as a whole of the banks' reluctance to become involved in the provision of long-term capital for industry, it is clear that they have preferred to remain aloof from this sort of business for much of the last century, and have prospered while doing so. The joint-stock banks preferred to concentrate on less risky short-term lending to industry, while the merchant banks were able to make a good living from their traditional business financing foreign trade and arranging loans for foreign governments and had little need to break new ground by moving into industrial finance and domestic new issues.[3] The merchant banks' attitude to the types of business that they either could or should undertake began to change in the early part of this century, but was only carried into effect after World War I, when changing conditions deprived them of much of their traditional business. The decline in world trade in the 1930s hit the merchant banks' accepting business by reducing the demand for trade finance, and their foreign issuing business also suffered in the turbulent economic conditions of the inter-war period. The post-war years saw a succession of embargoes on foreign new issues in London, both official and unofficial, aimed at protecting the pound and Britain's gold reserves, and they greatly restricted the merchant banks' scope to act as international issuing houses in their traditional way. As a result of these embargoes and growing competition from New York and Paris, foreign issues in London fell from an average of £130 million a year between 1921 and 1924, representing roughly 60 per cent of the new issues made. They then fell to an average of just over £104 million each year between 1925 and 1931, and fell again in the 1930s as falling demand and government controls took effect, to a low point of just under £21 million in 1935, when they made up only 38 per cent of the new issues arranged that year.[4] There was thus still foreign issuing business for the merchant banks to handle during the inter-war period, but it was a declining field and they were forced to begin arranging domestic new issues if they wanted to maintain the level of their issuing activity.

Fortunately for the merchant banks, this was a booming business in the years after 1918, with room for them to establish their presence, alongside the stockbrokers and company promoters who were active in the field. British industry had been starved of the opportunity to raise capital during the war, and when wartime restrictions were repealed in March 1919 the pent-up demand that was released resulted in a boom in domestic new issues on the London capital market, which was used to finance domestic industry to an extent that was unprecedented before the war. Domestic new issues raised £187.7 million in 1919 and £331 million in 1920, representing 85 per cent of the new issues made in London that year, as new companies were formed and many existing companies were converted from private to public status. Not only were more companies being formed and more domestic issues being made in London in the 1920s than before the war, all requiring the services of an issuing house, but the number of large companies capable of affording the services of the merchant banks in this role had also increased dramatically since the end of the nineteenth century, and with the wave of mergers and rationalization schemes that accompanied the birth of the corporate economy in the 1920s, moving into domestic issuing became a practical possibility for the merchant banks. They were also encouraged to develop in this direction by the Governor of the Bank of England, who believed that the merchant banks could play an important part in industrial rationalization as well as in company promotion.[5]

The merchant banks which had been most prominent in foreign issuing led the way in the merchant banks' move into domestic issuing. Morgan Grenfell and Lazards, for example, both arranged issues for a number of electrical companies, while Rothschilds and Baring Brothers became involved in several of Governor Norman's schemes to rationalize depressed sections of British industry. Competition among the London issuing houses brought down the cost of arranging new issues during the inter-war period, but the merchant banks continued to find it uneconomic to make small issues of the sort required by much of British industry at the time. Their issuing work was therefore predominantly on behalf of large-scale concerns, and their contribution to the financing of smaller companies (which the Macmillan Committee found experienced particular problems in raising capital) was only limited. The 'Macmillan Gap', as it became known, was a recurring theme in business development between the wars, but in so far as it was filled at all during this period, it was done by new investment bankers such as Sir Arthur Wheeler and Sir Nutcombe Hume of Charterhouse, Philip Hill and F. A. Szarvasy, rather than by the established merchant banks.[6] The merchant banks' involvement with domestic industry in this period was thus mainly concerned with channelling investment funds to companies through the Stock Market as they had always done, but increasingly they also took a hand in arranging new issues and company reorganizations for large industrial clients. These were unchartered waters for the merchant banks, however, and progress was slow. The Sperling Combine's attempt at reconstruction in the shipbuilding industry was one of the earliest ventures in this field to involve merchant bankers, and their experience emphasized the need for caution in moving into an unfamiliar type of business.

## The development of the Sperling Combine

The British shipbuilding industry was the largest in the world before 1914, and it expanded enormously during the war to meet the demand for ships. Shipbuilding companies made substantial profits during the war and expected their prosperity to continue when the fighting ended, as they made good the shortage of ships caused by wartime losses.[7] The mood of the industry was thus buoyant in the summer of 1918, and it appeared to contemporaries to be a promising industry in which to invest. With its diversified structure, the shipbuilding industry was also attractive to businessmen who had absorbed the ideas of the embryonic rationalization movement, and thought that there was scope for increased profitability in the industry through integration and economies of scale. The members of the Sperling Combine were clearly attracted by the profits to be made in the industry, and they were also enthusiastic about the gains to be made by forming a large, integrated ship and marine engine building group.

The Sperling Combine's attempt at rationalization in the shipbuilding industry centred upon the Northumberland Shipbuilding Company at Howdon on the Tyne. The company was set up in 1898 by Rowland Hodge (1859–1950) who bought an existing shipbuilding yard that year and renamed it. Hodge had trained as a shipbuilder, working successively for John Elder & Co. in Glasgow, and for Schlesinger Davis & Co. and Swan Hunter on the Tyne, before branching out at the age of thirty-nine and starting his own company. He modernized and expanded the yard at Howdon, and developed a valuable business building passenger ships and vessels for the Admiralty, but the firm's main business was in building large cargo steamers. Hodge soon found that he needed more capital to develop the business than he was able to provide himself and in 1901 he sold the controlling interest in the firm to the Furness Withy group, which was trying to expand its shipbuilding interests at the time. Hodge remained as managing director, however, and he continued to be a substantial shareholder in the company.[8]

The Northumberland Shipbuilding Company developed successfully as part of the growing Furness Withy shipping and shipbuilding group over the next few years, but its position was questioned in the changes in the structure of the group that took place after the first Baron Furness's death in 1912. His son Marmaduke Furness was more interested in shipbuilding than in shipping, and he soon set about putting his own ideas for the future of the group into effect. In 1916, he disposed of the greater part of Furness Withy's shipbuilding interests (although he retained the Northumberland Shipbuilding Company), and, in the spirit of wartime enthusiasm, he used the proceeds to finance the construction of a new, modern shipyard at Haverton on the Tees. The project proved an expensive one because of problems involved in building on the low-lying Haverton site and it precipitated friction over the future of the company between Furness and F. W. Lewis, who had been one of his father's senior advisers, and had remained with the firm. The situation deteriorated to the point where the only solution seemed to be to split the business in two, with the shipping and shipbuilding sections going their separate ways. Lewis arranged for the shipping subsidiaries to buy out the Furness family's interest in Furness Withy, and part of the £10 million purchase price was met by transferring the shipyard and the group's other industrial investments to Marmaduke Furness.[9] As part of the general re-organization Furness Withy decided to sell the Northumberland Shipbuilding Company. It was bought by Robert Workman, a London shipbroker who was also a member of the Belfast shipbuilding family involved in Workman, Clark & Co. Workman had considerable experience of the shipbuilding industry to draw on, but he lacked the financial resources to buy the company alone. He did, however, have contacts in the City of London which shared his optimistic view of the shipbuilding industry's future and was prepared to back him. With the City's support he was able to enter into negotiations with Furness Withy, and in July 1918 they signed an agreement for him to buy the Northumberland Shipbuilding Company for £830,000.[10]

Workman's financial backing came from the City firm of Sperling & Co. Sperlings began life in the early 1870s as a firm of stockbrokers, although they appear to have been outside brokers rather than members of the Stock Exchange. The firm became active in the relatively new field of company promotion, new issues and underwriting in the late nineteenth century, and continued to develop in this direction in the years before World War I. The firm became well known in this role, and between 1917 and 1925 it produced a quarterly periodical called *Sperling's Journal,* which contained articles by City figures on a range of financial issues, but dealing especially with the fortunes of the firm's share issues. The early twentieth-century partners in Sperling & Co. were not content to be stockbrokers and company promoters, however; they wanted to move into the wider financial world and, in 1915, they began to describe themselves as bankers, and a few years later as merchant bankers.[11]

This move was in line with what was happening in a number of other City stockbrokers at the time, as they too began to copy their country counterparts by taking more interest in company promotion and new issue work, rather than simply confining their interest to buying and selling existing shares. Panmure Gordon became well known as an issuing house at the end of the nineteenth century, and so too did Foster and Braithwaite who made a name for themselves as issuers of electricity companies in the 1880s and 1890s. Perhaps most strikingly of all, Helbert Wagg & Co., who had been Rothschilds' principal brokers at the Stock Exchange for most of the nineteenth century, also began to take an interest in company promotion in this period, and like Sperlings they too made the transition from stockbroking to a broader financial business and began to call themselves merchant bankers. [12] This was still a relatively novel step though, as H.O. O'Hagan made clear in his autobiography. O'Hagan was himself a successful company promoter and claimed to have introduced underwriting to the City for domestic industrial issues. Writing about Ellis & Co., another firm of stockbrokers who turned company promoters under the influence of a new partner, he said, 'so old fashioned was the firm's reputation that I never attempted to secure them for my underwriting list, new issues were the last thing I should have expected them to interest themselves in.'[13]

Sperling & Co. had five partners in 1918, only one of whom was a member of the Sperling family. The five were Eric Sperling, James Strong, Sir Ernest Paulet Stacey, Edward Welton and Edward Mackay Edgar. Neither Sperling nor Strong was particularly active in the firm's shipbuilding scheme, but the other three partners all played a part in the events associated with the Northumberland Shipbuilding Company. Mackay Edgar was the driving force behind much of what happened at Sperlings in the war years and the early 1920s, and he was the key figure in the shipbuilding initiative. Mackay Edgar was a Canadian and before moving to England in 1906 he had been a member of the Montreal Stock Exchange and active in the field of company promotion.[14] The early years of the twentieth century saw a wave of company formation and industrial amalgamations in Canada, influenced by the American example of corporate development through the close ties that existed between the Montreal and New York financial markets, and Edgar was only one of a series of Canadian entrepreneurs who put their experience of issuing in the New World to work in London, which was the major supplier of long-term capital for Canada at the time. Perhaps the most famous of this group was Max Aitken (later Lord Beaverbrook), who moved to London after a profitable career as a company promoter and arranger of industrial mergers, but there were many others who also made their mark in the City. Sir James Dunn, for example (who later became the chairman of the Algoma Steel Corporation), also moved to London before World War I, setting up his own banking business after his successful career in Canada working with Aitken, Mackay Edgar and F.S. Pearson as a company promoter. Sir Edward Peacock, who as a senior partner in Baring Brothers became one of the City's most respected figures and Montagu Norman's trusted aide in several rationalization schemes, was also a Canadian who started his business life selling stocks and shares as the manager of Dominion Securities, before he too moved to London in the years before World War I.[15]

Mackay Edgar moved to Britain intent on developing his Canadian interests, selling Dominion stocks and shares through the network of contacts he had already established among the London financial community. He spent two years working on his own, but then in 1908 he was invited to become a partner in Sperling & Co. He and Sperlings were already well acquainted, since the firm had long established interests in Canada.[16] Mackay Edgar quickly became a dominating influence in the firm, and he fostered the Canadian connection. Sperlings arranged a series of Canadian issues during 1908 and 1909, but they did little to enhance the firm's reputation in London. The Bank of England reported that the firm was 'not strong', having arranged the underwriting for these issues badly and recommended caution in dealing with them. Problems recurred two years later, when there were rumours circulating in the City that the firm had received help from their bankers, and although Sperlings strenuously denied this, they remained very much a second-rank firm of stockbrokers in this period. Brown Shipley turned down offers of participation in underwriting arranged by Sperlings because they regarded them as too speculative, while E.C. Grenfell of Morgan Grenfell noted very bluntly in 1914 that the firm was 'very second rate'.[17] Criticism of this sort may have barred Sperlings from some business opportunities, but the firm continued to expand even so. In 1912 the Bank of England told an enquirer that the partners had £250,000 in the business and as much again outside,[18] and within a few years they opened an American office, although on Broadway rather than the more conventional Wall Street. Led by Mackay Edgar, the Sperling partners became involved in domestic industrial issues, and by 1918 they were keen to expand this area of their activities.[19] It was against this background that they became involved in the shipbuilding industry with Robert Workman.

Mackay Edgar and his partners agreed to provide Robert Workman with the financial backing he needed for his deal with Furness Withy, but as the project required more cash than they could provide alone, they began to look around for another firm to join them in the scheme. Their attention turned to the merchant bank, Kleinwort, Sons & Co. Kleinworts were a well-known and successful merchant bank, established in London since the middle of the nineteenth century. They were primarily an accepting house, however, and had only very limited experience of issuing work to draw on. Nevertheless there were good reasons for turning to them on this occasion. The partners already knew one another, since the two firms had worked together in the past, and this was an important consideration in a business that depended heavily upon trust and personal contact. In addition, Kleinworts' youngest partner (the founder's grandson), Herman Andreae, was keen to develop his firm's interest in issuing and investment banking and could be expected to be sympathetic to the project.[20]

The connection between the two firms went back to the time of Mackay Edgar's arrival in London before 1914. Herman Andreae took a keen interest in Canadian investment and the potential of the Canadian economy before the war. His enthusiasm had been fired by a visit to the country in 1900, and it was encouraged by the Conservative MP Ian Hamilton Benn. Hamilton Benn was a partner in the London pulp and paper merchants Price and Pierce, and he became involved in the construction of a large pulp mill at Ocean Falls in British Columbia, as well as with a series of other projects in the country. He persuaded Andreae that Kleinworts should invest in the scheme, and despite the problems that were experienced when the company's capital proved to be grossly insufficient for the necessary construction work, Andreae's enthusiasm for the country continued.[21] Hamilton Benn's Canadian interests brought him into contact with Max Aitken and Mackay Edgar, and he subsequently worked with them in company promotion and share dealing, offering Aitken important backing when he first arrived in London. Hamilton Benn was able to introduce Andreae, Aitken and Mackay Edgar, and as a result the two Canadians were offered sub-underwriting participation by Kleinworts on several occasions. Mackay Edgar and Andreae became close friends, and Mackay Edgar was able to return the compliment when he became a partner in Sperlings, offering Kleinworts underwriting in a number of the issues arranged by his new firm, including the Cuban Ports issue in 1911, intended to raise money to improve the harbour facilities on the island.[22]

The links between the two firms were strengthened in 1919 when Sperlings took on Herman Andreae's younger brother Edward as a partner. Unlike his elder brother who had gone straight into the family bank as a young man, Edward Andreae trained as an industrial chemists in his father's native Germany. He returned to Britain after completing his PhD, and before the war had become managing director of British Glanstoff at Holywell, the British operation of a German company making artificial fibres. Despite his success as an industrialist, however, he wanted to follow his elder brother into the City, and finally achieved his ambition when he was offered a partnership by Sperling & Co., probably because of his brother's connection with the firm. His combination of industrial and banking experience was unusual in the City at the time, and his knowledge of industry was useful to his brother's firm and to Sperlings as they expanded their interests in industrial new issues. Andreae sat on the board of several of the Sperling Combine's shipbuilding companies during the 1920s and 1930s and played an important part in their development. His career as a merchant banker was not, however, an unqualified success. He was considered for the chairmanship of the Lancashire Steel Corporation in 1931 when it was set up as part of one of the Bank of England's rationalization schemes, and he might well have been given the job but for Montagu Norman's feeling that he had been 'rather blown upon by the Sperling affair'.[23]

Edgar persuaded Kleinworts to back Robert Workman in his purchase of the Northumberland Shipbuilding Company, which seemed a very sound business proposition. As well as the company's assets, valued by Workman at around £850,000, the company also had contracts to build ships for Italian and Norwegian shipowners after the war, which would bring the firm an income of £1.1 million in the first two or three years after the end of hostilities. Kleinworts were asked to lend Workman money to enable him to clinch the bargain with Furness Withy, but his interest in the company appears to have been short-term, at least initially, since Kleinworts were told that 'once secured he would sell the company to Hatry or others'.[24] Kleinworts agreed to lend Workman £50,000 as a deposit on the purchase price of the company, and they also agreed to buy 750,000 preference and ordinary shares for a total of £325,000,[25] while the balance of the money that Workman needed was provided by Sperlings themselves. The two firms were to be repaid in part from the profits of the Norwegian and Italian contracts, but part of the money was to be raised by selling the Northumberland Shipbuilding Company's shares to the public.[26] Plans to sell the shares went ahead very quickly, but in deference to wartime controls the promoters decided to try to place them privately through another Sperling-sponsored company, the Canadian and General Trust Ltd, rather than by a Stock Exchange flotation. Their methods attracted criticism from some quarters, including *The Times*, which reported that 'A correspondent complains to us of being made the recipient of uninvited circulars. . . hawking about the shares of the Northumberland Ship-building Company Ltd.' The paper's columnist warned that 'there are several mysterious points about the circular sufficient to give any investor pause'. There was no prospectus giving detailed information about the company, and in particular there was no mention of the company's issued capital. Most mysteriously of all, the Canadian and General Trust Ltd was offering the shares for sale at 3 shillings, but also offered to buy them back immediately for 4 shillings. In *The Times*' view this was 'certainly suggestive of catch penny finance rather than sound business'.[27]

## The expansion of the Northumberland Shipping Company

Workman bought the Northumberland Shipbuilding Company with Sperlings' support in July 1918, and whatever his original plans for selling out to someone else, he and Sperlings formed a close alliance and continued as proprietors of the company for the next few years. Not only that, but they also extended their interests in the industry, against the background of the growing boom in shipbuilding after the war, as the scarcity of shipping and high freight rates encouraged much new building and the purchase of old ships at inflated prices.[28] Over the next two years, Mackay Edgar and Robert Workman expanded their shipbuilding interests by buying up a series of other companies in an effort to build a large and profitable group. Their first puchases were made in 1919, when they acquired control of two well-known shipbuilding firms, William Doxford & Sons on the Wear and Fairfield Engineering on the Clyde. William Doxford began shipbuilding in 1840, and by 1905 – 7 its output figures of some 90,000 gross tons were the highest of any yard in the world. The company's success in the years before World War I was based on the popularity of its 'turret design', introduced in 1893. These ships were designed to reduce the tolls payable on passing through the Suez Canal, where tolls were calculated on the basis of the width of the ship, measured at the upper deck. The 'turret' ships were built with sloping sides, which left a very narrow upper deck and so reduced tolls in the Canal. By 1914 the company was making a profit of £161,000, with a capital of £450,000. It was thus an attractive proposition for Mackay Edgar and his colleagues. The Doxford family decided to realize the capital they had tied up in the business and sold out to the Northumberland Shipbuilding Company in February 1919. The firm paid £3 million for Doxfords, and the money was raised by issuing £3 million worth of 6 per cent mortgage debentures, with the Canadian and General Investment Company acting as trustees for the stock. The Doxford family took £500,000 of the debentures in part payment for their business, so that they retained a voice in its future, while £680,000 was offered privately to the existing shareholders in the Northumberland Shipbuilding Company. The remainder of the issue was offered to the public and was quickly taken up.[29]

Mackay Edgar and Workman moved on swiftly after this purchase to continue their policy of expansion as opportunities arose. During the summer of 1919 they entered into negotiations to buy the Fairfield Shipbuilding and Engineering Company. The firm was established in 1834, gradually moving from making machinery and marine engines into shipbuilding, and by the time of World War I the company had established itself as one of the few firms in the country building warships. The Northumberland Shipbuilding Company's opportunity to take over Fairfield came in 1919, when Lady Pearce (the widow of the founder's son) died and a large block of shares in the company came on the market. They were bought up by the Northumberland Company which then moved to put its own men on the board. Robert Workman became chairman of the company under its new owners, and he was joined by Mackay Edgar and several of their close associates.[30]

The group kept up the momentum of their policy of expansion, with a series of further purchases during 1920 that extended the geographical spread of the Sperling Combine's interests as well as increasing its shipbuilding capacity. The group acquired the Blythswood Shipbuilding Company on the Blyth, and also set up the Monmouth Shipbuilding Company to buy the government-owned National Ship-yards at Chepstow and the adjoining yard of Edward Finch & Co. Ltd. Both yards were relatively small by the standards of the group's earlier purchases, and the Monmouth Company was set up with a capital of £200,000, all held by the Northumberland Shipbuilding Company.[31] The Combine's biggest acquisition in 1920 was the purchase of Robert Workman's family business, the Workman Clark yards in Belfast, with a capital of just over £1 million. The firm was started in 1877 and specialized in medium-sized cargo boats and ships designed to carry both passengers and cargo. During the war, like most shipbuilders, they concentrated on Admiralty work, producing mainly smaller vessels such as patrol boats and sloops. Once again the combine followed its usual practice of putting in its own directors, while retaining as many of the original board as possible. Mackay Edgar and Robert Workman became directors, but the founder Frank Workman remained as a chairman until 1923.[32]

The Sperling Combine's efforts to create a shipbuilding empire went even further. They also attempted to buy Swan Hunter & Wigham Richardson in 1920, but this time their bid failed.[33] They succeeded in acquiring an interest in Irvine's Shipbuilding and Dry Dock Company in West Hartlepool, however, through a complicated exercise in cross-directorships, which brought the Combine into contact with Clarence Hatry, then embarking on the earliest of his famous industrial rationalization schemes. In 1917, Hatry and his partners in the Commercial Bank of London acquired control of a series of shipbuilding firms, including Joseph T. Eltringham & Co. on Tyneside and Irvine's Shipbuilding on the Tees. It is not clear whether these companies were intended to form the nucleus of a separate shipbuilding rationalization scheme, or whether they were intended to become part of Amalgamated Industrials, formed by Hatry in 1919 to bring together a diverse mixture of interests in cotton spinning, shipbuilding and pig farming.[34] Rowland Hodge, the founder of the Northumberland Shipbuilding Company and a director under Sperling's ownership, became the chairman of Eltringhams under the new Hatry regime, and he also became a director of Hatry's British Glass Industries.[35] Contacts between the two groups were closer at Irvine's Shipbuilding. The company was founded in 1860 by Robert Irvine who eventually sold out to Furness Withy. They sold their interest in the company in 1917, and it passed into the hands of Hatry and his partners, operating in conjunction with Robert Workman. Hatry and his associate Peter Haig Thomas became directors of Irvine's after the takeover, and they were joined on the board by Workman and Sir John Esplen, who was also a Sperling nominee on the boards of Northumberland, Doxfords, Fairfield and Workman Clark.[36]

As well as expanding their interests in shipbuilding during 1920, the Sperling Combine followed the example of a number of other shipbuilders at the time, and tried to move into steel making. The shipbuilders were worried about the rising price of steel as the post-war boom continued, and tried to diversify into steel manufacture in an attempt to reduce costs and secure supplies of this vital raw material.[37] Their first attempt came early in 1920, when they tried to buy the well-known steel manufacturers Baldwins. Acting as agents for the Northumberland Shipbuilding company they offered the shareholders £3 per share for the company, which was accepted. An agreement for the purchase was signed in February, but Sperlings backed out of the deal after the budget, when contrary to popular expectation, the rate of excess profit duty was increased from 40 to 60 per cent. Not surprisingly, Baldwin's took legal action against the company, but Mackay Edgar and his associates preferred to pay £845,000 in damages, rather than complete the purchase and take on a large excess profit duty liability. All was not entirely lost, however, since they were able to negotiate a contract for Baldwin's to supply the Northumberland Shipbuilding Company, with steel, as part of the wider discussions over damages.[38] Sperling's second attempt to acquire an interest in steel production was

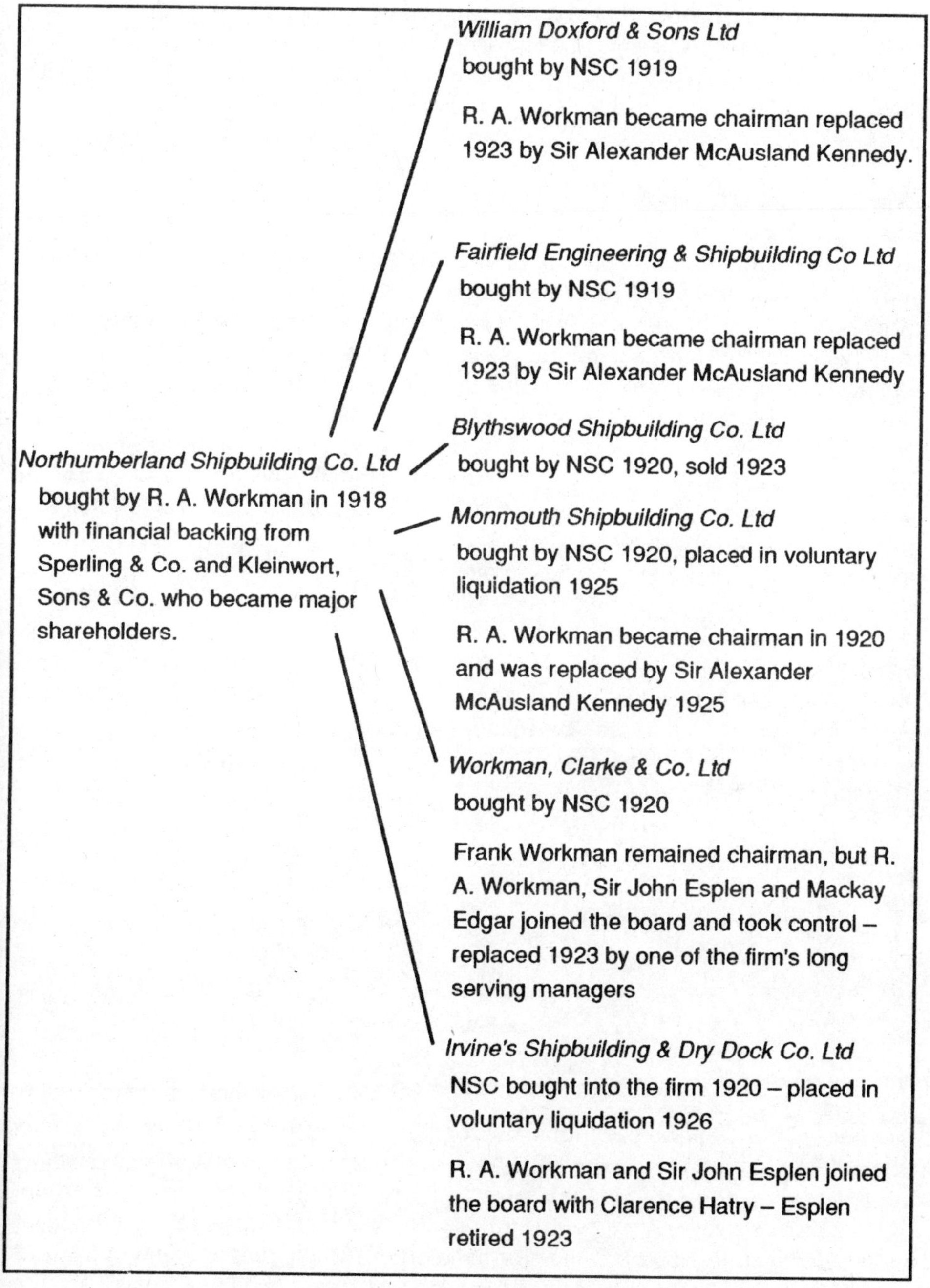

*William Doxford & Sons Ltd*
bought by NSC 1919

R. A. Workman became chairman replaced
1923 by Sir Alexander McAusland Kennedy.

*Fairfield Engineering & Shipbuilding Co Ltd*
bought by NSC 1919

R. A. Workman became chairman replaced
1923 by Sir Alexander McAusland Kennedy

*Blythswood Shipbuilding Co. Ltd*
bought by NSC 1920, sold 1923

*Northumberland Shipbuilding Co. Ltd*
bought by R. A. Workman in 1918
with financial backing from
Sperling & Co. and Kleinwort,
Sons & Co. who became major
shareholders.

*Monmouth Shipbuilding Co. Ltd*
bought by NSC 1920, placed in voluntary
liquidation 1925

R. A. Workman became chairman in 1920
and was replaced by Sir Alexander
McAusland Kennedy 1925

*Workman, Clarke & Co. Ltd*
bought by NSC 1920

Frank Workman remained chairman, but R.
A. Workman, Sir John Esplen and Mackay
Edgar joined the board and took control –
replaced 1923 by one of the firm's long
serving managers

*Irvine's Shipbuilding & Dry Dock Co. Ltd*
NSC bought into the firm 1920 – placed in
voluntary liquidation 1926

R. A. Workman and Sir John Esplen joined
the board with Clarence Hatry – Esplen
retired 1923

Figure 4.1   The Sperling Combine

much more straightforward. Towards the end of 1920 Workman Clark, acting on behalf of the group, took an interest in Lanarkshire Steel, and also helped to secure coal supplies by buying shares in colliery owners John Watson & Co. in Glasgow.[39] The purchases were paid for from the proceeds of an issue of debenture stock made that year, and this latter had serious repercussions for the firm.

## Depression and Difficulties

As a result of this vigorous policy of expansion, by the end of 1920 as well as its own yard at Howden on the Tyne, the Northumberland Shipbuilding company also owned a series of shipbuilding firms throughout the country, and had interests in steel manufacture and coal mining. The group of associated companies had a nominal capital of some £4 million that year, while Northumberland Shipbuilders alone produced 59,220 gross tonnage and made a profit of £150,000.[40] 1920 marked the high point of the company's achievement after the war, however, and thereafter problems began to multiply as the economic climate worsened. The post-war shipbuilding boom came to an end in 1920, and like the rest of the shipbuilding industry the Northumberland Shipbuilding Company found orders becoming scarcer. The firm's output fell markedly in 1921, to 14,704 gross tonnage, and although the situation improved slightly in 1922, the picture remained gloomy for the rest of the decade. The other members of the group were also badly affected by the fall in orders. Fairfields built only one cable ship in 1920 and two tankers in 1921, and the Washington Naval Treaty which severely limited naval building made the situation worse, by causing the cancellation of several Admiralty orders.[41]

Table 4.1   Gross tonnage built by the Northumberland Shipbuilding Company, 1919–31[42]

| 1919 | 45,078 | 1926 | nil |
|------|--------|------|--------|
| 1920 | 59,220 | 1927 | nil |
| 1921 | 14,704 | 1928 | 38,100 |
| 1922 | 17,420 | 1929 | 40,490 |
| 1923 | 11,200 | 1930 | 14,560 |
| 1924 | 25,517 | 1931 | nil |
| 1925 | 14,772 |      |        |

While all the Sperling Combine's companies experienced problems in the shipbuilding slump in the early 1920s, the Northumberland Shipbuilding Company itself was worst affected and drew support from the other members of the group, thereby further weakening their position. Group support of this kind became easier to coordinate after 1922 when the Northumberland Shipbuilding Company set up a general purpose committee, chaired by Mackay Edgar and recognized by the associated companies, to make decisions on finance and policy for the group as a whole.[43] The Northumberland Shipbuilding Company drew support from all the members of the group as orders dried up and it became harder to cover production overheads and the interest due on its fixed interest securities, with serious results. In 1928 it was claimed that Northumberland Shipbuilding had deprived Workman Clark of 'practically the entire assets of the company', while the Bank of England thought that it had 'ruined the financial position of Doxford's by denuding it of its liquid assets'.[44] The position at Fairfields, however, is best documented. Fairfields subscribed for £400,000 of the Northumberland Shipbuilding Company's 6 per cent non-cumulative preference shares in October 1921 to inject cash into the company, and also made a series of loans to the company, and to Sperlings, over the next two years. In 1923 Fairfields even bought an unfinished hull from the Northumberland company to provide them with cash. This constituted a serious drain on Fairfield's resources, at a time when the firm was already suffering from a severe decline in business. Profits fell and the firm paid dividends only on its preference shares from 1920 to 1924.[45]

Table 4.2   Fairfields profits, 1920–25[46]

|      | Available for distribution | Brought forward from the previous year | Earned that year |
|------|---------------------------|----------------------------------------|------------------|
| 1920 | 171,619                   | —                                      | —                |
| 1921 | 97,288                    | 75,699                                 | 21,589           |
| 1922 | 161,730                   | 46,038                                 | 115,692          |
| 1923 | 169,586                   | 110,480                                | —                |
| 1924 | 130,985                   | 130,985                                | 149              |

Support from the rest of the Sperling Combine helped to bolster the Northumberland Shipbuilding Company's position, but the situation was clearly becoming very serious by 1923. All the associated companies were having trouble in paying dividends, and Workman Clark's financial position was so serious that MacCullums, the steel stockholders, bought 2,500 of their own shares from the Belfast firm 'to relieve their cash shortage and by doing so keep their most important customer in business'.[47] The Northumberland Company itself had gone from a profit of £101,346 in June 1920 to a loss of £390,850 by the middle of 1923. The directors attributed the firm's position to losses on steel stockholdings and the cancellation of contracts, and the settlement with Baldwins which was paid in 1921 can hardly have helped the situation either.[48] By 1923 the Northumberland Shipbuilding Company held shares in the associated companies with a nominal value of £8.8 million, and had advanced £158,377 to the rest of the group, at the same time receiving £472,543 in advances from the other companies. Dividends, which had reached extraordinary levels at the height of the post-war boom, were now non-existent. The time had clearly come for action to try to recover the deteriorating situation.

The first obvious step was to sell off some of the assets of the group, and although it was not easy to find purchasers for shipyards at the time, the Combine did succeed in

*Table 4.3   Northumberland Shipbuilding Company dividends, 1918–23[49]*

|  | 10% part preference shares | B preference | Ordinary shares |
|---|---|---|---|
| 1918–19 | 15% | — | 70% |
| 1919–20 | 10 | — | 222½ |
| 1920–21 | 10 | — | 5 |
| 1921–22 | 5 | nil | nil |
| 1922–23 | nil | nil | nil |

finding a buyer for the Blythswood shipyard in September 1923. The Monmouth Shipbuilding Company was put into voluntary liquidation in an attempt to cut the group's losses in South Wales, although the company was subsequently bought back from the Board of Trade by Fairfields for £25,000.[50] Kleinworts had taken relatively little interest in the internal workings of the various shipbuilding companies in the Sperling group during the early 1920s. They had regarded their investment as just that, and had left the bulk of the work of managing the companies to Sperlings, and particularly to Mackay Edgar, who with Robert Workman, had taken the lead in the business. The Combine's financial difficulties in 1923 forced them to take a greater interest in what was going on to try to protect their position, and as the situation continued to deteriorate their involvement grew. The problems in 1923 precipitated serious differences between Kleinworts and Mackay Edgar and Workman, and as a result both he and Workman resigned from the boards of the Northumberland Shipbuilidng Company and the various associated companies during the autumn of 1923. They were replaced by Sir Alexander Kennedy, a naval architect turned shipyard manager, who had worked in the group for several years, and who soon became crucial in the management of the various companies.[51]

Mackay Edgar remained connected with the Northumberland Shipbuilding Company through his partnership in Sperling & Co., and Robert Workman kept up his interest in shipbuilding through his directorship of Irvine's Shipbuilding. This company also had problems during the slump in shipbuilding in the early 1920s. Irvine's paid no dividends on its ordinary shares after 1920 or on its preference shares after 1922, and the firm made a loss in 1924 which took its debit balance to £59,175. The company's financial position continued bleak and at the end of 1926 it was forced into liquidation by the holders of the company's debenture stock. The company was discharged in February 1927 when the debenture stock was redeemed, but the firm failed to prosper. A planned reconstruction scheme that involved writing off £583,000 of the company's capital was abandoned in 1929 after Hatry's arrest, and finally in 1930 the Middleton yard was sold to a local syndicate led by Stephen Furness and A.S. Purdon, the former managing director.[52]

Despite the disposal of Blythswood and Monmouth Shipbuilding, the Northumberland Shipbuilding Company's financial position continued to worsen after 1923 as the general low level of activity in the shipbuilding industry continued. The extent of cross-financing within the group began to worry Kleinworts, who saw it as an extremely destabilizing influence.[53] Despite this the firm continued to grant new loans to the Northumberland Company during 1924, to provide working capital and to keep the business going. They were careful to look for good security for their loans, however, and when they joined Fairfields and Sperlings in making £30,000 available to the company in the autumn that year, their £10,000 share of the loan was secured partly on ordinary shares in Fairfields and partly on a new class of £300,000 7 per cent prior lien debenture stock created by the Northumberland Shipbuilding Company.[54] The loan was originally fixed for a year but it was renewed for a further year, maturing at the beginning of November 1926: by then the company had other problems.

The first of these was relatively minor in terms of its direct effect on Northumberland Shipbuilding and its associated companies, but it affected the reputation of Sperling & Co., and by extension that of the Sperling Combine as a whole. The problem came in December 1925 when Sir Edward Mackay Edgar, the senior partner in Sperlings and the leading enthusiast in the firm for the shipbuilding venture, was made bankrupt after losing money when the value of the shares in his British Controlled Oilfields collapsed from 24 shillings to 3 shillings because of speculative activity organized by the company promoter James White. Mackay Edgar resigned from Sperling & Co. immediately, and although he cleared his debts of £66,462 very quickly, he did not rejoin the firm.[55] Even after his resignation from Sperlings at the end of 1925, however, Mackay Edgar continued to play a part in the discussions about the Northumberland Shipbuilding Company's future. The Company's position received a more serious blow earlier in the year, when a Nowegian firm, the Bergens Privat Bank, threatened to issue a writ to recover £15,000 that it was owed by the company. The Northumberland Company did not have the resources to pay the debt and risked bankruptcy if the bank forced the issue, but Kleinworts, who were by now involved in a close inspection of the firm's position, managed to persuade them to compromise. They agreed to accept prior lien debenture stock in settlement of their claim, rather than force the company into liquidation and thus acquired a continuing interest in the firm's development.[56]

## Liquidation and reconstruction

Matters at the Northumberland Shipbuilding Company were clearly coming to a head. Kleinworts were increasingly worried about the position of the firm, and without Mackay Edgar's enthusiasm the rest of the Sperling partners also took a less optimistic view of the future. By the early months of 1926, the financiers had decided that matters had gone too far and resolved to put the company into voluntary liquidation. Dissolving the company in this way had several advantages, since it would enable the company 'to get rid of the heavy liabilities both on account of income tax, inter-company finance and advances made by Sperlings', and the receiver would also be able to realize the underlying assets to cover the prior lien debentures. A new company could then be formed to acquire the Fairfield, Doxford and Workman Clark shares, and since the prior lien holders would receive their cash, they would need relatively little new money to restart the Howdon Yard. Sir Alexander Kennedy would also be in a much stronger position to attract orders without the old Northumberland name as a millstone around his neck.[57]

Sperlings were originally against the idea of winding up the Northumberland Shipbuilding Company, which they argued would damage their financial interest in the company and their reputation, but by early April 1926 they had come to agree with Kleinworts that it was the only way out and discussions began in earnest to decide the most appropriate methods to adopt. The new company that they planned to set up at Howdon would clearly need working capital, and the bid to the receiver for the assets of the remaining companies had to be large enough to forestall public criticism but both Kleinworts and Sperlings were keen to keep the bid as low as possible so as to involve a minimum of new money in addition to the proceeds of their prior lien debentures. Mackay Edgar proved an additional complication, since he had forged an alliance with Furness Withy and was keen to become involved in the reorganization. Any bid would therefore have to be large enough to discourage his interest.[58]

The Northumberland Shipbuilding Company was put into liquidation in July 1926 while discussions about the future continued, with Ernest Evan Spicer of City accountants Spicer & Pegler (who had acted for Kleinworts for many years) as receiver.[59] The situation was finally resolved when Kleinworts and Sperlings agreed to set up a new company to offer the receiver £320,000 for the assets of the Northumberland Shipbuilding Company, which would be used to cover the outstanding prior lien debentures, together with a further £125,000 for the shares in William Doxfords. Half the money was to be provided by Kleinworts and Sperlings, and the other half by the Doxford family who were keen to recover their family business. Kleinworts stood to receive £157,000 for their holding of prior lien debentures, while Sperlings would realize a further £18,000. They would have to provide £40,000 of new money to carry out the plan, £20,000 contributed by Kleinworts.[60] The offer was accepted by Spicer on behalf of the Northumberland Shipbuilding Company, and Kleinworts and Sperlings went ahead with setting up the new company which was to acquire the Northumberland assets.

The new company was registered in December 1926 as the Shipbuilders Investment Company Ltd, with an initial capital of £10,000. This was subsequently increased, and by the end of the 1927 the company had an authorized capital of 400,000 £1 shares, 279,932 of which were issued. The three directors of the new company respresented the interest groups that had been party to its formation: Sir Alexander Kennedy, the managing director of the Northumberland Company, Edward Andreae of Sperling's and George Strachan, a director of Doxfords. The shares were also taken up by the various interested parties, using a variety of nominees. The new company took over the assets of the old Northumberland company (the Northumberland Shipbuilding Company's Yard at Howdon, 24,580 of the 25,000 £10 ordinary shares in Fairfields, practically all of the issued 750,000 5 per cent preference, 6 per cent preference and ordinary shares in Doxfords, and 43,200 shares in Workman Clark) intending to try to rebuild the position of them all, but it was generally felt that the strongest element in the group was Fairfields, and that in its role as a holding company the Shipbuilders Investment Company would have to rely on Fairfields for most of its hope of profit.[61]

In fact, Kleinworts' and Sperling's hope for the future of their investment in shipbuilding very quickly ran into problems, when in the autumn of 1927, Workman Clark became involved in a protracted legal action arising out of the past activities of the Sperling Combine in cross-financing among members of the group. The case went back to Workman Clark's issue of £3 million of 7 per cent mortgage stock in 1920. One of the shareholders sued the then directors of Workham Clark and the partners in Sperling & Co who had acted as their agents, claiming damages for fraudulent misrepresentation in the prospectus and for conspiracy to defraud. The case was a complex and lengthy one, and reached the Northern Ireland Court of Appeal. Judgment was in favour of Workman Clark and Sperlings on the charge of conspiracy to defraud, but no judgment was reached on the misrepresentation charge. While still denying liability, they paid £130 into court and this was accepted by the plaintiff.[62] The court case further weakened Workman Clark's already precarious position and the company went into liquidation. It was restarted in 1928 by William Strachan, a former director of the company, without any involvement by Kleinworts or Sperlings, but it was unable to survive the economic problems of the early 1930s and was finally bought up by National Shipbuilders Security in 1935 as part of the programme to close down redundant yards.[63]

The Shipbuilders Investment Company thus lost one of its four major investments in shipbuilding at a time when the position of the Howdon Yard was also causing serious concern. The yard was being operated as the Northumberland Shipbuilding Company (1927) Ltd, but Kennedy and his colleagues were unable to find enough orders to keep it afloat. By February 1931 the position was 'utterly hopeless' according to Edward Andreae, with an overdraft at the National Provincial Bank of around £34,000 and an annual cost of £10 – 12,000 just for rates, taxes, rent and caretaking. The Company decided to cut their losses, and sold the yard to National Shipbuilders Security so that it too could be closed down as redundant capacity.[64]

Kleinworts' and Sperlings' interest in shipbuilding continued into the 1930s, however, through their shareholdings in Fairfields and Doxfords. They had expected Fairfields to be the most prosperous of the Shipbuilders Investment Company's investments, but in fact the firm had a difficult time in the late 1920s. At the AGM in 1930 the chairman complained of 'the curtailment of warship and high class passenger work and the great difficulty experienced in securing remunerative prices for the few orders;.[65] The situation continued to deteriorate and by 1933 Fairfields were only able to operate because of large overdraft facilities from the Bank of Scotland. In March that year the bank refused to increase its support beyond the £280,000 they had already made available, and the firm faced a crisis. They appealed to the Bank of England for help, and after canvassing opinion within the industry about Fairfields' value to the country as producers of specialist vessels, the Bank agreed to help the firm by providing up to £200,000.[66] The Company's West Yard was sold to National Shipbuilders Security as an economy measure, but then with the beginning of the rearmament programme the firm's position began to improve. Kleinworts must have begun to feel that their problems with the company were over, but then in 1935 the Anchor Line defaulted on bills of £133,000 and these were presented to Fairfields for payment. The company was unable to meet the bills, and with Bank overdrafts of nearly £300,000 Kleinworts agreed with the Bank of England that their best course of action was to sell Fairfields for the best price they could get. Sir James Lithgow had already made it clear to the Bank that he was prepared to make an offer for the Company, and in July 1935 he offered Kleinworts £50,000 for their Fairfield shares. The offer was accepted and he took over the company, paid off the Anchor Line bills and secured the bank overdraft.[67] The Shipbuilders Investment Company thus realized a loss of over £175,000 on the sale of their Fairfield shares, and began 1936 with only one remaining investment in the shipbuilding industry.[68]

Their shareholding in Doxfords was also proving troublesome. The company did relatively well in the late 1920s and, by 1931, in contrast with the situation at Fairfields and the Northumberland Shipbuilding Company, Andreae was able to report to Kleinworts as the major shareholders that Doxfords were 'financially quite able to look after themselves'.[69] Within four years, however, the company was in serious difficulties. Charles Doxford had remained manager of the company after he sold out in 1919, and although he had no financial stake in the firm, he and his family had hopes of recovering an interest in the business in the future. When the firm ran into trouble he therefore pledged his own credit to obtain orders for the company to try to ensure its survival. He died in January 1935 leaving several bills outstanding, endorsed by him to assist the company. His executors had to pay some £171,000 on these bills and wanted to recover the money from the company. The company did not have the money to pay them, and could only carry on in business if the executors agreed not to press their claim. The Doxford family decided to use the situation to try to regain control of the company and warned Kleinworts that unless they came to terms, they would force the company into liquidation, in which case the shareholders were unlikely to recover their investment.[70] Kleinworts finally agreed to pay them £150,000 to settle the claim, with the help of the National Provincial Bank which had acted as Doxfords bankers for many years.[71]

The Shipbuilders Investment Company thus became sole shareholders in Doxfords and with only this investment remaining, Kleinworts decided that the Company was no longer necessary, since the Doxford shares could be distributed quite easily among its shareholders. The company was put into voluntary liquidation in March 1937, and as the major shareholders (holding 328,482 of the 360,000 issued shares), Kleinworts received 456,224 of the 500,000 Doxford ordinary shares and some £220,000 from the sale of the preference shares.[72] Kleinworts intended to wait for a suitable opportunity to sell these shares and realize their investment, but in the event they were not finally able to dispose of them until the early 1950s.

## Conclusion

The Sperling Combine was an ambitious attempt to rationalize a geographically dispersed part of the British shipbuilding industry just after World War I, and its aims were very much in keeping with the spirit of times, when large integrated companies able to take advantage of economies of scale in production and finance were in vogue. The promoters seem to have given very little thought to the exact details of their amalgamation scheme, but the prospects of profits in the shipbuilding industry looked bright when they began operations in 1918. Like many of the other mergers that took place during the post-war boom, however, the Sperling Combine was not a success,[73] although it is hard to judge whether the outcome would have been different if the industry had not moved into deep depression almost immediately.

Kleinwort Sons & Co.'s original involvement in the shipbuilding scheme was intended to be a short-term measure in the usual banking manner, and it formed part of the firm's wider efforts to develop an issuing and investment business alongside its traditional acceptance activities. The situation developed rather differently, however, because of changes in conditions in the industry, and their commitment became a long-term one. It lasted over thirty years and took the firm far beyond straightforward investment and the usual work of an issuing house into detailed matters of industrial management. The firm's efforts to move into issuing were the result of the interest of one partner who became increasingly influential in the firm in the 1920s, as more senior partners grew older and retired. By the time Andreae wanted to move into this area, however, alliances had already been formed among the more established issuing houses and he took the firm into an alliance with what was generally thought to be a second-rate firm, as they too tried to move from their traditional stockbroking activity into company promotion. Andreae and Mackay Edgar were thus keen to develop their firms in a similar direction, and they both took a number of initiatives in the fields of company promotion and industrial investment. Under Andreae's influence Kleinworts became involved in Mackay Edgar's Sperling Combine and in Crosses & Winkworths (another of his promotions, this time in the cotton industry), and they also provided backing for Leslie Urquhart in his mining ventures in Russia and Australia, and for Clarence Hatry in his rationalization scheme in the City, none of which ventures proved a great success.[74] Mackay Edgar's interests meanwhile extended beyond shipbuilding and the cotton industry, and included oil exploration and production, electricity generation and mining.

Kleinworts' original involvement in the Sperling Combine took the form of a loan and the purchase of shares to enable the Combine to be set up. They saw the venture as an investment, and it was Mackay Edgar and his associates who developed the plans for establishing a large shipbuilding group. Their methods of financing, by cross-shareholdings and heavy borrowing at high interest rates, meant that when the slump in the industry came the Combine's companies were in a poor position to withstand the serious financial buffeting they received. By 1926 all of the group were experiencing serious problems. It was at this point that Edward Andreae was called in to act in a relatively new role in British industry as a company doctor, to try to retrieve the situation for his own firm and for Kleinworts. Their experience in shipbuilding was expensive and time-consuming, and clearly illustrated the dangers merchant bankers faced in moving into the uncharted waters of industrial finance in the inter-war period, particularly when they gave only limited initial attention to the project.

# Notes

1. The argument was developed in G. K. Ingham, *Capitalism Divided? The City and Industry in British Social Development* (London, 1984).
2. Macmillan, *Committee on Finance and Industry* (HMSO, 1931, Cmnd 3897); Radcliffe, *Committee on the Working of the Monetary System* (HMSO 1959, Cmnd 827); Wilson, *Committee to Review the Functioning of Financial Institutions* (HMSO, 1980, Cmnd 7937).
3. The joint-stock banks' role in industrial finance before World War I is discussed in P. L. Cottrell, *Industrial Finance, 1830–1914* (London, 1980), esp. pp. 236–44; the merchant banks' were primarily concerned with the provision of credit for international trade and also used their overseas contacts to develop as issuing houses, acting for foreign governments and public utilities, but only very rarely for domestic industrial concerns. Their development is described in S. D. Chapman, *The Rise of Merchant Banking* (London, 1984).
4. S. J. Diaper, 'Merchant banking in the inter-war period: the case of Kleinwort, Sons & Co.', *Business History*, Vol. XXVIII (1986), passim.
5. Ibid.
6. Ibid.
7. C. L. Mowat, *Britain Between The Wars* (London, 1968), p. 279; L. Jones, *Shipbuilding in Britain* (Cardiff, 1957), pp. 131–2.
8. *Shipbuilder*, Vol. 8 (1913), pp. 149–50; Vol. 18 (1918), p. 49; In 1903 the company's issued capital stood at £80,000, £22,140 held by Hodge and £25,360 held by Lord Furness, his son and his secretary. PRO BT31/15991/57516.
9. *Shipbuilding and Shipping Record*, Vol. 14 (1919), p. 417; *Dictionary of Business Biography* (DBB) entries *re* Christopher and Marmaduke Furness; S. Pollard and P. Robertson, *The British Shipbuilding Industry 1860–1914* (Cambridge, Mass., 1979), p. 96; D.J. Douglas, 'The history of north-east shipbuilding', MA thesis Durham (1968), p.156.
10. *Post Office London Directories*, 1920–50; Furness Withy Archives, Agreement 30 July 1918, between Furness Withy and R.A. Workman.
11. *Post Office London Directories*, (1874–1915); *Stock Exchange Lists of Members* (1914–1920); *Bankers' Almanac; Sperlings Journal* was distributed to holders of shares in companies promoted by the firm, and contained details of their performances. Several of the regular contributors to the *Journal* were business connections of the firm, including Herman Andreae of Kleinwort, Sons & Co. (writing as Acceptor), and Leslie Urquhart, the mining engineer. The British Library of Political and Economic Science has a nearly complete run of the *Journal* between 1917 and 1924.
12. W. J. Reader, *A House in the City* (London, 1979), p. 93; W. L. Fraser, *All to the Good* (London, 1963), passim; *DBB* entry *re* Harry Panmure Gordon; H. O. O'Hagan, *Leaves From My Life* (2 vols, London, 1929), Vol. 1, pp. 367–75.
13. H. O. O'Hagan, *Leaves*, Vol. 2, p. 335. Ellis & Co. went into company promotion under the influence of Gerald Lee Bevan, who became senior partner in 1912, and went bankrupt in 1922 as a result of his activities,

particularly in conection with the collapse of the City Equitable Fire Insurance Company. *DBB* entry *re* Gerald Lee Bevan; P. S. Manley, 'Gerald Lee Bevan and the City equitable companies', *Abacus*, Vol. 9 (1973), pp. 107–15.

14. Furness Withy Archives, Letters from Sperling & Co. give details of the partners; Obituary for Sir Edward Mackay Edgar, *The Times*, 9 October 1934, p. 19a.

15. C. P. Kindleberger, 'The Formation of Financial Centres' in *Princeton Studies in International Finance*, 36 (1974), p. 47; R. T. Naylor, *The History of Canadian Business, 1867–1914* (Toronto, 1975) pp. 216–17; W. Kilbourn, *The Elements Combined, A History of the Steel Company of Canada* (Toronto, 1960), pp. 63–79; A. J. P. Taylor, *Beaverbrook* (London, 1972) passim; Lord Beaverbrook, *Courage, the Story of Sir James Dunn* (London, 1962), passim; C. Armstrong and H. V. Nelles, 'A curious capital flow: Canadian investment in Mexico, 1902–1910', *Business History Review*, Vol. 58 (1984), pp. 186, 194; *DBB* entries *re* Sir Edward Peacock and James Frater Taylor.

16. Edgar had wide-ranging interests, from public utilities in the United States to brewing in British Columbia, and including oil exploration and production, insurance, cotton manufacture and gold mining, as well as shipbuilding. He also had literary pretensions and owned the *Saturday Review* at one time. *Shipbuilder*, Vol. 24 (1921), pp. 182–3; PRO FO371/5625, FO371/5639, *Times* obituary, op. cit. A long series of articles in *Sperlings Journal* and the *Saturday Review* gave details of the progress of the companies in which Mackay Edgar was involved. Sperlings were responsible for the promotion of the British Columbian Electric Railway Company for example. P. E. Roy, 'Direct management from abroad', *Business History Review*, Vol. XLVII (1973), pp. 241, 247.

17. Bank of England, supervision department record card. Guildhall Library, Ms. 20, 120, Brown Shipley 'Private and Confidential Memoranda *re* Business Meetings and Transactions, Share Issues etc.', and Ms.21,799, Morgan Grenfell, 'Extracts of Correspondence of E. C. Grenfell, 1900–1936'.

18. Bank of England, supervision department record card.

19. *Saturday Review*, Vol. CXXXV (1923), p. 64; *Shipbuilder*, Vol. 24 (1921), p. 182.

20. Diaper, 'Merchant Banking', passim. 'The brothers Kleinwort took in nephew H. André [sic] who developed the business on more speculative lines apart from the old merchant acceptance business'. Guildhall Library, Ms. 21, 799, Extracts of Corres. of E. C. Grenfell, p. 92.

21. House of Lords Record Office, Beaverbrook Papers Series A Canadian Corres. Business and General, esp. Benn to Aitken, 27 November 1909; Obituary for I. H. Benn, *The Times*, 14th August 1961, p. 13c. G. W. Taylor, *Builders of British Columbia* (Victoria B.C., 1982), discusses the history of Ocean Falls.

22. A. J. P. Taylor, *Beaverbrook*, pp. 55–8; S. J. Diaper, 'The History of Kleinwort, Sons and & Co. in merchant banking, 1855–1961,' (PhD thesis, Nottingham, 1983), pp. 265–71; Guildhall Library, Ms. 21, 799, Extracts of

Corres. of E. C. Grenfell, p. 92; *The Times*, 1 October 1913, p. 18b.

23.  Information from the Andreae family; Bank of England, SMT 9/1 memo. 23 February 1931.

24.  Kleinwort Benson Archive (KBA), memo 21 June 1918. Hatry, a one time partner in Ellis & Co., was one of the most prominent financiers and company promoters of his generation. He arranged a series of industrial mergers before resorting to fraud to help carry through his scheme to rationalise the steel industry. He was arrested in 1929, and subsequently jailed. *DBB* entry *re* Clarence Hatry. R. G.Walker, 'The Hatry affair', *Abacus*, Vol. 13 (1977), pp. 78–82; P. S. Manley, 'Clarence Hatry', *Abacus*, Vol. 12 (1976), pp. 49–60.

25.  They agreed to buy 250,000 £1 10 per cent cumulative preference shares and 500,000 1 shilling deferred ordinary shares: KBA, Kleinworts to R.A. Workman, 11 July 1918.

26.  KBA, E. E. Spicer to H. A. Andreae, 31 July 1918.

27.  *The Times*, 7 October 1918, p. 12c.

28.  Mowatt, *Britain between the Wars*, p. 279.

29.  *Shipbuilder*, Vol. 9 (1913), p. 131; Vol. 20 (1919), pp. 143–4; *Stock Exchange Year Book*, 1920; *DBB* entry *re* Sir William Doxford; *The Times*, 18 February 1919, p. 15b.

30.  *Shipbuilder*, Vol. 32 (1925), p. 71; Pollard and Robertson, *British Shipbuilding* p. 84; M. S. Moss and J. R. Hume, *Workshop of the British Empire. Engineering and Shipbuilding in the West of Scotland* (London, 1977), passim, esp. p. 131; *Stock Exchange Yearbook* (1919 and 1920).

31.  Moss and Hume, *Workshop*, p. 131; *Stock Exchange Year Book* (1921).

32.  *DBB* entry *re* Sir George Clark; *Stock Exchange Year Book* (1921–23).

33.  *Shipbuilder*, Vol. 22 (1920), p. 201.

34.  *Shipbuilder*, Vol. 18 (1919), pp. 134–5; Vol. 19 (1918), p. 174; *Shipbuilding and Shipping Record*, Vol. 11 (1918), p. 669; *Stock Exchange Year Book* (1918–20); *DBB* entry *re* C. C.Hatry.

35.  *Directory of Directors* (1920).

36.  *Shipbuilding and Shipping Record*. Vol. 10 (1917), p. 113; *Stock Exchange Year Book* (1918–23); PRO BT15776/52429, BT31260/168723. Haigh Thomas was the nephew of Lord Rhondda of Cambrian Coal and an associate of Hatry's from the days of Ellis & Co. He became a director of Hatry's Commercial Corporation of London, and was involved in many of his rationalisation schemes. *DBB* entry *re* G. L. Bevan; *Directory of Directors*. Sir John Esplen was a naval architect, orginally from Liverpool, who enjoyed a successful career as a shipbuilder, serving on the boards of a series of companies, including several owned by Lord Furness. *Shipbuilder*, Vol. 19 (1918), p. 116; Vol. 33 (1926), p. 286.

37.  Harland & Wolff bought David Colville & Sons in this period, for example, while Lithgows bought the Calderbank steel works of James Dunlop & Co. in an effort to safeguard their position. J. R. Hume and M. S. Moss, *A Bed of Nails. The History of P. MacCallum & Sons Ltd of Greenock, 1781–1981, a Study in Survival* (Greenock, 1983), p. 69.

38. Strathclyde Regional Archives, Fairfield Shipbuilding and Engineering Directors' Minutes, 22 June 1921; J. C. Carr and W. Taplin, *History of the British Steel Industry* (Oxford, 1962), p. 359, D. L. Burn, *The Economic History of Steelmaking, 1867–1939* (Cambridge, 1940), pp. 384–90.
39. Hume and Moss, *Bed of Nails*, p. 69; *Shipbuilding and Shipping Record*, Vol. 30 (1927), pp. 568–9.
40. *Stock Exchange Year Book* (1920).
41. Fairfield Minutes, 19 May 1921; Moss and Hume, *Workshop*, p. 134.
42. Information very kindly supplied by Mr Joe Clark of Newcastle Polytechnic.
43. Fairfield Minutes, 29 August 1922.
44. *Northern Ireland Law Reports* (1928), pp. 176–7; Bank of England, G1/395 memo, undated 1936.
45. Fairfield Minutes, 18 October 1921, 26 April 1922, 26 June and 15 October 1923, *Stock Exchange Year Book* (1925).
46. Fairfield Report and Accounts (1920–4).
47. Hume and Moss, *Bed of Nails*, p. 72.
48. *The Times*, 25 September 1923.
49. *Stock Exchange Year Book* (1925).
50. Fairfield Minutes, 15 October 1923, 6 August and 24 October 1924.
51. *Stock Exchange Year Book* (1923–24), *Shipbuilding and Shipping Record*, Vol. 16 (1920), p. 53.
52. *Shipbuilder*, Vol. 33 (1926), pp. 286–287, Vol. 37 (1930), p. 717, *Stock Exchange Year Book* (1930).
53. KBA, memo., October 1924.
54. KBA, Sperlings to Kleinworts, 10 November 1924, Fairfield Minutes, 12 August 1924.
55. White was another flamboyant company promoter in the nineteenth century tradition. He became the managing director of the Beecham Trust, which dealt in property, and he made large profits from refinancing cotton manufacturers, leaving them watered capital. His greatest notoriety, however, came from his speculative activity on the Stock Market, organizing pools in Dunlop Rubber, Eagle Oil and British Controlled Oilfields. A. Vallance, *Very Private Enterprise. An Anatomy of Fraud and High Finance* (London, 1955), pp. 88–90. *The Times*, 11 December 1925, p. 5b, 6 January 1926, p. 19d, 9 October 1934, p. 19a.
56. KBA, memo., 5 August 1925, Kleinworts to Bergens Privatbank, 11 August 1925.
57. KBA, memo., 18 March 1926.
58. KBA, memo., 30 March 1926, 18 March, 30 March, 1 April, 27 April, 24 November 1926.
59. KBA, memo., 29 June 1926.
60. KBA, memo., 31 December 1926.
61. PRO BT31/32792/18009, *Shipbuilder*, Vol. 34 (1927), p. 356, *Investors' Chronicle*, 21 May 1927, p. 1, 202.

62. Northern Ireland Law Reports (1928), pp. 162–177, *Shipbuilding and Shipping Record*, Vol. 30 (1927), pp. 568–69.
63. *The Times*, 7 April 1928, p. 18b, L. Kennedy and P. Ollerenshaw (eds), *An Economic History of Ulster* (Manchester, 1985), p. 193.
64. KBA, E. P. Andreae to Kleinworts, 20 February 1931.
65. Quoted in Moss and Hume, *Workshop*, p. 138.
66. Bank of England, SMT 3/282, C. Bruce Gardiner to B. G. Catterns, 21 July 1932.
67. Bank of England, SMT 2/4, E. D. Skinner to Sir Alexander D. Kleinwort, 16 April 1935, SMT 2/5, Sir Alexander Kleinwort to M. Norman, 10 April 1935 and Sir James Lithgow to Kleinworts, 6 July 1935, Moss and Hume, *Workshop*, p. 138.
68. PRO BT31/32792/218009, Balance Sheet 31 December 1935.
69. KBA, E. P. Andreae to Kleinworts, 20 February 1931.
70. Bank of England, G1/395, Inland Revenue to Hopkins, 25 January 1936. The Inland Revenue became involved in the discussions because Doxfords owed income tax from 1927. The company was unable to pay the debt and the Revenue accepted preference shares in lieu of their claim. Kleinworts bought the 24,783 shares for £50,000 to strengthen their hand in dealing with the executors by becoming sole shareholder. Bank of England, G1/395, H. A. Andreae to M. Norman, 11 May 1936, memorandum of 'phone call E. P. Andreae to M. Norman, 15 April 1936.
71. Bank of England, G1/395, E. P. Andreae to M. Norman, 25 June 1936 and report of the Doxford directors, October 1935; KBA, E. P. Andreae to Kleinworts, 9 July 1936.
72. PRO BT31/32792/218009; KBA, Kleinworts to S.I.C., 17 March 1937, undated memorandum *re* Doxfords; Kleinworts to the S.I.C. Liquidator, 12 March 1937 and the Liquidator to Kleinworts, 16 March 1937.
73. The fortunes of the post-war merger boom are discussed in L. Hannah, *The Rise of the Corporate Economy* (London 1976, 2nd edn 1983), esp. pp. 27–53.
74. *Saturday Review*, Vol. CXXXV (1923), p. 755. Sperling & Co. arranged the issue of shares in the companies set up to develop Urquhart's mining interests, details of which appear in G. H. Nash, *The Life of Herbert Hoover, The Engineer, 1874–1914* (New York; London, 1983), and G. Blainey, *Mines in the Spinifex, The Story of the Mount Isa Mines* (1960).

# 5 The Stock Exchange and the British economy, 1870–1939

*Ranald C. Michie*

## Introduction

On 5 November 1929, the Chancellor of the Exchequer appointed a committee to inquire into the relationship between finance and the economy. This committee, chaired by a lawyer, Lord Macmillan, consisted of fifteen members, including some of the most talented people of the day, such as Keynes, McKenna and Bevin, as well as other economists, industrialists and financiers. Between November 1929 and February 1931, at a time of international economic crisis, this Committee took extensive evidence, closely questioning 57 witnesses and receiving submissions from 31 further people and 15 associations and institutions. These represented the broad spectrum of informed opinion in the country ranging from the Governor of the Bank of England through the representatives of clearing and merchant banks to individual industrialists, trade unionists and politicians. Groups as diverse as the TUC, the FBI, the Central Landowners Association and the Economic Freedom League all ensured that their views were presented. However, there was one group from whom no evidence was taken and none given and that was the Stock Exchange and its membership. The activities, functions and importance of these institutions received scant attention and little sustained analysis or discussion. From the few references that were made the consensus emerges that the Stock Exchange was considered of little significance in the whole question of finance and the economy. On the positive side praise was given to provincial brokers who were regarded as playing a role in mobilizing capital for small companies. Conversely, on the negative side criticisms were made of the Stock Exchange's diversion of funds into valueless bouts of speculation and fraudulent company promotion. Altogether the Stock Exchange was seen as making a marginal contribution to either prosperity or depression.[1]

It can only be said that the viewpoint which saw the Stock Exchange as either an irrelevancy or corrupting influence was commonplace throughout the nineteenth century itself. As one writer wrote rhetorically in 1851:[2] 'how is it that no serious attempt has ever been made to impose a check upon that most fruitful cause of crime and misery – the Stock Exchange?'

The fiction of the time abounds with references to the ease with which money could be lost on the Stock Exchange, as in the novel, *The Dynamiter*, by Robert Louis Stevenson: 'A hundred pounds will with difficulty support you for a year; with somewhat more difficulty you may spend it in a night; and without any difficulty at all you may lose it in five minutes on the Stock Exchange.'[3] Reinforced by the conclusions of the Macmillan Committee, it is this opinion that has prevailed in the twentieth century, with most of the historical literature highlighting the apparent long-standing division between the Stock Exchange on the one hand, and the finance of the economy on the other. Whatever else the Stock Exchange did, it was not felt to contribute much to meeting the capital requirements of the economy, which is regarded by most writers as being synonymous with manufacturing industry, and it certainly did not promote structural change. Recently Ingham has suggested, in the aptly titled book *Capitalism Divided*, that 'Britain's movement towards modern mass production industry was impeded by the structure of the domestic financial system. This was not simply a matter of the export of capital, but also the absence of any close institutional links between finance and industry.'[4] These conclusions characterize the work of numerous scholars who have investigated the Stock Exchange from the perspective of either the finance of business of the development of the economy.[5]

### Importance of the Stock Exchange

There are two simple measures of the importance of the Stock Exchange in the British economy in this period. The first is to compare the paid-up value of quoted securities with the estimated capital stock. This is done in Table 5.1. From these crude statistics it can be seen that quoted securities were equivalent to 36 per cent of the capital stock in 1853/5, rising to 46 per cent in 1873 and 132 per cent in 1913, before falling back to half that level – 64 per cent – in 1920, and then recovering to 120 per cent in 1933. However, among the securities quoted a high proportion represented foreign rather than domestic capital, while another major constituent comprised government debt, mostly created neither to capitalize assets nor fund capital projects but to finance current expenditure, especially during periods of war. If these two categories – foreign and government – are excluded from the securities quoted on the Stock Exchange then its significance assumes a somewhat different complexion. In 1853/5 the domestic non-government securities quoted were equivalent to only 7 per cent of the capital stock, but there was substantial subsequent growth for the proportion reached 11 per cent in 1873 and 37 per cent in 1913. In contrast, by 1920 the Stock Exchange's contribution to the capital stock had fallen dramatically to 14 per cent, with inflation and wartime expenditure. Even by 1933 the proportion was only 30 per cent, despite a major decline in the capital stock due to deflation, depression and the loss of Southern Ireland. Thus, in aggregate terms it is clear that from the mid-nineteenth century onwards, the Stock Exchange was steadily increasing its involvement with the domestic capital stock but that trend was spectacularly reversed between 1914 and 1918, before resuming its previous course. Under peacetime conditions the Stock Exchange was coming to play a more

*Table 5.1   Securities quoted on the Stock Exchange, 1853–1933[b]*

| Year | Gross capital stock[a] | Total | Domestic[c] | Foreign[d] | Domestic (excl. gov.)[e] |
|------|------|------|------|------|------|
| 1853 | — | £1.22 bn | £1.11 bn | £0.11 bn | £0.25 bn |
| 1856 | £3.43 bn | — | — | — | — |
| 1873 | 4.94 | 2.26 | 1.41 | 0.85 | 0.56 |
| 1913 | 8.50 | 11.26 | 4.47 | 6.79 | 3.18 |
| 1920 | 25.86 | 16.58 | 9.46 | 7.11 | 3.71 |
| 1933 | 15.42 | 18.48 | 11.55 | 6.93 | 4.55 |

*Notes:*
a. Gross reproducible capital (cost at current replacement cost).
b. Paid-up value not current market value.
c. Consists of the following categories – domestic government; domestic railways; other transport and communications; gas, electricity and water; manufacturing and commerce. Over time the last four categories came to include overseas assets so that the domestic total is a maximum one.
d. Consists of foreign governments; foreign railways; agriculture, fishing and forestry; mining. The last two were almost entirely foreign.
e. Domestic minus all securities issued by central, local and municipal government. (Part of this was issued to finance capital projects or acquire assets).

*Sources:*
Capital Stock: C. H. Feinstein, *Statistical Table of National Income, Expenditure and output of the U.K., 1855–1965* (Cambridge, 1972), Table T103.
E. V. Morgan and W. A. Thomas, *The Stock Exchange. Its History and Functions* (London, 1962), pp. 282–3.

important role in the finance of economic activity through the growing securitization of both debt and capital, though other means remained of greater importance throughout.

The second measure is to compare the sectoral distribution of the paid-up capital of quoted securities with the composition of the capital stock, here used as a proxy for the demand for finance within the economy (cf. Tables 5.2 and 5.3).

From these rough estimates it is obvious that the securities quoted on the Stock Exchange were not all representative of the British economy's demand for capital. Quoted securities were dominated by government debt, only a small proportion of which was reflected in the capital stock, through such operations as the Post Office or municipal enterprise. At the same time the Stock Exchange was increasingly oriented towards foreign securities before World War I, for they reached 60 per cent of the total paid-up capital by 1913, and then declined in the inter-war years.

However, on more detailed examination certain trends become obvious. In terms of domestic securities the 60 years before World War I witnessed a major expansion in the non-government element, which was only 23 per cent in 1853 but 71 per cent in

*Table 5.2   Securities quoted on the Stock Exchange*

| A) *Proportion by sector* | | | | | |
|---|---|---|---|---|---|
| Category | 1853 | 1873 | 1913 | 1920 | 1933 |
| Government Domestic | 70% | 38% | 11% | 35% | 38% |
| Foreign | 6 | 22 | 33 | 19 | 21 |
| Total | 76 | 60 | 45 | 53 | 59 |
| Railways Domestic | 16 | 17 | 11 | 8 | 6 |
| Foreign | 3 | 16 | 26 | 23 | 14 |
| Total | 19 | 32 | 37 | 31 | 21 |
| Other transport and communications | 1 | 1 | 3 | 2 | 4 |
| Gas, electricity and water | 1 | 1 | 1 | 1 | 2 |
| Financial services | 1 | 5 | 5 | 4 | 4 |
| Manufacturing and commerce | 2 | 1 | 8 | 7 | 10 |
| Agriculture, fishing and forestry | — | — | — | — | — |
| Mining | 1 | — | 1 | 1 | 1 |
| B) *Proportion by location*[a] | | | | | |
| Domestic | 90 | 62 | 40 | 57 | 64 |
| Foreign | 10 | 38 | 60 | 43 | 36 |
| C) *Proportion by source* | | | | | |
| Domestic Government | 77 | 61 | 29 | 61 | 61 |
| Domestic Non-government | 23 | 39 | 71 | 39 | 39 |
| D) *Proportion by economic activity*[b] | | | | | |
| Domestic Manufacturing & commerce | 9 | 5 | 27 | 32 | 39 |
| Transport & communications | 83 | 73 | 48 | 43 | 39 |
| Gas, water, electricity | 3 | 3 | 5 | 5 | 7 |
| Services | 5 | 19 | 19 | 19 | 15 |

*Notes:* See Table 5.4, p. 104
*Source:*
Morgan and Thomas, *The Stock Exchange*, pp. 282–3.

1913. It took the war and subsequent government policies to alter the balance to its former position, with government debt comprising 61 per cent of the paid-up capital of domestic quoted securities in both 1920 and 1933. Excluding government debt entirely from domestic securities it can be seen that the Stock Exchange was becoming involved in more diverse areas of the British economy, expanding beyond the railways into manufacturing industry, distribution and services. These trends continued throughout, despite the war and the subsequent economic difficulties, with the share of manufacturing and commerce growing from 5 per cent in 1873 to 27 per cent in 1913, 32 per cent in 1920 and 39 per cent in 1933. Nevertheless, large and important sectors of the British economy appear to have made no call whatsoever on the Stock Exchange, most notably agriculture and housing, which, between them, were responsible for 46 per cent of the capital stock in 1856 and 34 per cent in 1937.

*Table 5.3  Gross capital stock, 1856–1937*

|  | (excludes inventories) | | | (includes inventories) | | |
| --- | --- | --- | --- | --- | --- | --- |
| Category | 1856 | 1873 | 1913 | 1913 | 1924 | 1937 |
| Agriculture | 19.1% | 15.4% | 6.2% | 9.2% | 8.2% | 6.1% |
| Mining | 1.6 | 2.2 | 2.1 | 2.0 | 2.2 | 1.9 |
| Manufacturing and commerce | 25.3 | 25.8 | 28.3 | 33.2 | 33.0 | 31.0 |
| Housing | 27.3 | 25.1 | 24.1 | 21.0 | 23.1 | 27.5 |
| Transport and communications | 18.5 | 22.6 | 23.4 | 20.5 | 19.5 | 16.5 |
| Gas, water and electricity | 1.7 | 2.7 | 4.8 | 4.4 | 4.5 | 7.0 |
| Public and professional services | 6.5 | 6.2 | 11.1 | 9.7 | 9.5 | 10.0 |

*Source:*
R. C. O. Matthews, C. H. Feinstein and G. J. C. Odling-Smee, *British Economic Growth, 1855–1973* (Oxford, 1982), pp. 222–3.

Generally, from this evidence there do appear to be grounds for criticizing the Stock Exchange on its contribution to the British economy: on the one hand, a diversion of funds overseas and, on the other, a failure to become more fully involved in the industrial sector. There was clearly a growing commitment to foreign securities, the paid-up capital of which was greater than domestic by 1913, though this movement was reversed during and after the war. Within the domestic securities quoted those issued by government at all levels were of major significance, and though that position was lost by 1913 the war restored it. Apart from government securities the Stock Exchange's main involvement was in areas of social overhead capital such as the provision of transport and the supply of gas, electricity and water, rather than agriculture, mining, manufacturing, retailing or construction. The Stock Exchange was tied to the finance of domestic and foreign governments, railways and utilities, and though its participation in domestic industry was growing this remained of minor significance throughout the period. Contemporary impression and government investigation are borne out by statistical analysis, or so it might seem.

It is this weakness in the links between formal capital markets – principally the Stock Exchange – and industry that is used by many authors to suggest that here lay the principal cause of Britain's relatively slow economic growth since 1870. As the securities market came to play an increasingly central role in the allocation of financial resources, it diverted the stream of finance away from the potentially productive areas of the economy, like engineering, chemicals, energy and communications, into much less dynamic sectors such as overseas railways and foreign government borrowing. In particular, Kennedy has compared Britain unfavourably with its major industrial competitors in the relative size of its advanced industrial sectors, with serious long-term repercussions for the economy, and suggested strongly that the cause of this lay in the London capital market

the operations of British capital markets played a central role in first creating, and then maintaining an industrial structure capable of only limited growth . . .

because possibilities for diversifying risks across financial assets representing both industrial and social overhead capital were so limited in London, risk-taking was inhibited and this was reflected in low rates of return on the majority of widely traded British financial assets.[6]

Essentially, his findings indicate that the London Stock Exchange was an excellent market in which investors could trace government stocks, railroad securities, municipal and public utility bonds, and the shores of mining and real estate enterprise, many of which operated abroad, but a very poor place to buy and sell industrial securities. As such, it transmitted the wrong signals to investors and hence was largely responsible for Britain's economic decline.[7]

## The Financial Network

However, before accepting the conventional analysis it is important to review the way the various components of the British economy were financed and the extent to which their demand for capital was satisfied. The Stock Exchange's lack of involvement may perhaps be explained by a lack of demand for the services it could provide rather than its failure to supply. Kennedy himself recognizes this position for the United States in this period when he suggests that,

> In a sense, because of the greater level and wider distribution of wealth and the generally buoyant economic environment which this created, formal financial markets were less necessary in the late nineteenth century in promoting a given rate of economic growth in the U.S. than in Europe.[8]

He even accepts that such informal channels existed in Britain at the same time, and that they contributed substantially to the provision of finance. However, whereas in the case of the United States the lack of demand for all the services of the formal financial market is used to explain its lack of involvement, such an excuse is not allowable in the British case, according to Kennedy.[9]

Demand for capital within the British economy was differentiated in terms of amount, location, use and risk. At one extreme was the provision of a railway network which was both largely indivisible and substantial, necessitating the commitment of a large amount of funds for a long period at one time, and producing a guaranteed return over many years. At the other extreme were many manufacturing or commercial ventures in which the initial capital requirement was both small and divisible, with considerable scope for further expansion financed by reinvestment over time, assisted by bank and trade credit or the issue of securities once success had been established. Between these two extremes existed complete diversity, creating scope for different methods of financing, ranging from the public flotation of a major new enterprise to self-finance out of personal savings. At the same time financing itself was becoming more complex as demand for intermediation expanded with the growing scale of operations and the increasing separation of borrower and lender in a heavily populated, sophisticated economy. There was a constant need to switch finance between different sectors and regions in response to demand, as some declined and others expanded. As the nature of the demand for capital was so varied it would be unrealistic to expect that it would be supplied in only one way.

Within the British economy, for example, the simple most important demand came from housing, which absorbed around a quarter of the available supply throughout (cf. Table 5.3.). However, virtually none of this came via the Stock Exchange, being provided on either an individual basis or by government (cf. Table 5.2). Does this indicate a failure of even greater dimension than the lack of a close involvement with manufacturing? As an investment house property required constant management in order to ensure that responsible tenants were found, rents were regularly collected and the necessary maintenance was undertaken. This was more easily done if the owners themselves were able to exercise personal supervision, giving a bias to local and individual investment. Housing was also an easily divisible investment as each house could earn a return as soon as completed. There was thus no need to mobilize finance on a national basis to construct a complete housing stock, and then manage it as one enterprise. Instead, there existed a devolved structure through which the finance for housing could be obtained on a local basis from interested investors. This centred on the local solicitor who, through his clients, was in touch both with those interested in investing in house property, such as the local business community, and those with prospective or existing property for sale, such as another client or small-scale speculative builder. The solicitor was also in a position to arrange for a mortgage on the property, using the funds placed with him by other clients, though banks, building societies and insurance companies became increasingly involved, attracted by the prospect of a secure, long-term return on real heritable property. It was by these methods that almost all Britain's housing stock was financed before World War I, with around one million investors supplying the capital required.[10]

This did not mean that housing finance was not part of the national capital market or uninfluenced by events elsewhere in the economy. Investors in house property could easily find alternatives, both in their own locality or elsewhere, and this became progressively easier as the capital market became more integrated. According to Stimson & Sons, a firm of London estate agents, writing in 1896, 'Bank rate governs sale of properties – when low incentive to invest in property, when high people content with bank interest.'[11]

In the 1890s, for instance, a shortage of suitable alternative investments led to a rise in property prices and a boom in housing construction, which lasted until 1904, after which a reaction set in due to an accumulation of unsold and unlet property, uncertainty about future demand, higher interest rates, and better investment opportunities elsewhere. The capital market was rationing supply efficiently in response to the price the housing sector was willing to pay in the form of rent and mortgage interest. As this price was bid up in the years immediately before the war, and the attractiveness of alternative investments waned, so the level of house building rose. Housing was not a social service but a business and the cry of the homeless was only heeded by a few charities and municipal authorities. However, with the cessation of construction during World War I, and the rent controls that were established as a result, the nature of housing finance changed fundamentally. The amount of new housing, the construction of which required to be financed, was very large but the low rents neither generated sufficient funds within the housing sector nor attracted funds from outside. One solution would have been to abandon fixed rents but this was not done, forcing housing to be provided either as a social service or by the individual for himself. Consequently,the limited involvement of the Stock Exchange with the finance of housing reflected the nature of demand before 1914, the success of traditional mechanisms and the lack of returns in the post-war years to all but home owners.[12]

In a similar fashion to housing and for the same reasons, other substantial sectors of the British economy had their financial needs wholly or partially met without any involvement of the Stock Exchange, whether it was agriculture, mining, manu- facturing or most services. In agriculture, for example, there was a division between the landowner who provided the fixed capital, in the form of improved land and buildings, often with the assistance of a mortgage, and the individual farmer who ran the farm and provided the working capital. The mechanism in manufacturing can be seen clearly through the development of the Coventry cycle/motor-cycle/motor-car industry from the 1890s. Initially, the capital requirements were tiny as each part of the manufacturing process could be subdivided and distributed over numerous individual firms, and then the parts collected together and assembled to produce the final product. Cooperation reduced the scale of operations to a level that was accessible for any individual with only modest savings. The fixed capital required came from the individual himself supported by business and family connections, with the working capital being provided by banks and suppliers. Success then generated the finance for future expansion in either expanding output or diversifying into motor-cycles or, later, motor-cars. These profits were also a signal to outside investors that the industry was prospering, and so it was relatively easy to obtain further funds from a wider investing public as a tangible business, rather than an entrepreneur's dream, was now in existence. The likes of Austin and Daimler followed this path, and successful firms in growth industries never found themselves deprived of finance either from re-invested profits or public issues of securities, even during the generally more difficult inter-war years.[13]

Though the capital requirements of individual enterprises were continuously on the increase, putting increased pressure on the savings of the community, so was both collective and individual wealth. It remained a fairly simple matter for an entrepreneur with a successful record or with the right contacts among family, friends and business associates, to obtain the necessary finance for any promising new venture, without the need to attempt a public issue of shares. The Macmillan Committee was informed that £50,000 could be raised with little difficulty. Generally, for every activity there existed an interested and informed group who could be called upon to supply the necessary finance if they were convinced of the merits of either the proposal or the proposer. This element of familiarity was vital for bankruptcy, fraud and failure were commonplace, and only intimate knowledge could reduce the risks to a level which made the investment a matter of calculation rather than a gamble.

Industries as diverse as coal mining, shipping and cotton spinning obtained their finance from their own localities, as it was there that the greatest concentration of informed investors existed. For example, of the 1,650 companies that appealed for funds from the investors of north-east Scotland between 1845 and 1895, those that were successful in obtaining support (and most were not) were those operating in the region, being promoted by individuals respected locally or pursuing activities with which local investors were both familiar and in which they were successful.[14]

## Demand for external finance

Despite the existence of these methods by which industry was financed numerous companies were publicly floated in such fields as manufacturing, mining and commerce. This happened not only at the local level, with the securities of numerous such firms being quoted in the provincial stock exchanges, but also nationally, where the London Stock Exchange and its members played a role of increasing importance. Between 1853 and 1933 the paid-up capital of the industrial and commercial companies listed on British stock exchanges rose from £21.9 million to £1,773.7 million, and most of these operated domestically (cf. Table 5.4). However, it was rarely the need to raise capital that led to their adoption of the joint-stock form and the acquisition of a stock exchange quotation, but other requirements for almost all were the conversion of established private businesses into public enterprises. For example, the need to facilitate the division between ownership and management on the retirement of the founder or the merging of individual firms so as to reorganize production were among the principal forces behind the flotation of manufacturing concerns. The growth of these joint-stock manufacturing companies did not indicate an abandonment of the informal means of finance because of its inadequacies but an awareness of the flexibility and convenience of the joint-stock form for established business at a certain stage of their development. A public issue of shares and a Stock Exchange quotation were important in facilitating further expansion in the fields of manufacturing, commerce and allied areas rather than a necessity from the outset. Certainly, the timing of company flotations, especially those involving conversions of established firms, coincide far more with a desire and ability of investors to purchase the securities being issued than a need by the industries concerned, or the vendors, to raise new capital or to realize assets. This was obviously true of the immediate post-war flotation boom when the market responded to the confident mood of investors and helped to create the securities they wanted to purchase.[15]

Whereas before World War I there was little sign that informal means were failing to provide new enterprises in novel and diverse fields with the capital they required, and thus encourage the growth of intermediation, hints of difficulties did emerge in the inter-war years. E.L. Payton, representative of the National Union of Manufacturers, with 3,000 small firms nationwide, told the Macmillan Committee that, because of the depressed state of the economy, 'most of your friends have got their own commercial difficulties and have not their money free to put into that business, and so you retard it.'[16] Even Sir Robert Kindersley, director of the City merchant bank, Lazard Bros & Co., admitted before the same committee, 'I think

*Table 5.4  Securities quoted on British stock exchanges, 1853–1933*[a]

| Category | 1853 (£millions) | 1873 (£millions) | 1913 (£millions) | 1920 (£millions) | 1933 (£millions) |
|---|---|---|---|---|---|
| Government[b] Domestic | 853.6 | 858.9 | 1,290.1 | 5,753.2 | 6,992.1 |
|     Foreign | 69.7 | 486.5 | 3,746.1 | 3,094.2 | 3,963.9 |
|     Total | 923.3 | 1,345.4 | 5,036.2 | 8,847.4 | 10,956.0 |
| Railways Domestic | 193.7 | 374.0 | 1,217.3 | 1,259.5 | 1,125.4 |
|     Foreign | 31.3 | 353.3 | 2,930.5 | 3,888.8 | 2,665.8 |
|     Total | 225.0 | 727.3 | 4,147.8 | 5,148.3 | 3,791.2 |
| Other transport and comm.[c] | 16.6 | 30.8 | 323.8 | 347.3 | 659.1 |
| Gas, electricity and water | 7.8 | 18.9 | 156.7 | 185.2 | 311.3 |
| Financial services[d] | 13.1 | 105.9 | 609.5 | 715.0 | 683.6 |
| Manufacturing and commerce[e] | 21.9 | 25.5 | 872.2 | 1,203.1 | 1,773.7 |
| Agriculture, fishing and forestry[f] | — | 1.1 | 24.9 | 32.3 | 59.1 |
| Mining[g] | 7.4 | 7.6 | 91.4 | 97.5 | 242.2 |
| Total | 1,215.5 | 2,262.5 | 11,262.5 | 16,576.1 | 18,476.2 |

*Notes:*
a.  These were compiled from the *Stock Exchange Official Intelligence* (originally *Burdett's*) and included provincial as well as London quoted stocks.
b.  All levels of government.
c.  Canals, docks, shipping, telegraphs, telephones, tramways and omnibus. Many of these were foreign.
d.  Banks, discount houses, insurance, financial trusts, investment companies, land and property. Many of these were foreign and the sector was dominated initially by banks, but later investment companies, with an orientation overseas, became the largest sector.
e.  Including coal and copper mining companies some of which would be foreign.
f.  Rubber, tea and coffee plantations. Hence, entirely foreign.
g.  Metal mining. Hence almost entirely foreign.
*Source:*
E. V. Morgan and G. W. A. Thomas, *The Stock Exchange: Its History and Functions* (London, 1962), pp. 282–3.

for small concerns the probability is that there is something lacking in our financial organisation.'[17] However, even in the inter-war years firms in growth areas, like motor vehicles, do not appear to have experienced any real problems in raising funds through both informal and formal avenues.[18] It was Sir Mark Webster Jenkinson, an accountant with extensive experience of company finance, who clearly identified in his evidence to the Macmillan Committee, the central problem that arose after the war: 'I think new industries generally can find the capital. I am thinking more particularly of some of the older industries.'[19]

World War I made a major impact on the British economy because of its long-term impact on the international economy with which Britain was closely integrated, and its slowing-down of the necessary process of adjustment within Britain. This resulted in a depressed economy for Britain in the 1920s, with its worst manifestations concentrated in those sectors most dependent upon international trade.[20] One consequence of this was a prolonged fall in business income, with the gross profit rate between 1924 and 1937 averaging around one-third the pre-war level, at constant prices. Inevitably this reduced the supply of funds available for self-financed growth, especially in those sectors most badly affected, like shipbuilding in the 1920s. Added to this contraction in profits was the increased level of taxation owing to the need to service the vastly increased National Debt with which Britain emerged from the war. Thus, even out of the profits that were being made, less was left at the disposal of the business sector to fund either new projects or established firms. Overall, after depreciation, net savings were just over half the 1873–1913 level between 1925 and 1937.[21]

Even the act of taxation itself, though it may be regarded as merely redistributing income from one group in society to another, undermined the mechanism of self-finance, as Sir Josiah Stamp pointed out:

> You cannot expect these private businesses to be financed as they were by people who knew them once the money has left them by high taxation and gets into the hands of rentiers who do not know them, and if it is bid for by home enterprise it goes into the very large concerns. No *rentier* getting his war loan return and looking round for further investment is going to put the money into the business of John Jones or Tom Smith whose securities are not marketable, he will put them into the securities of some large combine. You have altered the whole direction of savings by that very fact.[22]

Consequently, by the mid-1920s, companies in the major sectors of British manufacturing, most notably the export industries, were being forced to look for external finance for the first time if they were to avoid bankruptcy and closure, as they had exhausted the traditional sources. The difficulty was that the very firms looking to solve their financial problems, by the issue of securities, were the ones least attractive to investors because of the commercial difficulties they were in. Sir Roland Nugent, of the Federation of British Industry, explained the problem:

> I think you are in a vicious circle, you cannot go to the public for capital, because your dividend or profit record is pretty bad, for the same reason you have not accumulated reserves, yet you cannot get on the profit earning scale again until you re-condition your plant, and there you are.[23]

From all the basic industries the complaint was the same – depression and taxation had undermined the means of finance that had served them well until the war, but now they could not obtain the funds they required to modernize their plant and keep their businesses going.[24]

Therefore, the 'Macmillan Gap' was only incidentally the problem of financing new manufacturing enterprises. More importantly, it was the question of what to do with long-established and once-successful firms that could no longer generate profits, had exhausted their reserves and were a poor risk for further lending. To suggest that the Macmillan Gap was anything different is a misreading of evidence. Between financiers and industrialists the only quarrel was not over the degree of assistance already extended to the industries concerned but whether the condition they were in was sufficiently temporary to justify extraordinary financial aid until the economic upturn came. Certainly by 1930, the prospect of recovery was receding fast, with Sir W. N. Goschen, Chairman of the National Provincial Bank, concluding: 'I think when the industry has reached such a point that it has exhausted all its capital and credit that it is entitled to have there is only one thing – to disappear.'

Harsh as this viewpoint was it was shared by both other bankers, like J. W. Beaumont Pease of Lloyds Bank, and industrialists like the shipbuilders Sir William Lithgow and W. L. Hickens.[25] Any efforts by the Stock Exchange or its members could not have persuaded investors to buy securities inssued by firms with a record of losses and little prospect of future success, no matter their prosperity in the past. The Stock Exchange did respond to demand, for issues of securities were of growing importance to British industry between the wars. However, neither the Stock Exchange nor any other financial institution was capable of rescuing those concerns which could no longer find a market for their products at prevailing prices.[26] The responsibility for the economic conditions that led to their downfall lay with the war and its aftermath, both internally and externally, and the policies adopted by successive governments, not the financial system in general or the Stock Exchange in particular.

In complete contrast to the financing of such activities as manufacturing industry, where the Stock Exchange's role grew gradually, it was of major importance from the outset in meeting the financial requirements of government, infrastructure projects or most forms of overseas investment. Either the amounts required were too large, the time available too short or the necessary contacts lacking for the informal market and accumulated revenue to suffice. For example, informal means could not provide the government with the finance needed to support the war effort between 1914 and 1918, nor the funds required to develop railway and tramway networks; telegraph and telephone systems; and electricity, gas and water supplies. As the economy's need for more and larger capital projects grew so did the pressure put on the Stock Exchange to mobilize savings for long-term investment on an impersonal basis in contrast to short-term and personal. Therefore, it was in the twin fields of government funding and infrastructure finance that the Stock Exchange could make its greatest contribution by facilitating what was not otherwise possible.

However, in the sale of the securities issued by governments and corporate enterprise stockbrokers played a relatively minor role. Government issues, whether home or overseas, were largely in the hands of the banks, both merchant and commercial, with growing competition from the investment trusts. In the field of corporate enterprise brokers were more active, especially outside London where financial intermediation was less specialized. There the stockbroker was one of the few experts resident in the community, particularly with banking amalgamation eliminating the independent local banker. Even there, though, there was competition from the ubiquitous solicitor as well as the emerging accountants. Generally, stockbrokers were only one among many groups and individuals who undertook

106

company promotion and they were by no means the most important. There was never any shortage of those willing to enter the arena of company promotion in response to the public's demand for attractive and topical investments. As foreign borrowers declined in the inter-war years the merchant banks turned increasingly to the issue of domestic securities, at the expense of less well-established groups.[27]

Consequently, in the business of persuading the investing public to purchase the securities being issued by both governments and companies, the brokers were of only minor significance, frequently acting in a subsidiary role to merchant bankers who used brokers as a means of establishing contact with investors. It was only in the provinces that the brokers were important participants in the new issue market, because the volume of business could not support specialist intermediaries either in total or for each individual issue. Admittedly there were a few London brokerage firms, like Sperling & Co., that did undertake an extensive new issue business, but they appear to be exceptions.[28]

## Role of the Stock Exchange

Though the members of the Stock Exchange were involved in a variety of activities, including company promotion, their prime function as a collective body, and the purpose of the institutions to which they belonged, was to provide a market for the securities whose issue was largely the preserve of others. The Stock Exchange's contribution to and importance in the British economy cannot be assessed by an examination of the marginal activities of its members but only by an evaluation of this prime function. The type of institutions or enterprises that made principal use of the Stock Exchange, through the issue of securities and their subsequent quotation, were those which required long-term capital (cf. Table 5.4). Governments required to fund debts that they had already incurred and could not pay for out of current revenue, but which they could service by way of interest payments and eventually repay. Similarly, infrastructure projects involved large-scale and permanent capital expenditure with a return being obtained over a long period out of the revenue generated. Both types offered no prospect of a rapid return and quick repayment, which severely curtailed the supply of funds available for such an investment. Few investors were confident enough of the future and in a strong enough position to alienate permanently their savings, irrespective of the return offered. Over time institutions like insurance companies, investment trusts and banks became adept at forecasting the demands on their assets, so releasing funds for long-term investment. However, the demands for such funds also grew rapidly as economic activity became more capital-intensive.

The importance of the Stock Exchange was that by providing a market for securities it became easier to persuade investors to purchase new securities and thus facilitate the finance of long-term projects. With the possibility – or, even better, the certainty – that securities could easily be converted into money, and money into securities, access was obtained to the much larger pool of short-term savings. Those requiring finance could obtain it for the time required while those providing it could realize their investment at will not by withdrawal but by the sale to another investor. Thus, the contribution made by the Stock Exchange was to separate the needs of the borrower and the lender, provide each with the finance or investment they wanted, and so increase the supply of funds available by mobilizing total savings for productive use. As the Stock Exchange operated behind the scenes of finance rather than channelling funds directly into particular sectors of the economy, its importance is both easily missed by contemporaries and later commentators and not easily explained by simple reference to the finance it provided.[29]

As the market provided by the Stock Exchange improved and came to embrace different types of securities, so did the employment of short-term funds in the holding of long-term investments. It was reported to the London Stock Exchange in 1909, for instance, that 'the large English Banks, Discount and Insurance Trust Companies . . . continually enter into large transactions in stock exchange securities for short periods at rates calculated to give only a slight profit over the Bill rates for money'.[30]

A further refinement that was more common was for banks and other financial institutions to lend to investors, brokers and jobbers on the strength of the securities they held. This represented employment for the most liquid of the bank's assets as the loans could be easily and quickly recalled in the near certainty that the money would be repaid either by obtaining a replacement loan or by the sale of the securities. Between the banks and their vast holdings of short-term deposits and the securities representing long-term debt there thus existed a close relationship through the increasing use of quoted securities as collateral for loans. As F. Hyde, Managing Director of the Midland Bank, observed: 'We cannot lend our money direct for capital purposes, but we can lend our money on a marketable share. The effect of lending money on a marketable share may be that we are finding money for capital purposes that we would not find in the shape of a capital advance.'[31]

The growing sophistication of, and specialization within, the British financial system not only allowed the banker to lend long-term but encouraged him to do so, safe in the knowledge that the underlying asset, in the form of a share or debenture, could be realized at will via the Stock Exchange. German bankers, faced with a much smaller and less active Stock Exchange, were envious of their British counterparts, and were worried by the risks direct participation in industry exposed them to because they did not possess such an easy alternative for employing their deposits. During the questioning of the Macmillan Committee Jakob Goldschmidt, of the Darmstadter und National bank, was asked by the Chairman, 'Do I understand that the German banker, like the English banker, does not like to have his money tied up permanently in industry?' To which he replied, 'No, the German banker dislikes that as much as any banker anywhere else in the world.'[32]

While many in Britain looked with envy on the German banking system, both before and after the war – and since – because of its close connections with industry, the Germans themselves were well aware of the necessities which had forced such actions upon them and the problems it caused by locking up funds that could be withdrawn at short notice by depositors in unrealizable assets.

Not all securities offered suitable collateral for loans for it was necessary that they should possess an active market and be widely held, so that they could be easily bought and sold without dramatic price fluctuations or serious delays. For much of the nineteenth century only the National Debt met these criteria but, increasingly, a variety of other securities came to do so, including the issues of the major railway companies and industrial concerns, as well as some from overseas. Thus, the Stock Exchange's ability to mobilize domestic savings for investment gradually pervaded more areas of the economy. Before 1914 this change was greatly aided by the decline in the size of the National Debt in relation to quoted securities, even with the growth of local authority borrowing (cf. Table 5.4). However, this tendency was reversed with the quadrupling of the government debt during the war. This provided investors with an attractive alternative investment to the variety of domestic and foreign issues they had turned to before the war. With subsequent deflation and currency instability these sterling-denominated fixed interest securities, secured on government revenues, provided an atractive home for the funds of investors, with possibly detrimental consequences for both overseas issues and the stocks and shares of domestic enterprise (cf. Table 5.4).[33]

The success of the London Stock Exchange, in particular, in developing the largest and most active market in securities attracted not only the otherwise idle balances of British banks and financial institutions but also a growing volume of such funds from abroad before 1914. As banking became more sophisticated, more competitive and more international banks sought ways to employ safely and remuneratively all the funds at their disposal, above the level that prudence dictated. Hence the attractions of either investment in securities quoted in London or lending on their collateral. As a result, whereas net UK bank deposits rose from £501.7 million in 1877 to £1,062.7 million in 1914, those of foreign and colonial banks present in London climbed from £106.9 million to £1,855.2 million or from 21 per cent to 157 per cent of the UK level. Obviously, not all this was available for direct or indirect investment in securities, but it does indicate the rapidly growing pool of savings, which the existence and efficient operation of the Stock Exchange allowed British borrowers to tap. The Stock Exchange may have been channelling British funds overseas before 1914 but it was also attracting cheap finance from abroad, including such countries as Germany, as part-recompense, as well as mobilizing savings at home.[34]

As with other developments in securities the war also affected the supply of short-term funds available for investments in, or lending upon, securities. The war itself, and the instabilities it caused, led to a partial shift away from London as the focus of the world's money market, thereby reducing the supply of foreign funds which had helped underpin demand for securities. In particular, international attention switched to New York. Additionally, in order to meet its increased expenses after the war, the British government resorted to the issue of Treasury Bills in large amounts. These were short-dated and self-liquidating and proved to be attractive and remunerative investments for the funds that previously had been lent on the collateral of securities or employed in holding finance and commercial bills. The result was to reduce further the demand for quoted stocks and shares in comparison to pre-war levels. Therefore, the altered international position of the inter-war years deprived the Stock Exchange of part of the short-term funds upon which it relied while the government itself became a major competitor for those that remained with the issue of Treasury Bills.[35]

Overall, therefore, one can detect a major divide with World War I in the contribution made by the Stock Exchange to the British economy. Before the war economic development was financed in a variety of distinct ways with the importance of the Stock Exchange steadily growing. Self-finance was commonplace in commerce, manufacturing, construction, agriculture and numerous other activities, where the scale of operations was insufficient to justify the need for intermediation of any kind. The securities that were issued tended to capitalize assets already in existence, for reasons of convenience and flexibility, rather than finance further development. Finance obtained through the issue of securities could be characterized largely as the prerogative of government and infrastructure at home and, increasingly abroad, with the Stock Exchange acting to increase the demand for such securities by expanding the supply of funds available for investment. In that the Stock Exchange played a complex but dynamic role for, by removing the distinction between short- and long-term investment, it mobilized funds world-wide that would otherwise have remained idle. It was this pressure of funds looking for investments in securities that led the joint-stock form to pervade even more areas of the British economy rather than inadequacies of finance by traditional means leading to an increasing resort to public flotation and new issues. In turn, this analysis suggests that the Stock Exchange was not only responding to the economy's demand for capital, where that required the facilities of a Stock Exchange, but that its success was forcing the pace of change by competing with the traditional means of finance and gradually supplanting them, as with the conversion of established private businesses into public companies.

With the war something of a change in direction occurred because of the rapid rise in government debt, government borrowing and the level of taxation, and the steep fall in the general profitability of British industry, reflecting the altered international environment. The war upset the delicate but slowly changing ways by which the various components of the economy were financed. In particular, the lower level of profits reduced the importance of accumulated reserves as a source of capital for industry at the very time when the government's requirements for both short- and long-term funding curtailed the Stock Exchange's ability to increase the supply of funds available for investment in securities. Some adjustment had to take place and it was overseas investment that was squeezed out in the end, adding further complications for the already depressed export industries like shipbuilding, coal-mining and textiles (cf. Table 5.4).

## Conclusion

This is not to say that the Stock Exchange itself did not make a contribution to the way the supply of finance was organized. In particular, the Stock Exchange was not a unified body but consisted of distinct and separate components, each with their own authorities, aims and privileges. There were for example, eighteen formally organized Exchanges in addition to London, as well as such specialist markets as that in Oldham for cotton spinning companies and in Mincing Lane for tea and rubber shares. Until the years immediately before World War I all these different Exchanges had existed in relative harmony, mainly because London did not impose any minimum commission rates and was lax in the implementation of the rules which would have restricted inter-market dealing, such as that forbidding jobbers to transact business with non-members. Thus an integrated securities market had developed which facilitated active nationwide trading in all types of securities, including increasingly numerous industrial and commercial issues. However, the membership of the London Stock Exchange began to fear that business was ebbing away from their market as telephonic communication removed its previous monopoly position on certain types of business. Its response was to erect barriers between itself and the other Exchanges, first by preventing jobbers making a market for outside brokers (1909) and, second, by establishing minimum commission rates which discriminated against non-members (1912). These were passed against considerable opposition and might have been reversed, but the war, which undermined much of the London Stock Exchange's international position, made the membership determined to preserve their position against all rivals. In addition, the London Stock Exchange emerged from the war as a more generally restrictive institution, outlawing certain practices which had made it attractive in the past, like dealings for the account in gilt-edged stock and the use of 3-month options. All this helped to reduce the service offered by the premier Stock Exchange – London – and create divisions within the market as a whole. The provincial Exchanges, for example, developed their own parallel market-making mechanisms to that existing in London because of the high commission charges and the prohibition. Inevitably, the result was to weaken the securities market by raising costs and increasing dealing times, which decreased the ability of securities to offer a safe haven for short-term funds.[36]

Nevertheless, though the quality of the service provided by the Stock Exchange did deteriorate between the wars, because of the restrictive practices imposed by London, this was of marginal importance in terms of the provision of finance. Of far greater significance was the relative reduction in the supply of funds for investment because of low profitability, taxation and London's diminished international role, and the unattractiveness of many of the available domestic investments. As W. L. Hichens observed, 'You cannot expect financial institutions to take interest in an industry which is being run at a loss. It is not reasonable.'[37]

The Stock Exchange was by no means perfect. It did perform a vital role that was largely unrecognized because it was neither direct nor obvious. The contribution it was making to economic life was growing before World War I. It did respond to the demand placed upon it as exhibited in the changes in the securities it quoted. However, it was very much a passive force circumscribed by economic conditions, international events and government policy, and it is in these areas – and especially the latter – that the causes of economic decline and the inter-war depression have to be sought rather than seeing the Stock Exchange and its membership as scapegoats. Britain between 1870 and 1939 was a large, advanced and complex economy with a major place in the international economy. The operation of the Stock Exchange reflected that position and its success or failure can only be judged in the context of the demands made of it and the environment within which it was allowed to operate. The service provided by the Stock Exchange after World War I certainly deteriorated but that hardly explains either the areas of technological failure before 1914 or the depressed state of the economy afterwards.


## Notes

1. Committee on Finance and Industry (Macmillan Committee), Report and Minutes of Evidence (HMSO 1931, Cmnd 3897).
2. Dot, *The Stock Exchange and its Victims* (London, 1851), p. 3.
3. Robert Louis Stevenson, *The Dynamiter* (London, 1885), p. 2.
4. G. Ingham, *Capitalism Divided?: The City and Industry in British Social Development* (London, 1984), p. 169, cf. pp. 10, 35, 153, 227–8, 241–2.
5. M. J. Wiener, *English Culture and the Decline of the Industrial Spirit, 1850–1980* (Cambridge, 1981), pp. 129, 166; A. K. Cairncross, *Home and Foreign Investment, 1870–1913* (Cambridge, 1953), pp. 90, 95–6; P. L. Cottrell, *Industrial Finance, 1830–1914* (London, 1980), pp. 146–53, 189; W. A. Thomas, *The Finance of British Industry, 1918–1976* (London, 1978), pp. 7, 102, 107; W. P. Kennedy, 'Economic growth and structural change in the United Kingdom, 1870–1914', *Journal of Economic History*, Vol.42 (1982), p. 112; M. H. Best and J. Humphries, 'The City and industrial decline', in B. Elbaum and W. Lazonick (eds), *The Decline of the British Economy* (Oxford, 1986), pp. 223, 236; W. P. Kennedy, *Industrial Structure, Capital Markets and the Origins of British Economic Decline* (Cambridge, 1987), pp. 56, 148–9.
6. Kennedy, *Industrial Structure*, p. 56.
7. Ibid., pp. 6, 8, 17–18, 27, 79, 110, 116, 117–18, 120, 123–5, 128–9, 132, 139–41, 148–9, 160, 162–3.
8. Ibid., p. 117.
9. Ibid., p. 124.
10. A. Offer, *Property and Politics: A Study of Landed and Urban Property in England between the 1880s and the Great War* (D.Phil, Oxford University, 1978), pp. 34, 36, 83–4, 330; *The Land: The Report of the Land Enquiry Committee* (London, 1914), Vol. II (urban), pp. 82–4; E. J. Cleary, *The Building Society Movement* (London, 1965), p. 151; R. J. Springett, *The Mechanics of Urban Land Development in Huddersfield* (PhD thesis, Leeds University, 1979), pp. 209, 271, 275, 352.
11. *Estates Gazette, 26 December 1896.*
12. S. B. Saul, 'House building in England, 1890–1914', *Economic History Review* Vol. 15 (1962/3), p. 133; Offer, *Property and Politics*, pp. 32, 192, 205, 214, 231.
13. D. Thomas and T. Donnelly, *The Motor Car Industry in Coventry since the 1890s* (London, 1985), pp. 17, 20, 23–4, 50–5, 58–9, 105; cf. Macmillan Committee: Minutes QQ3921, 6760, 7901, 7976, 8351, 8742.

14. J. B. Jeffreys, *Trends in Business Organisation in Great Britain since 1856* (PhD thesis, London University, 1938), p. 130; A. Essex-Crosby, *Joint-Stock Companies in Great Britain, 1890–1930* (M.Com, London University, 1938), pp. 228–30, D. H. MacGregor, 'Joint-stock companies and the risk factor', *Economic Journal*, Vol. 39 (1929), pp. 495–6; J. Scott and M. Hughes, *The Anatomy of Scottish Capital* (London, 1980), pp. 20, 37, 44, 46; R. C. Michie, *Money, Mania and Markets: Investment, Company Formation and the Stock Exchange in Nineteenth-Century Scotland* (Edinburgh, 1981), pp. 232–4; R. C. Michie, *The London and New York Stock Exchanges, 1850–1914* (London, 1987), ch.4.

15. G. L. Ayres, *Fluctuations in New Capital Issues on the London Money Market, 1899 to 1913* (MSc, London University, 1934), pp. 188–9, 202; A. R. Hall, *The London Capital Market and Australia, 1870–1914* (Canberra, 1963), p. 21; Cairncross, *Home and Foreign Investment*, p. 95; cf. chapters by Armstrong and Diaper in this volume.

16. Macmillan Committee, Minutes Q 22511.

17. Macmillan Committee, Minutes Q 1530.

18. Thomas, *Finance of British Industry*, pp. 91–2, 102.

19. Macmillan Committee, Minutes Q 3607.

20. Evidence of Professor Henry Clay to the Macmillan Committee Minutes QQ 8527, 8548.

21. R. C. O. Matthews, C. H. Feinstein and J. C. Odling-Smee, *British Economic Growth, 1856–1973* (Oxford, 1982), pp. 140, 149, 178, 190–2, 383–6, 518, 527; W. A. Thomas, *The Provincial Stock Exchanges* (London, 1973), pp. 256, 317; Thomas, *Finance of British Industry*, pp. 91–2, 96, 102, 107, 115, 117.

22. Macmillan Committee Minutes Q 3950.

23. Macmillan Committee Minutes Q 8380.

24. Macmillan Committee Minutes QQ 1530, 1537, 2511, 2536, 3607, 3651–3, 3695, 3706, 6760, 7976, 7980, 8351, 8365, 8372, 8382, 8400, 8494, 8548, 8576, 8694, 8696, 8742, 9267. Statements by Sir Mark Webster Jenkinson, 27 March 1930, *Central Landowners' Association*, 27 March 1930, H. Lakin-Smith, 11 July 1930.

25. Macmillan Committee Minutes QQ 1934 of 2257, 2271, 7980, 8382, 8494.

26. Cf. Thomas, *Finance of British Industry*.

27. W. J. Reader, *A House in the City* (London, 1979), pp. 98–100, S. Chapman, *The Rise of Merchant Banking* (London, 1984), pp. 16, 25, 96, 158; J. Sykes, *The Amalgamation Movement in English Banking, 1825–1924* (London, 1926), p. 186; cf. chapters by Armstrong, Cassis and Diaper in this volume.

28. Thomas, *Finance of British Industry*, pp. 42, 48–50; Thomas, *Provincial Stock Exchanges*, pp. 254–6, 318; cf. Diaper in this volume.

29. F. Machlup, *The Stock Market, Credit and Capital Formation* (London, 1940), p. 23; E. T. Powell, *The Evolution of the Money Market 1385–1915* (London, 1915), p. 576.

30. London Stock Exchange: Committee of General Purposes, 4 October 1909; cf. 8 July 1912, C. A. E. Goodhart, *The Business of Banking* (London, 1972), p.

131; R. S. Sayers, *The Bank of England 1891–1940* (Cambridge, 1976), pp. 25, 38–41; Michie, *London and New York Stock Exchanges*, ch. 5.

31. Macmillan Committee, Minutes Q 913 of QQ870–90.

32. Macmillan Committee Minutes Q 7285 of QQ 7283–4, Q 6760.

33. Macmillan Committee, Q 6971; National Monetary Commission, *Interviews on the Banking and Currency Systems* (Washington, 1910), pp. 108, 120, 134, 180; cf. R. C. Michie, 'The London Stock Exchange and the British securities market, 1850–1914', *Economic History Review*, Vol. 38 (1985).

34. F. Capie and Webber, *A Monetary History of the United Kingdom, 1870–1982* (London, 1983), Vol. 1, pp. 130, 254; League of Nations, *Memorandum on Commercial Banks, 1913–1929* (Genoa, 1931), pp. 294, 297.

35. Capie and Webber, *Monetary History*, pp. 130, 254; Macmillan Committee Minutes QQ 401, 494, 512, 560, 7598, 7603.

36. E. V. Morgan and W. A. Thomas, *The Stock Exchange: Its History and Functions* (London, 1962), pp. 221–6; Thomas, *The Provincial Stock Exchanges*, pp. 214–38; Michie, 'London Stock Exchange', pp. 75–82; D. Kynaston *The London Stock Exchange, 1870–1914: An Institutional History* (PhD London University, 1983), p. 261.

37. Macmillan Committee, Minutes Q 7980.

# 6 The rise and fall of the company promoter and the financing of British industry

*John Armstrong*

The period 1870 to 1914 was the heyday of the individual company promoter working on domestic industrial flotations. A number of features made these years golden for that breed. Before 1870 few manufacturing companies had adopted joint-stock limited liability and even fewer had become public companies. There was a much greater willingness to adopt these protective legal devices after 1880 and this provided numerous opportunities for the promoter to exploit. Since this was a novel phenomenon there were few formulas for firms to follow and thus the manufacturing company was at the mercy of the promoter's apparently greater expertise and knowledge. The promoter profited from this naivety. There were few rules. Neither company law nor the regulations of the Stock Exchange placed many restrictions on the methods the predatory promoter might employ. Snares that by modern standards would be illegal or unacceptable were fair game. The astute company promoter used the victim's own avarice to his advantage. By holding out the prospect of dazzling short-term gains to the owners, he was able to blind them to the fact that this was at the expense of their longer-term interests. This chapter examines why this was such a good time for the unscrupulous company promoter, the methods that were used, the effects they had on British industry, and why the period from the outbreak of World War I saw a decline in their importance.

Company promoters did not float only home industrials. They were willing to make a profit from any available source. Some promoters are particularly associated with the flotation of domestic manufacturing firms but they also dabbled in foreign issues as did E.T. Hooley and Horatio Bottomley, or local government bonds as did Clarence Hatry. Others were mainly promoters of foreign securities, but at times moved into domestic flotations, for instance Birch Crisp, Davison Dalziel and Sir Ernest Cassel. Although some promoters specialized in home industrials at certain periods of their careers, the methods they used, their motivation and morality was applied in a very similar fashion to their other issuing activities.

The individual company promoter was not the only agency for converting a private to a public company. Merchant banks occasionally deigned to be involved in the flotation of large, famous, manufacturing companies. Guinness, for instance, in 1886 used Baring Bros to convert them from a partnership to a public company.[1] Barings floated a number of other famous brewers including Whitbread & Co. and Combe & Co.[2] Sometimes the services of a stockbroker alone were used and the middleman – the promoter – who in any case needed to use a broker, cut out. Harry Panmure Gordon, the flamboyant Hatton Court broker, made quite a business out of floating home industrials. His most famous was Liptons in 1898,[3] and he was involved with a number of breweries including Ind Coope, Newcastle Breweries and Plymouth Breweries.[4] Foster and Braithwaite, another firm of brokers, made something of a speciality in British manufacturing firms, especially electrical engineering.[5] An alternative was for the firm to employ no outside specialists other than their regular advisers such as their bankers, solicitor and accountant. Harrison has shown this was not unusual in the cycle and motor car industries, and O'Hagan mentions one or two examples,[6] but there is little evidence that it was in widespread use elsewhere. Using an intermediary often increased the return to the vendor as well as increasing the probability of a successful flotation. Given these incentives and the novelty of the exercise most firms preferred to use a specialist.

## The functions of company promoters

What precisely were the functions of a company promoter? In brief they were to find a suitable business activity and turn it into a joint-stock, limited-liability company the shares of which were quoted on the Stock Exchange. The business might already be in existence in the form of a partnership, as Guinness was before Barings floated them in 1886,[7] or a 'private' limited-liability company as Schweppes was before Hooley floated them in 1897;[8] or it could be a brand new venture, though this was less common. Converting a partnership into a joint-stock limited-liability company was straightforward and relatively cheap. Under the Companies Act 1862, which was effective with minor amendments until the recodification of 1908, all that was needed was to file with the registrar a memorandum of association signed by seven shareholders stating the company's name and objects.[9] Subsequently, the company was required to send in a number of returns, such as the registered address, details of members and their shareholders, articles of association and a list of the directors. However, none of these was particularly onerous and it required no special skill to complete these tasks. Many firms carried them out on their own or with minor assistance from their solicitor or banker. Similarly, once the company was up and running the regular returns required by the registrar were minimal and well within the capability of the average company secretary. It was certainly not necessary to engage the services of a professional promoter for this stage of the process.

The Stock Exchange required a little more information than the registrar of companies. In order for a company's shares to be traded on the Stock Exchange the committee had to appoint a 'special settlement day'. This was the date on which the shares could first be officially traded and included in the list of bargains.[10] To obtain a special settlement day the committee laid down that the secretary of the share and loan department had to receive a number of documents including the prospectus and articles of association of the company, the applications for shares, the allotment book, the amount of shares to be allotted to the public, the amount of deposit paid and a certificate from the bankers confirming that the deposits had been received. If the company also wanted an official quotation, that is, it wished its shares included in the official list with the prices at which they were traded, it had to conform to additional conditions. The firm had to be 'of sufficient magnitude and importance'; the prospectus had to be publicly advertised and to agree substantially with the articles of association. At least one half of the nominal capital had to be issued and at least two-thirds of the shares intended for the public had to be subscribed for and allotted. The company also had to reveal how many of the shares were being issued other than for cash, for example, to the original owners as 'vendors' shares, or to others for services rendered. All agreements between the company and any other party had to be revealed, such as agents appointed abroad who had exclusive rights, service contracts and customers with special privileges. Additionally, the intangible assets of the company were usually listed, the patents, trade marks, and brand names which it owned.[11] Although it was not difficult to comply with these conditions they were somewhat more onerous than those imposed by the Registrar of companies. They required the company to have 'a member of the stock exchange . . . authorized . . . to give full information as to the formation of the undertaking, and . . . able to furnish the committee with all particulars they may require'.[12] Hence the need for a broker who usually appeared on the prospectus. However, none of the stipulations was so complex as to require a specialist intermediary. Any businessman capable of carrying out the normal day-to-day record-keeping of a firm could cope with these conditions, and, as Harrison has shown for the bicycle business, often did.[13] A company promoter could not fill the role of the informed sponsor inside the Stock Exchange unless he was a member of the exchange.

What then were the specialist services the promoter offered? Floating the company was primarily a marketing exercise. Thus an appreciation of the mood of the market was essential to know what was likely to 'sell' to the investor. However a market could be stimulated, in shares as in any other commodity, and the company promoter needed to be adept at this if he was to be successful. Although company law before 1900 did not insist that a prospectus be issued when shares were offered to the public the Stock Exchange did, and the company promoter normally used this device as one way of 'puffing' his shares. Although there were various attempts to make prospectuses truthful before 1900, the law did not specify what had to be included and the company promoter had a fairly free rein to indulge his creative-writing talents.[14] It was not unusual for fiction writers and journalists to be employed to turn out an appealing prospectus. The other method of publicity the professional promoter utilized was the press. By judicious sweeteners he not merely minimized adverse comments but also ensured favourable mention in editorial matter to complement the advertisements he paid for. In this he was aided by the 'new financial journalism' emerging in the 1880s, which was critical, outspoken, and opinionated. At its best it exposed frauds and cheats, but at its worst the acceptance of bribes to puff shares or not to reveal a racket was common.[15] The astute company promoter also ensured that his promotions were a success by formal or informal underwriting.

This was often achieved by having a circle of well-heeled acquaintances who put their money into the speculations on the say of the promoter, irrespective of their real merit. By virtue of previous track-record the promoter was credited with the Croesus touch and his cronies and colleagues believed everything he promoted would be a success.

Thus the real expertise of the company promoter was not financial or technical, but rather marketing and publicity. If he could sell the particular company to the investors, prices would rise to a premium, the issue would be wholly or preferably over-subscribed and the flotation would be deemed a success. In theory the role of the company promoter was to aid the business wishing to raise additional capital by going public. In practice, this was not always the case. As will be discussed later the motivations for going public were varied, and raising additional capital for the business was not the sole or in some cases main motive.

### The reasons for flotation

The Stock Exchange before 1880 dealt in the shares of relatively few domestic industrial companies. The mainstays of its operations were home government stock, home railways, overseas investments, again often in governments or for railway construction, plus a smaller market in utilities. However, this situation changed drastically after the 1880s when a significant number of home manufacturing concerns took corporate form and went public.[16] There were a number of reasons for this movement. Some businesses perceived the advantages of limited liability in providing security for their families and allowing them to establish private wealth outside the business remote from any fluctuations in its fortunes. This was reinforced by the well-publicized examples of unlimited companies which failed and in so doing required large sums from the hapless shareholders. The crash of the City of Glasgow Bank in the autumn of 1878 rammed this home. The shareholders had to find 27.5 times their original shareholding to pay off the company's liabilities. The vast majority, unable to do so, were declared bankrupt.[17] However, the acquisition of limited liability did not require that the company go public, though the reverse was true. The reasons for going public included a desire to place an objective value on the shareholdings of family members and to make that asset more easily realizable by creating an active market in the shares. Many private family firms insisted that shares be offered first to existing members[18] and this was conducive to price-fixing rather than the shareholder receiving the market value. Professor Coleman has suggested that by the late nineteenth century a number of families which had founded firms in the industrial revolution, because status in Britain was not based on mere wealth but title and life style, were seeking to realize some of the capital tied up in their business in order to buy country houses, land estates and titles and adopt the life-style of a gentleman.[19] There is certainly evidence of this occurring and not just among second- or third-generation entrepreneurs;[20] it served as one motive. Some families certainly seemed keen to disengage themselves from active business and spread their capital more widely in a range of types of security.[21] The onset of a more effective

118

form of inheritance tax also played a part. Although it was an entirely avoidable tax before World War I, to do so usually required that business wealth be held in corporate form which allowed the shareholding to be placed in a trust. Sometimes a company went public to raise additional capital to expand its activities. Although a firm might go public and raise no additional capital,[22] in the majority of cases this was a significant motive, even if the founder or family retained most of the equity and issued mainly debentures or preference shares. The increasing competition from foreign firms in traditional British markets, continuous production beginning to replace batch-production with concomitant larger quantities of capital equipment and raw materials, and the intensity of competition between numerous producers with a newly-emerged national market, all led to requirements for additional finance which a Stock Exchange quotation could provide. Finally, some firms went public through deficiencies in family stamina. Where the founder or main family entrepreneur was not enjoying robust health he offered to sell the company. Alfred H. Harman, the founder of Ilford, offered to sell out to H. Osborne O'Hagan because of 'poor health' and his doctor telling him to 'give up business altogether' and John Lawson Johnston, the founder of Bovril, sold out to Hooley partly because he was in ill health.[23]

### Diversification from traditional investments

A number of factors combined to cause investors to consider holding domestic industrial paper in the last quarter of the nineteenth century. A marked and unprecedented fall in the income to be derived from government stock, as measured by the yield on Consols, occurred.

*Table 6.1    Yield on Consols, 1863–1902 (per cent, per annum, decade average)*

|  | Old 3% Consols | New 2.5% Consols |
|---|---|---|
| 1863–72 | 3.25 | 3.25 |
| 1873–82 | 3.12 | 3.12 |
| 1883–92 | 2.72 | 2.70 |
| 1893–1902 | 2.35 | 2.22 |

*Sources:*
B. R. Mitchell and P. Deane, *Abstract of British Historical Statistics* (Cambridge University Press, 1962) p. 455; C. K. Harley, 'Goschen's conversion of the National Debt and the yield on Consols', *Economic History Review*, 2nd series, Vol. XXIX, No. 1 (1976), pp. 101–6.

The money income from his source fell between 27 and 32 per cent over the whole period. Thus *rentiers* who depended on Consols as their sole or main source of income saw a continuous and worrying decline in money income. It might be argued that this perceived reduction was not real, since prices were declining at the same time. Although any measure of price movement in this period has to be treated with a degree of scepticism, and different measures abound, all agree that prices were falling and there is rough agreement that for the period 1863/72 to 1893/1902 it was between 30 and 40 per cent.

Table 6.2  Price indices, 1863–1902

|  | Rousseaux | Sauerbeck-Statist | Saul Wholesale | BoT Wholesale |
|---|---|---|---|---|
| 1868–72 | 117 | 111 | 135 | 140[a] |
| 1893–1902 | 71 | 66 | 85 | 94 |
| Per cent reduction | 39 | 40 | 37 | 33 |

Note:
a. 1871–2 only.
Sources:
Rousseaux, Sauerbeck, Statist and BoT Wholesale: Mitchell and Deane, *Abstract* pp. 472–6; Saul Wholesale: S.B. Saul, *The Myth of the Great Depression 1873–1896* (Macmillan, 1969), p. 12.

Thus although the yield on Consols was falling in money terms prices were falling faster so that the real yield on government stock was in fact rising slightly. However, if the concept of money illusion, used to explain spiralling inflation in the 1960s and 1970s,[24] is conceded to have some validity there is an even stronger case for its occurring in reverse in a less sophisticated stage of economic development. If mid-twentieth- century American and English workers bombarded by economic analysis, of a sort, via television, and the press believed that rising money wages were a guarantee of economic success without considering the equal or greater rise in retail prices, then how much more likely that the late-nineteenth-century investor with fewer news media and a less formalized economic understanding should believe that a fall in money income was equivalent to a drop in real income. This belief was compounded by the increasing variety of consumer goods that were becoming available, ranging from the luxury foods of jam and chocolate through soap[25] to the consumer durables initially aimed at a middle-class market, viz. bicycles and sewing machines.[26] The growth of department stores using the relatively new technology of plate glass, electric illumination and lifts to display this cornucopia provided the middle class with the opportunity to examine and lust after these products. At the same time, the costs of child-rearing for the middle class were rising in terms of the growing need for a public school education. This was often followed by several years when the male child was earning little or nothing because he was studying in one of the professions, such as law, accountancy or medicine increasingly requiring education and a period of articles, made doubly expensive by the normal entry requirement of the payment of a premium. Therefore, in a number of ways, the late nineteenth century put pressure on the middle classes to augment their income. One response for those living solely on unearned income was to seek respectable employment to supplement their interest payments. Another, in a period of falling yield on Consols, was to look for alternative investment opportunities. As Cottrell says: 'The investment policies of the insurance companies and the domestic banks, as well as of private investors, were strongly affected by the decline in yield on Consols . . . This led to more adventurous attitudes.'[27] One of the 'adventures' some *rentiers* were willing to consider was to dabble in home industrials. This movement was demonstrated by one Major Best, who 'until the middle of the 1870s . . . had been investing steadily in Consols; then he began to diversify his portfolio.' The fictional Misses Schlegal followed a similar investment path, each having determined to 'shift her money out of Consols'.[28]

Not merely were home government bonds looking less attractive in the late-nineteenth century, but that other stalwart receptacle of spare capital, especially for aristocrats and peasants, land was losing some of its attraction. Although there has been dispute over the degree of depression in the later nineteenth century one recent authority wrote 'the last quarter of the nineteenth century . . . was certainly one of agricultural depression, of falling prices, more numerous bankruptcies, lower rents and untenanted farms.[29] Estimates vary but there is general agreement that rents fell sharply in this period. Fletcher believes rents in Cambridgeshire fell about 35 per cent between 1870 and 1896.[30] Ashworth suggests the reduction was about 29 per cent on average in England and Wales between 1870–4 and 1900–4.[31] Perry agrees the rough magnitude: 'one analysis made in 1907 suggested a figure of 25 per cent between the early seventies and the mid-nineties.'[32] Of course, the average figures conceal great local variations, ranging, Perry suggests, from over 50 per cent to scarcely 10 per cent but all agree that 'tenants sought relief in rent reductions, or temporary abatements . . . many tenants gave up their farms even at reduced rentals.[33] The result was that 'the landlord class as a whole had suffered a permanent loss of capital and income . . . it was reckoned that they could not in general hope to receive a net income of more than 3 per cent on the reduced capital value of their estates'.[34] Faced with falling rental income, lower capital values, defaults on rents and difficulties in attracting new tenants, the landlord certainly lost any motive to invest further in land and indeed in many cases attempted to extricate his capital to put it where he might receive a higher return. As the *Times* put it 'they mistrust the security which land offers in present circumstances in England'.[35] The result was that 'from the 1880s onwards there was a general movement by landowners to spread their assets through investment in stock exchange securities'.[36] Here was a source not only of potential investors in speculations which promised a high yield, such as foreign gold mines or domestic manufacturing companies, but also of disgruntled aristocrats and gentry who looked favourably upon the offer of a 'guinea pig' directorship and a chance to make up in fees what had been lost in rents: 'a considerable section of the landed interest was acquiring the habit of frequent dealings with stockbrokers and was becoming increasingly familiar with the world in which the great financial magnates of the day, Beit, Cassel, Speyer and Wernher, had their being.'[37]

If Consols offered a low yield and land looked risky as well as a poor return the capitalist seeking a safe haven for surplus funds had to look further afield. In the period 1870–1914 much of this spare capital went abroad: Britain's capital exports totalled about £3,500 million[38] multiplying seven-fold the existing level of overseas investments. However, this was not a steady process but rather went in long waves punctuated by various crises of confidence caused by foreign governments defaulting on interest, severe falls in foreign stock exchanges, or a sharp drop in the price of commodities. For example, the autumn 1873 Wall Street crash created a climate inimicable to overseas investments.[39] The coincidence of a number of factors in the early 1890s made for an even greater slump: 'the Baring Crisis [of 1890], the Wall Street panic [of 1893], the end of the land boom in Australia and the collapse of the banking system in 1893 [based on wool incomes failing to cover sheep station outgoings] were sufficient to shake confidence in all foreign securities and consequently overseas investment fell to a low ebb during the 1890s'.[40] This was compounded by the collapse of the 'kaffir boom' in South African gold mining shares in late 1895.[41] It was during these periods of disillusion with foreign investment, 1874 to 1879 and 1888 to 1900,[42] that attention was turned to British industrial companies as an alternative source of income. For example, in 1894, 'This was a period of general uncertainty in overseas markets and Cassel had become especially disillusioned with American railroad ventures . . . he decided upon . . . becoming more closely involved in British business finance' and was involved in the promotion of the Electric Traction Co. and the sale of Maxim-Nordenfelt to Vickers.[43] Cassel was not alone in his thinking: other lesser capitalists also took more interest in domestic industrials when foreign investment looked risky.

Finally, yet another standby for the investor was looking less attractive after 1870. Railway shares had given a significant impetus to both the London and provincial stock exchanges from the 1830s and had been responsible for drawing capital out of hoards and increasing the size of the investing public.[44] Trade in railway paper comprised a very large proportion of the activities of the markets and the securities of the larger companies were seen as blue-chip investments suitable for even the fabled widows and orphans. However after 1870 'the profitability of the railways was declining throughout the period'.[45] The net receipts of the railways as a percentage of paid up capital fell steadily from about 4.44 in 1870 to 3.40 in 1900.[46] As a result 'the ordinary shares of the leading railway companies no longer justified any hopes of high dividends.'[47] Indeed by the 1880s, 'even the most successful lines were having to cut back dividends on their ordinary stock'.[48] One response of the traditional railway shareholder was to move more into debentures which had a fixed rate of interest, priority over equity and a cumulative payment. The other response was to look beyond the railway companies at a wider portfolio of shares including home industrials.

Thus a number of features of the late nineteenth-century economy combined to make traditional investments less attractive. This impelled investors to look for alternatives as there were forces urging them to maximize their income. This greater

122

intrepidness embraced foreign stocks and shares and also home industrials. The company promoter thus had a potentially large customer-base for his activities.

### The promoter's marketing methods

The company promoter needed a good eye for the type of undertaking which would be attractive to the investor. The selection of an appropriate business was the first key aspect. Different promoters tackled this in similar ways. One method was to promote existing businesses manufacturing consumer goods which were already well known by virtue of being heavily advertised. Given that the last thirty years of the nineteenth century saw a steady rise in average real incomes and the beginnings of a mass market[49] there were a number of products that were becoming household names – Sunlight soap, Woodbine cigarettes, Mazzawatee tea. The company promoter saw that knowledge of the product would transfer to the firm and make the shares of the company attractive. Hooley, for instance, promoted Bovril and Schweppes, both well-known and advertised consumer items in the 1890s.[50] Bottomley played on the likelihood of the name of the parliamentary reporter – Hansard – being well known when floating his Hansard Printing Union in 1888, and O'Hagan began negotiations with Horlicks and Ilford, both well-publicized names.[51] They used the goodwill which had been established for the product to sell the shares in the company which manufactured it.

Another technique was to identify any type of share that was in high favour with the investing public. The company promoter then jumped on the bandwagon and floated companies of a similar kind, trusting that the general enthusiasm and unsatisfied demand would carry over to his pet project. The original cause of the popularity of the class of security, one company announcing high profits or dividends, a 'new' product that seemed 'high-tech', or a sudden breakthrough in production methods, was immaterial. The promoter spotted the craze and hitched his wagon to it. Hooley exemplified this in the 1890's when he floated bicycles and their components, earlier O'Hagan was heavily into breweries, Lawson floated the early car companies, and Clarence Hatry pushed companies setting up automatic photography booths in the 1920s.[52] At the time each of these products excited investors who were willing to buy the type of share in large quantities.

A related method was to float companies formed to exploit patents, inventions or exclusive privileges. These operations had even more glamour as they hinted at huge opportunities arising from technical breakthroughs. At a time when the investing public was becoming aware of the great opportunities in science-based industries, such as electricity or chemicals, the lure of patents and inventions was particularly high. This technique was used by Hooley in conjunction with the cycle boom – the Pederson Cycle Frames Company – and the use of hydraulic power – the Hydraulic Joint Syndicate Ltd – both of which were formed to exploit patents bought by Hooley from the inventors; O'Hagan bought patents on automatic oilers and cement mixers and then tried to float companies based on them, with little success.[53] Thus the choice of the type of company to be promoted was important. Promoters sought good names assiduously and approached many more potential clients than they actually floated – Hooley, for instance, tried to get Boots, Liptons and Ilford, but was unsuccessful.[54]

Once chosen the company needed to be given maximum publicity. The formal method for this was the prospectus. As well as being printed and made widely available in banks, brokers, solicitors, and being sent out to any prospects – a form of early mail 'shot' – an abridged version was put into a wide range of newspapers and journals, especially those likely to be read by the target audience. If the promotion was a gold mine the prospectus was likely to appear in the mining journals, if for Schweppes or Bovril in the *Chemist and Druggist Grocer,* and *Hotel Proprietors Review*, for the cycle companies in its trade press such as *Cycling*. The prospectus also appeared in the financial press, the large circulation dailies, the major weeklies and any other organ which was aimed at the middle and upper-class investor.

Drafting the prospectus was a work of art and often owed more to the novelist than the lawyer.[55] Flowery phrases intended to attract the investor and persuade of the profitability of the venture were common. It usually contained a brief history of the company, an appraisal of the market in which it was operating, encouraging descriptions of the past growth in output and profits and the anticipated future growth. Thus the Humber Cycle Company prospectus emphasized the firm's pedigree in cycle manufacture and its past growth in output: 'it has been found quite impossible to keep pace with the orders . . . the Humber factories have been kept running early and late, to endeavour to cope with demand'. The market for cycles was evaluated: 'cycles are daily becoming more and more a necessity of every household', and future prospects were detailed in glowing terms: 'immediate and exceptional results are guaranteed to this Company'.[56]

Some prospectuses went into details of the manufacturing process presumably to impress the putative investor by its complexity, modernity, or sophistication. Some firms also made a great play of the quality of their product or service which differentiated if from other like products or services and thus cause the consumer to want to buy it. Another ploy used by writers of prospectuses, as a means of engendering enthusiasm for their wares, was to use local colour, exotic locations or customs to attract attention. Thus when Bovril sought investors in 1896 it made much of the location from which the raw material came: 'hundreds of miles of the most luxurious pasturage in the world. . . . Much of the herbage of the South American *pampa* is known as 'alfalfa' and in this country as 'lucerne' and it is in reality clover grass of the best quality . . . regularly sown . . . giving no fewer than five or six crops a year'.[57] This passage was intended to attract investors by the lush location and the related concept of rich pickings from the investment. Similar techniques were employed in other prospectuses.

The prospectus, however, was only one link in the chain of publicity. Before it had been issued, the company promoter fed journalists with informal press releases, entertained the gentlemen of Fleet Street, often paid for good editorial comment or to prevent the publication of adverse remarks. Hooley in particular complained loudly at his bankruptcy of the number of journalists he had had to bribe.[58] Bottomley was on the other side for much of the period, for with his various newspapers, especially *John Bull*, he accepted payments *not* to reveal information.[59] In some cases the company promoter went even further and owned or controlled his own newspaper which, not surprisingly, gave glowing puffs for the company dressed up as editorial or an independent article. Edward Beall, who floated the London and Scottish Banking & Discount Corporation Ltd in 1892, used the *Financial Gazette*, which he owned, to push his company's shares.[60] A number of other promoters endeavoured to ensure helpful publicity through ownership of organs of the press. Sir Edgar Vincent, interested in the promotion of the Reliance Taxi Cab Co. in 1908 and a company to make commercial fuel out of peat in 1912, owned the *Statist* from 1892 to 1898.[61] Sir Geoffrey Isaacs had interests in Welsh granite and gold mining, and Irish zinc and copper. In 1900, he started *British Mining* which carried laudatory articles on the prospects for Welsh gold mining companies, especially the St Davids Gold and Copper Mines, of which Isaacs was a director and shareholder. In 1902, when the paper was retitled *Sovereign*, it continued to run items praising the St David's concern.[62] Davison Dalziel, promoter of many companies, went one better and started his own news agency in 1891.[63] By such methods the promoters ensured ample publicity to whet the public's appetite for the prospectus.

To bolster this publicity the company promoter tended to lead a newsworthy life. Some were positively flamboyant. Bottomley, Hatry and Hooley all ran racing stables and led in winners to classic races, bringing them to the notice of the sporting fraternity. They owned large mansions in the country as well as elegant town houses at which they regularly entertained lavishly, so catching the attention of the social columnists, e.g. Whitaker Wright. Some had political aspirations, Bottomley was an MP for ten years and an unsuccessful candidate on two previous occasions, using the House of Commons as a platform for self-publicity and ensuring that his presence was well known around his constituency at election time.[64] This brought him to the notice of many and also provided exposure in the political columns in the press. Membership of the House of Commons was also useful for spotting prominent public figures who might be persuaded onto the boards of companies. Sir Edward Watkin certainly used it in this way to recruit Lord Cranborne, later the Marquess of Salisbury to the chair of the Great Eastern Railway in 1868.[65] Dalziel, who was MP for Brixton from 1910 and involved in promoting taxi-cab companies and the British Pullman Palace Car Co., used it to cultivate powerful political connections such as Sir Alexander Henderson.[66] Some promoters, such as Birch Crisp, did not even need to be successful in elections. Being a regular parliamentary candidate gave access to politically influential people who could aid his promotions – mainly loans to China and Russia – such as Sir Henry Brittain, MP for Acton, Almeric Paget MP, later Lord Queenborough, and helped him acquire Siemens in 1917 from the Public Trustee.[67] Although not all publicity was necessarily beneficial, and most of the dubious promoters experienced this when they appeared in court on bankruptcy, libel or fraud charges, most was. Even court appearances could be turned to the promoter's advantage if he was able to come out unconvicted, as Bottomley did on a number of occasions.[68] Some publicity was adverse or tended to denigrate the promoter for merely turning a fast buck: the *Economist* was one of the more outspoken critical journals.[69] So the promoter needed to engender an ethos of respectability about himself and his promotions. One way of doing this was to use 'guinea pig' directors – titled or famous people who put their names to the prospectus and attended board meetings. Many were there solely for pecuniary gain and had little experience or knowledge of business. The promoters could be very damning of them. Bottomley described such a person as 'one who devotes such time as he can spare from the pursuit of his pleasures to the neglect of his duties'.[70] Frequently, the shares needed to qualify as a director were given to them. Bottomley recruited for his Hansard Printing Union Kegan Paul, the publisher, Sir Henry Isaacs, Lord Mayor of London in 1889–90, uncle of Rufus Isaacs the future Attorney General and Viceroy of India, and Sir Roper Lethbridge, who made his name in India as editor of the *Calcutta Review* and Indian Political Agent, later MP for North Kensington.[71] Whitaker Wright recruited a galaxy of aristocrats to his London & Globe Finance Corporation: the Marquess of Dufferin and Ava, Lord Loch and Lord Edward Pelham-Clinton.[72] Hooley had regular guinea pigs, including the Duke of Somerset, Earls De La Warr, Albemarle, March, and Winchilsea,[73] and Harrison has shown the large number involved in the cycle, motor vehicle and related industries.[74] In an age of deference and respect for aristocracy, class and status, the titled head provided a cachet of respectability, permanence and solidity to otherwise dubious concerns.

To some extent the promoter's life-style was also intended to serve a similar purpose. The lavishness of his entertaining, the magnificence of his stables, mansion and cellar showed how successful he had been in making money and helped to overcome investor reluctance. If the promoter could accumulate the capital to live so regally, the logic seemed to be, why should the investor not make similar gains? The rich and titled circles in which he moved, his political connections all provided an image of respectability, success and above all wealth. If him, why not me also, was the response it evoked in many punters.

In order to maximize the potential market for his shares the company promoter offered a range of products to cater for a number of segments of the market. Because home industrials were a novelty promoters appreciated many investors were not yet ready to move on to equity. Their experience of government stock, made some prefer a low-risk, low-return security. Thus promoters offered various options in which risk was traded against yield. Lower yield debentures or preference shares theoretically had greater security as they received their dividend first, and it was often cumulative, while ordinary shares and deferred shares came lower down the pecking order for payment but were claimed to be likely to receive higher rates of return. A typical example of this in action was Hooley's float of Bovril in 1896 which used 4.5 per cent debenture stock, 5.5 per cent preference shares, 7 per cent ordinary shares and deferred shares 'likely to receive' about 10 per cent.[75]

Underwriting was another method of ensuring the flotation was a success. Before 1900 it was considered illegal for a company to employ an underwriter, because it was not allowed to issue shares at a discount.[76] The astute promoter got around this. He arranged the underwriting between himself and the underwriter. As an individual the legal restrictions did not apply. Hooley encouraged his wealthy friends to underwrite his promotions by offering them shares at a discount, or payment in shares of another of his companies.[77] Some promoters gave underwriters options on shares at attractive prices at some date in the future.[78] Others seem to have rarely resorted to such expedients. Bottomley, for instance, does not appear to have been a great user of formal underwriting, nor does Hatry. Harrison found a mixed response in the cycle and motor industries some companies being underwritten wholly or in part others boasting that they were not.[79] O'Hagan had no problems in recruiting underwriters 'before I could get the prospectus even into skeleton form' using 'some of the larger trust and investment companies [and] any person of means who was prepared to put up one or two thousand pounds of capital . . . for a substantial commission'. O'Hagan's close association with the stockbroking firm of Panmure Gordon 'gave me a greatly increased underwriting connexion'.[80] Even when there was no formal underwriting, the promoter attempted to ensure the success of his issue by having wealthy friends who agreed to subscribe even before a prospectus was issued, drummed up support among their friends and clients, circularized likely investors and generally acted to ensure a strong demand for the scrip. This circle of friends was crucial to a promoter's success. As Davenport-Hines and Van Helten said of Edgar Vincent, 'his progress was based on the range and quality of his social contacts'[81] and Thane of Sir Ernest Cassel 'he had very close family friends who were also close and regular business associates'.[82] Although some company promoters lacked the class of these City worthies, their social contacts were equally important in ensuring good flotations and they went out of their way to cultivate and keep sweet such useful friends and so maintain their place in the 'social web of investment' as it has recently been called.[83]

Promoters had other ways of ensuring that the shares of the company which they were floating went to a premium. This encouraged the public to buy them in expectation of a further rise, and also allowed the promoter to sell his own holding at a good profit. This was especially true as many promoters allotted themselves scrip gratis for their efforts in floating the company. Whitaker Wright, for example, gave himself free deferred founders shares in the West Australian Finance Corporation and London & Globe Company in 1894 and 1895. When these were taken over in 1897 by the London & Globe Finance Corporation he allotted himself £322,000 worth of equity as compensation. He then slowly sold these so that by 1900 he held only 2,500.[84] Another ploy was for the promoter to spread rumours around the exchange which pushed up the price of shares he was holding: 'Wright had made in November [1900] some market profit by sedulously spreading rumours that Le Roy (No. 1) was on the point of declaring a bumper dividend with the result that the £5 shares jumped to £9' and Wright made a killing.[85] If this did not work, an alternative method of pushing up the share price was for the company, soon after flotation, to declare a profit and announce the payment of a high dividend. Bottomley in 1890 arranged for the Hansard Printing Union to declare a dividend of 8 per cent on the preference shares and twelve on the ordinary. Not surprisingly 'the shares of the Union at this date were very much in demand, the result being that they became marketable at a substantial premium'.[86] Beall used the same tactic in 1892 when demand for the shares of his London & Scottish Banking & Discount Corporation Ltd was slack. He declared a dividend of 7 per cent, although the company had in fact made a loss, and then offered equity at a premium of 10 shillings

(50p) per share on the strength of this.[87] Even O'Hagan, one of the more scrupulous promoters, was not above such techniques. When floating the Sheffield special steel firm, Kayser Ellison & Co., he announced in the prospectus that the ordinary shares 'should pay 15 to 20 per cent' so that they soon went to a premium and O'Hagan was able to sell them at 'a profit of from £4 to £5 per share'.[88]

If a flotation looked as though it was going to be heavily under-subscribed the canny promoter did not despair of pushing the share price to a premium. He could exploit the fact that he was in control of the allotment process to corner the market in the shares and then deny the 'bears', who had sold short, the opportunity to get hold of any to settle their account. Wright used this technique when a mine he was promoting, Le Roy Mining (No. 2), failed to attract the public. A number of stock market operators, hearing on the grapevine that the float was not a success, sold short. By settlement day they had found it impossible to purchase shares, since Wright had cornered the vast majority, with the result that the share price soared to £15.[89] Hooley used similar tactics. Because the Humber Company had been so oversubscribed in 1894, Hooley jumped on the bandwagon and launched four other Humber variants.[90] However, Humber (Portugal) did not look as though it would do well, the public having sobered up a little at the prospect of a Humber company for every country from Austria to Zanzibar. So Hooley gave his brokers orders to buy shares before allotment. When, as expected, the issue was hopelessly under-subscribed Hooley brazened it out, put a notice in the press saying it had been fully subscribed and sent letters of regret to some of the few applicants. The shares went to a premium. Many stockbrokers believing, correctly, the issue was likely to be a flop had sold shares to Hooley at par expecting to be able to pick them up at a heavy discount. Because Hooley had cornered the market they were unable to deliver the shares they had sold and the price rocketed to over £13 each before Hooley sold them what they needed to complete their bargains.[91]

If these methods did not push the shares to a premium the company promoter had yet another weapon in his armoury. This was to stimulate the price by getting his cronies or companies to create an active market in the shares, although this was quite false and in fact only inter-company transfers. Thus, as there were no rules to outlaw dealing in shares before allotment,[92] the unscrupulous promoter, who controlled the allotment process and who was not constrained by rules about insider dealing, could manipulate the market. Similarly, if he controlled the company so that he could decide when and how much dividend was to be paid, and the law did not consider this necessarily illegal even if there were doubts about the accuracy of the 'profit' figure, this too ensured that he could push the share price up, attracting investors and at the same time make himself a handsome profit.

## Their deleterious impact

The effects of the individual company promoter in this period, on the whole, were mainly deleterious. Many of them did *not* provide finance for industry. If the promoter bought the business outright from the vendors, as Hooley tended and

O'Hagan did on occasions,[93] then the cash paid for the company went to the previous shareholders or partners. No capital was put into the actual business. Similarly, when the promoter relaunched the firm as a public company the cash he collected from the investors in payment for their shares went not into the company but into his pocket, since he was merely selling a piece of his property – the business – to another group of owners – the new shareholders. The same was true when a promoter launched a company to exploit a patent or invention he had purchased. The money he received was his payment for selling the 'valuable' rights or ideas to the new shareholders and the cash subscribed went to him not into the firm. Thus in many cases there was no direct input of fresh capital to the business to increase its productive capability.

It might be argued that going public was only the first step in the process of raising additional external capital. The promoter enabled the firm to go public and subsequently it returned to the market to raise new finance which went into the business and allowed it to expand its manufacturing and marketing activities. In some cases this occurred. A firm was launched, its shares traded and quoted, and a few years later it raised fresh capital via the Stock Exchange. In many cases this was not possible. If the business failed to make 'good' profits it could not seek funds from the market as investors, basing their judgement on its indifferent track record, would choose not to subscribe. The ability to go back to the market depended crucially on the company being profitable, paying anticipated dividends and thus keeping its share price high. If it failed in this it did not get a second bite at the cherry.

The company promoter frequently did not facilitate the generation of a high share price in the long term but rather retarded it. Although often no additional capital was put into the business there was a much increased capital structure. There was no wherewithal to generate increments of profit but more was needed simply to service the increased capital. In this circumstance the company was unlikely to be able to fulfil the expectations of the shareholders, especially those whose securities were not cumulative or were last in the line for payment. The price of these classes of share was therefore likely to drop as investors grew disillusioned with the poor yields. The company could not then go back to the market because the promoter had excessively increased the company's capital structure. It was in his interest to promote the company at as high a price as possible to maximize his income especially where the promoter bought and resold the firm outright.

A further factor likely to depress the share price was the high proportion of shares taken up by 'stags'. The company promoters themselves often unloaded their own holdings soon after flotation when the shares had achieved a profitable premium. This practice was also followed by some of the original vendors who were paid in part in shares, but who, following the float, realized some of their assets, especially if the shares went to a premium. Similarly, the promoter's friends, colleagues and cronies who had been so invaluable in ensuring a good launch by taking up shares beforehand were mostly only concerned to make a short-term killing and so followed suit and unloaded their shares fairly fast after flotation.[94] The net effects of these various groups selling large parcels of shares was to drive the share price down.

Also likely to push the share price down was the degree of 'watering' of the capital. It was quite normal for the promoter to capitalize the company at a figure well above the asset value of the operation. At the extreme some companies had virtually no tangible assets, merely a collection of patents or inventions. The less radical companies always had large elements of goodwill written into them as well as a valuation placed on their intangible assets such as trademarks, brand names and patents. This is quite contrary to modern accounting practice but was common at the time. Admittedly with the uninformative balance sheets usually issued the shareholders might never appreciate the degree of variance between balance-sheet valuation and asset value. However, if they did perceive this, and they were more likely to investigate when dividends did not live up to expectations, it would not reassure them and might tip the balance encouraging them to sell, so reducing the share price.

Company promoters did more than simply leaving the individual companies they promoted over-capitalized, under-resourced and unattractive to the investor. The lack of appeal of one or two companies could spread to the shares of that type of industry so disillusioning shareholders from the whole sector. Bicycles and motorcars were puffed and pushed in the 1890s so extravagantly that investors were wary of any company of this type for some time. Breweries suffered a similar fate following the rush into them in the late 1880s and drapery firms in the early 1890s.[95] When this trend of hectic promotion in the boom, followed by falling share prices, disappointing profits and disillusion, had occurred several times some investors began to shy away from industrials entirely, or at least see them as a much more speculative and risky class of share than they had appeared previously. Additionally, the spate of adverse publicity which followed these booms and busts[96] made owners of respectable companies shy away from the stock exchange as too like a casino. It reinforced their resolve to remain as private companies, which restricted their ability to raise fresh capital and so expand to meet large-scale foreign competition. In this way the company promoter did a disservice to British industry and made it more difficult for it to raise capital. They cannot be blamed wholly for the imperfections in the British capital market in the forty years before World War I but they did more to exaggerate the imperfections than help remove them.

Firms did not need to come to London for a flotation, nor did they need to use a company promoter. As explained in the introduction to this chapter, there were a number of other individuals and institutions willing and able to help convert a business from a partnership to a company. Firms could and did use the provincial stock exchanges rather than London. One of the most famous of the groups of shares floated on the provincial stock exchanges were the 'Oldham Limiteds', cotton spinning and weaving businesses formed during the 1870s and 1880s.[97] Similarly, Harrison has shown that many cycle companies used private placings in Birmingham, Coventry, Nottingham and Wolverhampton in the 1880s and 1890s.[98] O'Hagan too used this method to place shares in Stanhope Main Colliery in Barnsley and a timber merchant at Cardiff.[99] Hooley, of course, commenced his promotional career in Nottingham in the 1880s,[100] and David Chadwick conducted a large business in placings and promotions from Manchester in the 1860s and 1870s.[101] Provincial placings were better suited to smaller companies with a limited track record. The London market was fine for nationally known companies, such as

Bovril, Dunlop and Schweppes with large capital – say over £500,000 – which had been established for some time. It was not suitable for small, local businesses, which London intermediaries were very reluctant to handle.

It is difficult to generalize about the cost of a London promotion. At the top end of the market, Chapman believed merchant banks charged between 6 and 10 per cent commission for the whole process.[102] Cairncross broadly agrees, suggesting 5–6 per cent was not unusual but occasionally being much more.[103] One example of this is the South Staffordshire Iron Works which paid a Throgmorton Street firm, Jay and Co., £10,000 in the 1870s for forming a company with a total capital of only £70,000.[104] This is over 14 per cent. O'Hagan, who considered himself a model of probity, charged about 2½–3 per cent on private placings and rather more for flotations: he received 4½ per cent for promoting International Tea Stores, on capital of nearly £1 million.[105] The charges on the provincial exchanges, which expanded in the 1870s to cater for smaller, domestic, industrial floats, were lower because of single dealing (whereas there were both jobbers and dealers in London) and because the costs of printing, advertising and underwriting were less or avoided entirely. Chadwick claimed to charge 1 per cent of nominal capital plus actual expenses – 'a mere trifling cost',[106] though the total could be up to 8 per cent of the subscribed capital.[107] The apparent advantage to the business of allowing a company promoter to buy it outright was that all such flotation expenses were avoided, as they were borne by the promoter; and the original partners or shareholders of the firm received an immediate cash value on their shares, usually much in excess of the current market value. The hidden cost was, of course, that the long-run earnings of the business were likely to be impaired to the extent that the capital was watered.

It is not easy to assess the significance of the company promoters in numerical terms. We cannot even identify them conclusively for many were only incidentally promoters earning their income from a range of financial services, although some individuals stand out from the crowd. Thus it is difficult to calculate the aggregate number of companies promoted by them and the proportion this represents of all domestic flotations. Hooley promoted about thirty domestic companies in five years (1894–8) with a nominal capital of around £20 million;[108] Bottomley promoted only a handful of domestic industrial companies in the late 1880s with a capital of just over £1 million, but launched over forty companies engaged in overseas mining, especially Australian gold fields between 1894 and 1903 with a nominal capital in excess of £12 million.[109] O'Hagan, in his long City career, claims to have promoted dozens of domestic industrial companies with a large nominal capital as well as many overseas. Chadwick, the Manchester-based promoter, was involved in at least 47 limited companies between 1862 and 1874.[110] However, the company promoters' significance is to be measured not only by their numerical impact. The worst of them thrived on massive publicity leaving the less newsworthy but more honest in the shade. This self-advertisement exaggerated their impact in the public mind. Company promoters were most active in the upswings of economic activity and fuelled these booms through their efforts. Because of the unscrupulous activities of the least honourable promoters many of 'their' firms failed in the downswing or at least failed to live up to expectations. This tarnished individual firms' financial reputations and permeated whole groups of businesses – breweries, bicycles, motorcars – making it more difficult for well-run undertakings to raise capital. Indeed, at times, there were a general distrust of domestic industrial shares as a whole, the group being perceived as high risk. Much of this poor press can be laid at the doors of a clutch of unprincipled company promoters.


### Decline

World War I spelt the end of the golden age of the individual company promoter. On the outbreak of war in 1914 the committee of the London Stock Exchange closed the Exchange indefinitely and postponed settlements.[111] This was followed by an Act suspending payment for all business transactions for several months.[112] When the Exchange re-opened it was on a very limited scale. All new issues required approval of both the committee of the Stock Exchange and the Treasury. In order to prevent the demand for private capital from crowding out increasingly large sums required by the government for the war effort the Treasury, after initial laxity in 1914 and 1915, refused to authorize any new issue other than those positively needed 'in the national interest'.[113] This effectively put an end to any aspirations on the part of the individual company promoter for the duration. The end of the Great War did not bring a return to pre-war conditions in issuing, as in many other areas. Although domestic issues became possible again in 1919[114] 'a web of restrictions on the activities of international financiers in London began to emerge'.[115] The Bank of England, on the Treasury's behalf, retained control of foreign issues requiring would-be issuers to seek its approval. In the 1920s it was most generous with such licences when the loan looked likely to help the reconstruction of war-torn Europe.[116] This embargo made the issuing of foreign government bonds or industrial capital more complex. External conditions had also changed. Some countries, such as Russia, were no longer acceptable to investors given the nature of the regime which emerged in 1917. The vast weight of international indebtedness which had been brought about by the war, the problems of reparations, the frequent freezes on payments and plans for rescheduling created an ethos of uncertainty and high risk which made investors more wary of overseas investments. This was compounded by the 1929 Wall Street Crash, the banking collapse in both Europe and America precipitated by it, and the disappearance of any resemblance of free exchanges.[117] Additionally, whereas before 1914 Britain had been the unchallenged centre of world finance, after the war other centres developed, especially the US with its new-won creditor status. With investors more wary of overseas investment, the merchant banks which before 1914 had specialized in issuing foreign bonds and stock found this part of their business sharply curtailed. Barings, for example, before the war had issued mostly for four countries: Argentina, Canada, Russia and the United States. For different reasons all four countries no longer called upon Barings' services.[118] As a result Barings foreign issues fell to nineteen between 1918 and 1928 and eleven between 1929 and 1939. 'As these issues declined, so issues for United Kingdom borrowers rose . . . For Barings the finance of British Industry was becoming increasingly important.'[119]

Thus one of the reasons for the decline of the individual company promoter was that alternative institutions such as the merchant banks were more prepared to undertake this activity: 'a rapprochement began between British industry and the City, with merchant banks providing investment capital for home industries as opportunities for sound overseas investment vanished.'[120] The decline in the possibilities of overseas issuing were compounded by a reduction in the other staple of the merchant bank: acceptance. Both world trade and Britain's portion of it stagnated at best and by some measures declined in the inter war years. This meant a concomitant reduction in the amount of finance needed for overseas trade and this further breach in the traditional activities of the merchant banks caused them to look more favourably to issuing British industrials. The government's concern for amal- gamation and rationalization in Britain's staple industries was indicative of a greater willingness to be involved, even if at one remove, in the financing and structure of industry. This, plus the involvement of the Bank of England in various schemes to restructure some industries, such as cotton or shipbuilding, gave greater respect- ability and impetus to merchant banks to be involved in British industrial finance.

The merchant banks were not the only competition faced by the individual company promoter. A number of finance houses developed in the inter-war period whose main function was to raise capital for domestic issues. Among the more active were British Shareholders Trust, Charterhouse Investment Trust and Standard Industrial Trust.[121] Because they were concerned to build up a long-term reputation they were likely to be rather more careful in their choice of business and so gave the public some guarantee of the firm's probity. Of course, this greater use of formal institutions should not be exaggerated. The merchant banks were only really keen to be involved in large scale issues and as the Macmillan Committee pointed out there remained many imperfections in the capital market. There was still scope for the individual company promoter to operate. Among the more notorious in this period was Clarence Hatry, before his trial in 1930, using similar techniques to Bottomley or Hooley in the 1890s.[122] However their scope had diminished as alternative institutions were available, some of the more blatant abuses had been made illegal, and the investing public had gained a modicum of caution.

## Conclusion

In terms of the wider debate over Britain's industrial retardation in the late nineteenth century, the company promoter was a contributory factor. In as much as investors were turned off home industrials and some sound firms shied away from going public because of the adverse publicity surrounding 'company promotion', especially after the scandalous Hooley bankruptcy hearing of 1898, so British manufacturing was likely to stay small-scale and family-dominated. This contributed to its poor response in meeting competition from larger-scale, more professionally managed, foreign firms. Those companies that had been 'promoted' were often simultaneously over-capitalized and short of working and fixed capital and thus restricted in their ability to grow and compete. A crucial period in Britain's industrial history when large-scale foreign firms were beginning to compete some aspects of Britain's formal capital markets were found severely wanting.


## Notes

I am grateful to the members of a seminar held at the Business History Unit who made a number of helpful suggestions, especially Phil Cottrell for improving Table 6.2 and for other ideas, and Richard Davenport-Hines who supplied me with many valuable references and went out of his way to improve the draft.

1. M .J. Orbell, *Baring Brothers & Co. Limited: A History to 1939* (priv. pub., 1985) pp. 53–4.
2. Ibid.
3. B. H .D. MacDermot, *Panmure Gordon & Co. 1876–1976, A Century of Stockbroking* (priv. pub., 1976), pp. 38–40; A. Waugh, *The Lipton Story* (New York: Doubleday, 1950), pp. 95–6; D. J. Jeremy (ed.), *Dictionary of Business Biography*, Vol. II (London: Butterworths, 1984), p. 612.
4. MacDermot, *Panmure Gordon*, p. 38.
5. E. V. Morgan and W. A. Thomas, *The Stock Exchange, Its History and Functions* (London: Elek, 1962), p. 111.
6. A. E. Harrison, 'Joint stock company flotation in the cycle, motor vehicle and related industries, 1882–1914', *Business History*, Vol. XXIII, No. 2 (1981), p. 171; H. Osborne O'Hagan, *Leaves from My Life* (London, 1929), Vol. II, p. 23, states of the Pease coal and iron concern 'the parties responsible for the flotation . . . were the lawyers and accountants of the firm'.
7. Orbell, *Baring Brothers*, pp. 53–4; Morgan and Thomas, *Stock Exchange*, p. 133.
8. D. A. Simmons, *Schweppes: The First 200 Years* (Illinois: Springwood, 1983), p. 52.
9. Morgan and Thomas, *Stock Exchange*, p. 130; P .L. Cottrell, *Industrial Finance 1830–1914: The Finance and Organisation of English Manufacturing Industry* (London: Methuen, 1980), p. 54.
10. Morgan and Thomas, *Stock Exchange*, p. 152; W. J. Reader, *A House in the City: A Study of the City and of the Stock Exchange Based on the Records of Foster & Braithwaite 1825–1975* (London: Batsford, 1979), p. 70.
11. Guildhall Library, London (GHL) ST 122, *Rules and Regulations of the Stock Exchange* (1888), p. 60, clauses 130–2.
12. GHL, ST 122.
13. Harrison, 'Joint-stock company flotation', p. 172.
14. Cottrell, *Industrial Finance*, pp. 62, 68, 73–4.
15. D. Porter, ' "A trusted guide of the investing public": Harry Marks and the Financial News 1884–1916', *Business History*, Vol. XXVIII, No.1 (1986), pp. 1–17.
16. Hannah suggests the number of firms in domestic manufacturing and distribution quoted on the London Stock Exchange rose from 60 to 600

134

between 1885 and 1907: L. Hannah, *The Rise of the Corporate Economy* (London: Methuen, 1983), p. 20.

17. R. N. Forbes, 'Some contemporary reactions to a banking failure', *Three Banks Review*, No. 121 (1979), p. 54.

18. For example, the Ocean Steam Ship Co. had this in its articles of association: F. E. Hyde, *Blue Funnel: A History of Alfred Holt & Company of Liverpool 1865–1914* (Liverpool: Liverpool University Press, 1956) p. 143.

19. D. C. Coleman, 'Gentlemen and players', *Economic History Review*, 2nd series Vol. XXVI, No. 1 (1973).

20. Lever and Boot, both founders of their business bought titles and substantial mansions: W. P. Jolly, *Lord Leverhulme* (London: Constable, 1976), pp. 34, 57, 167, 212; S. D. Chapman, *Jesse Boot of Boots the Chemist* (London: Hodder & Stoughton, 1974), p. 177.

21. Hannah, *Corporate Economy*, pp. 54–5.

22. J. Armstrong, 'Hooley and the Bovril Company', *Business History*, Vol. XXVIII, No. 1 (1986), p. 30.

23. O'Hagan, *Leaves*, p. 401; Armstrong, 'Hooley', p. 21.

24. T. Congdon and D. McWilliams, *Basic Economics* (London: Arrow, 1976), p. 144; R. L. Heilbroner, *Understanding Macro Economics* (PHI, 4th edn, Englewood Cliffs, 1972), p. 47.

25. C. Wilson, 'Economy and society in late Victorian Britain', *Economic History Review*, 2nd series, Vol. XVIII, No. 1 (1965).

26. A. E. Harrison, 'The competitiveness of the British cycle industry 1890–1914', *Economic History Review*, 2nd series Vol. XXII, No. 2 (1969); R. Brandon, *Singer and the Sewing Machine: A Capitalist Romance* (London: Barrie & Jenkins, 1977), pp. 135–40.

27. P. L. Cottrell, *British Overseas Investment in the Nineteenth Century* (London: Macmillan, 1975) p. 28; E. M. Forster, *Howards End* (Harmondsworth: Penguin Books, 1978), p. 28.

28. F. M .L. Thompson, *English Landed Society in the Nineteenth Century* (London: Routledge & Kegan Paul, 1971) p. 308.

29. P. J. Perry (ed.), *British Agriculture 1875–1914* (London: Methuen, 1973), pp. xi-xii.

30. T. W. Fletcher, 'The great depression of British agriculture, 1875–1896, *Economic History Review*, 2nd series Vol. XIII, No. 3 (1961), p. 421.

31. W. Ashworth, *An Economic History of England 1820–1939* (London: Methuen, 1960), p. 61.

32. Perry, *British Agriculture*, p. xxvi.

33. Ibid., pp. xxv-xxvi.

34. Ashworth, *Economic History*, p. 70.

35. *Times*, 14 October 1887.

36. Thompson, *English Landed Society*, p. 307; D. Spring, 'Land and politics in Edwardian England', *Agricultural History*, Vol. LVIII, No. 1 (1984), pp. 22–4.

37. Thompson, *English Landed Society*, p. 308.

38. A. R. Hall (ed.), *The Export of Capital from Britain 1870–1914* (London: Methuen, 1968), p. 1.

39. R. Sobel, *Panic on Wall Street: A History of America's Financial Disasters* (London: Macmillan, 1968), pp. 154–96.

40. Cottrell, *British Overseas Investment*, p. 39.

41. S. F. Van Oss, 'The gold mining madness in the City', *Nineteenth Century,* Vol. CCXXIV, No. 224 (1895) pp. 537-47.

42. A. G. Ford, 'Overseas lending and international fluctuations 1870–1914', *Yorkshire Bulletin of Economic and Social Research,* Vol. XVII, No. 1 (1965).

43. P. Thane, 'Financiers and the British state: the case of Sir Ernest Cassel', *Business History*, Vol. XXVIII, No. 1 (1986), p. 85.

44. J .R. Killick and W. A. Thomas, 'The provincial stock exchanges, 1830–1870', *Economic History Review*, 2nd series, Vol. XXIII, No. 1 (1970), pp. 103–6.

45. H. J. Dyos and D. H. Aldcroft, *British Transport: An Economic Survey from the Seventeenth Century to the Twentieth* (Leicester: Leicester University Press, 1969) p. 172.

46. D. H. Aldcroft, *British Railways in Transition* (London: Macmillan, 1968), p. 7.

47. Dyos and Aldcroft, *British Transport*, p. 193.

48. Ibid., p. 184.

49. W. Hamish Fraser, *The Coming of the Mass Market 1850–1914* (London: Macmillan, 1981).

50. E .T. Hooley, *Hooley's Confessions* (Simpkin, Marshall & Co., 1925), p. 158; Armstrong, 'Hooley', p. 18; Simmons, *Schweppes,* pp. 52–3.

51. H. W. Bottomley, *Bottomley's Book* (London: Odhams, 1909) p. 150; O'Hagan *Leaves,* Vol. I, p. 401, Vol. II, pp. 21–3.

52. Cottrell, *Industrial Finance*, pp. 173–6; O'Hagan *Leaves*, Vol. I, pp. 245–56; T. R. Nicholson, *The Birth of the British Motor Car 1769–1897,* Vol. 3 (London: Macmillan, 1982), pp. 365–6; Jeremy, *DBB*, Vol. 3, p. 112.

53. A Vallance, *Very Private Enterprise: An Anatomy of Fraud and High Finance* (London: Thames & Hudson, 1955), p. 73; O'Hagan, *Leaves*, pp. 480–1.

54. *Edinburgh Evening Despatch*, 29 June 1956; Waugh, *Lipton Story*, p. 90; O'Hagan, *Leaves*, p. 405.

55. These paragraphs are largely based on J. Armstrong and S. K. Jones, *Business Documents* (Mansell, 1987), ch. 1.

56. *Saturday Review,* 28 March 1896.

57. *Saturday Review,* 21 November 1896.

58. Hooley, *Hooley's Confessions*, p. 161; *Cycling*, 18 June 1898, p. 544.

59. P. Brent, *The Edwardians* (London: BBC, 1972), p. 55.

60. Lord Reading, *Rufus Isaacs, First Marquess of Reading* (London: Hutchinson, 1942), p. 75.

61. R. P. T. Davenport-Hines and J. J. Van Helten, 'Edgar Vincent, Viscount D'Abernon, and the Eastern Investment Company in London, Constantinople and Johannesburg', *Business History*, Vol. XXVIII, No. 1 (1986), pp. 46, 54.

62. Jeremy, *DBB*, Vol. 3, p. 447; *British Mining*, Vol. 1, No. 2 (1 September 1910), p. 21; No. 8 (13 October 1900), p. 154; No. 15 (1 December 1900), pp. 286–8; *Sovereign*, Vol. IV, No. 90 (8 May 1902), p. 28.
63. Jeremy, *DBB*, Vol. 2, pp. 6–8.
64. Bottomley, *Bottomley's Book*, pp. 51, 55, 59; O'Hagan, *Leaves*, p. 281.
65. T. C. Barker, 'Lord Salisbury, Chairman of the Great Eastern Railway 1868–72', in S. Marriner (ed.), *Business and Businessmen: Studies in Business, Economic and Accounting History* (Liverpool: Liverpool University Press, 1979) pp. 87–9.
66. Jeremy, *DBB*, Vol. 2, pp. 7–9.
67. Ibid., Vol. 1, pp. 822–5.
68. H. Bottomley, *Hys Booke* (Neville, 1892), pp. 25–43, 175–8.
69. For example 30 November 1895, p. 1557; 30 January 1904, p. 165.
70. Bottomley, *Bottomley's Book*, p. 144.
71. Ibid., p. 151; *Who Was Who*, Vol. 2 (Edinburgh: A. & C. Black, 1967), p. 625.
72. Vallance, *Very Private Enterprise*, p. 55.
73. Ibid., p. 73.
74. Harrison, 'Joint stock company flotation', pp. 174–6.
75. Armstrong, 'Hooley', p. 30.
76. Cottrell, *Industrial Finance*, p. 70; 63 and 64 Vict., c. 48, clause 8(1).
77. Cottrell, *Industrial Finance*, p. 185; Armstrong, 'Hooley', p. 25.
78. For example, the Ashanti Goldfields Corporation paid their underwriters in options on equity at favourable prices : GHL, Ms 14, 164, Vol. 3, pp. 199, 271.
79. Harrison, 'Joint stock company flotation', p. 171.
80. O'Hagan, *Leaves*, pp. 150, 256, 368.
81. Davenport-Hines and Van Helten, 'Edgar Vincent', p. 56.
82. Thane, 'Financiers', p. 81.
83. R. C. Mitchie, 'The social web of investment in the nineteenth century', *Revue Internationale d'Histoire de la Banque*, Vol XVIII (1979).
84. Vallance, *Very Private Enterprise*, pp. 54–6: Jeremy, *DBB*, Vol. 5, p. 903.
85. Vallance, *Very Private Enterprise*, p. 61.
86. Bottomley, *Bottomley's Book*, p. 152; R. A. Haldane, *With Intent to Deceive: Frauds Famous and Infamous* (Edinburgh: Blackwood, 1970), p. 135.
87. Haldane, *With Intent*, p. 76.
88. O'Hagan, *Leaves*, pp. 269–70.
89. Vallance, *Very Private Enterprise*, p. 59.
90. Hooley, *Hooley's Confessions*, pp. 73–4.
91. Ibid., pp. 74–8.
92. O'Hagan, *Leaves*, pp. 270–2.
93. Ibid., pp. 245–8.
94. O'Hagan has numerous examples: pp. 266, 270, 399.
95. W. R. Lawson, 'Company promoting *à la mode*', *National Review*, No. 32 (1898), p. 104.
96. For example: H. E. M. Stutfield, 'The company monger's Elysium', *National Review*, No. 26 (1895) pp. 836–48; S. F. Van Oss, 'The limited company

craze', *Nineteenth Century*, No. 43 (1898), pp. 731–44.
97.  Cottrell, *Industrial Finance*, pp. 107–112.
98.  Harrison, 'Joint stock company flotation', p. 171.
99.  O'Hagan, *Leaves*, pp. 84–5, 442.
100. Jeremy, *DBB*, Vol. III, p. 330.
101. Ibid., Vol. I, pp. 625–31.
102. S. Chapman, *The Rise of Merchant Banking* (London: Allen & Unwin, 1984), p. 100.
103. A. K. Cairncross, *Home and Foreign Investment 1870–1913* (Cambridge: Cambridge University Press, 1953) p. 100.
104. Cottrell, *Industrial Finance*, p. 140.
105. O'Hagan, *Leaves*, p. 399.
106. Cottrell, *Industrial Finance*, p. 115.
107. Ibid., pp. 128–9.
108. John Dicks, *The Hooley Book* (London, 1904), pp. 16–17.
109. 'Tenax', *The Gentle Art of Exploiting Gullibility* (David Weir, 1923), pp. 287–9.
110. Cottrell, *Industrial Finance*, p. 114.
111. Morgan and Thomas, *Stock Exchange*, p. 217; J. Atkin, 'Official regulation of British overseas investment, 1914–31' *Economic History Review*, 2nd series, Vol. XXIII, No. 2 (1970), p. 325.
112. 4 & 5 Geo. V, c. 11, Postponement of Payment Act.
113. Morgan and Thomas, *Stock Exchange*, pp. 219–20.
114. Ibid., p. 222; W. A. Thomas, *The Finance of British Industry 1918–1976* (London: Methuen, 1978) p. 26.
115. Orbell, *Baring Brothers*, p. 76.
116. Ibid., pp. 79–80; Atkin, 'Official regulation', p. 326; Thomas, *Finance of British Industry,* p. 24.
117. J. S. Foreman-Peck, *A History of the World Economy* (Brighton: Wheatsheaf, 1983), Chapters 7 and 8.
118. Orbell, *Baring Brothers*, p. 79.
119. Ibid., p. 81.
120. R. P. T. Davenport-Hines, *Dudley Docker: The Life and Times of a Trade Warrior*, (Cambridge: Cambridge University Press 1984), p. 153.
121. Thomas, *Finance of British Industry,* p. 49; Davenport-Hines, *Dudley Docker*, p. 263.
122. Jeremy, *DBB*, Vol. 3, pp. 110–14.

# 7 The emergence of a new financial institution: investment trusts in Britain, 1870–1939

*Youssef Cassis*

Writing in 1923, the American expert on investment trusts, Leland Rex Robinson, observed that 'the English and Scottish investment trusts have been the most important factor in the export of capital from the United Kingdom.' And in assessing their role in the British economy after World War I, he added:

> It becomes more and more apparent that British finance, apart from the joint-stock banks, will be urgently called upon to support the efforts of British industry to regain and maintain its pre-eminent position in the world's trade, and it is particularly in respect of issues that will assist to this end that the [British Trusts] Association will play an important role.[1]

The export of capital and the relationships between finance and industry are among the central themes of this volume. Yet, despite their alleged importance, little is known about the precise role of investment trusts. They have been much less studied than other financial institutions such as banks, insurance companies or the Stock Exchange. There is still no general study of investment trusts that considers their role in the financial market, estimates the funds at their disposal and the direction of their investments or identifies financial interests that they represented.

This relative lack of interest may be due to the very nature of investment trusts' business, namely investment, which is not associated with another financial activity, as in the case of bank or insurance companies, or to the fact that there were a great many investment companies – over 200 in the 1930s – all very similar in size and business policy. Their relative importance, as compared to banks and insurance companies, and more recently to building societies and pension funds, might also have relegated them to the background.

The available literature on investment trusts dates principally from the inter-war period and is mainly written by American and European economists interested in investment trusts which, until the early 1920s, were specifically British.[2] There is one recent study of investment and unit trusts from their origins to the 1960s.[3] The case studies are also rare: a few anniversary histories[4] and recently an analysis of the operation of the British Assets Trust between 1897 and 1914 by Ranald C. Michie.[5] Similarly, with a few exceptions,[6] little mention of investment trust is made in the vast literature on financial markets and institutions, the export of British capital before 1914 or the financing of industry by the City of London.

Rather than attempt to provide a comprehensive account of the history of investment trusts from the 1870s to 1939, I shall concentrate on only four key factors of their development. Firstly, I shall consider the origins of investment trust, the main reasons of the appearance of this type of financial institution at the end of the nineteenth century and the differences between investment trust and the various types of finance companies which emerged during the same period. Secondly, I shall assess the relative importance of investment trusts, paying particular attention to the total assets at their disposal, as compared with those of banks, insurance companies or building societies. I shall then examine the investments of investment trusts within the broader context of the debate on the export of capital from Britain and the relationships between finance and industry. Finally, I shall consider the place of investment trusts within the City of London.

### Origins

The first investment trust is generally considered to have been the Société Générale des Pays-Bas pour favoriser l'Industrie Nationale, founded in 1822 in Brussels by King William I of the Netherlands. After the separation of Belgium from the Netherlands, this company was called the Société Générale de Belgique. In Britain, the London Financial Association and the International Financial Society, both formed in 1863, showed the same concerns for the finance of industry, but were too close to the Crédit Mobilier model to be considered as investment trusts.[7] The Colonial and Foreign Investment Trust, formerly the Colonial and Foreign Government Trust, founded in 1868, was the first to apply the principle of an investment trust, namely to spread risks over a number of investments without seeking to exert any control over the companies in which it had equity interests. The trust's founders claimed that their objective was to give the investor of moderate means the same advantages as the large capitalist. Specializing in foreign and colonial government stock, it simply spread its investments over a number of different stocks, using a portion of the extra interest as a sinking fund to pay off the original capital. According to its prospectus:

> A capitalist who at any time within the last twenty or thirty years had invested, say £1,000,000 in 10 or 12 stocks selected with ordinary prudence, would, on the above plan, not only have received a high rate of interest, but by this time have received back his original capital by the action of the drawings and sinking fund, and held the greater part of his stocks for nothing.[8]

Despite these promises, the success enjoyed by the Colonial and Foreign Government Trust and other trusts was limited during the next twenty years. In 1886, only twelve such companies were quoted on the London Stock Exchange.

140

Investment trusts enjoyed a remarkable success in Scotland during the 1870s, symbolized, as it were, by the foundation in 1873 of the Scottish American Investment Trust, the secretary of which was Robert Fleming, (1843–1933), considered as the 'father of investment trusts'. While Robert Fleming did not invent the concept of investment trust, he played a decisive role in establishing sound principles of investment trust management and remains the most remarkable figure in the history of this industry. The son of a Dundee shopkeeper, Robert Fleming went to work, at thirteen, for Messrs Edward Baxter and Son, a local textile firm that had built a family fortune in factory production of linen. By the time he was twenty-one he was chosen to be private clerk for the senior partner of the firm, Edward Baxter. The Baxters held extensive American securities, and Robert Fleming was tutored in investment procedures by Edward Baxter and given the responsibility, in time, for the management of his American holdings. In 1870, he was sent to the United States as Baxter's agent. When the Scottish American Investment Trust was founded in 1873, Robert Fleming became its secretary, but was, in fact, the driving spirit behind the enterprise, securing the services of four well-known Dundee businessmen as trustees. A second and a third Scottish American Investment Trust were formed in 1879. Following his initial success, Robert Fleming founded the Investment Trust Corporation in London in 1888. In 1890, he asked the trustees of the three Scottish American Investment Trusts to relieve him of the secretaryship, though arrangements were made for him to continue as advising secretary. In 1900, Robert Fleming opened a London office that eventually became Robert Fleming & Co., an agency offering to various investment trusts the advantages of cooperative management, purchasing and underwriting of financial activities, with the net result that by 1928, he was able to influence some 66 trusts that together controlled £114.8 million worth of funds. At his death in 1933, he left over £2 million.[9]

Robert Fleming's arrival in London in the 1880s coincided with a wave of formations of investment trusts. On the London Stock Exchange, their total nominal capital rose from £5 million in 1887 to some £50 million in 1890 and 70 new trust companies were formed during the same period.[10] However, investment trusts suffered severely in the aftermath of the Baring crisis. According to the *Bankers' Magazine*, in 1893, the net depreciation of their ordinary and preference capital was 14.45 per cent; for the companies formed after 1880, this depreciation of their ordinary capital was 29.19 per cent.[11] The *Bankers' Magazine* considered investment trusts as one of the fashions of the City, acting as a front of company promoters making their fortunes through the manipulation of founders' shares, the watering of stock and the underwriting of doubtful companies.[12] There is no doubt that alongside the formation of genuine investment trusts, modelled on the Colonial and Foreign Government Trust, the late 1880s saw the formation of numerous doubtful companies, that called themselves investment trusts, but that were little more than fraudulent operations. From the outset, *The Economist* was sceptical, noting that, despite their popularity with the public, few of them had been able to start in business and had experienced great difficulty in acquiring proper investments. It claimed that this was due to the fact that many trusts shared to a large extent the same directors and bought, on the whole, the same securities, thus forcing prices up against

141

themselves.[13] Shortly before the Baring crisis, *The Economist* warned that the investments of the investment trusts' capital in established undertakings could not suffice to pay a dividend of 7 per cent on ordinary shares boasted by most companies, and that they had therefore gone into promoting and underwriting doubtful concerns.[14] The result was that out of 101 investment trust companies registered in 1890, 50 went into liquidation, 30 of these before 1901.[15]

From 1896 on, with the general improvement of business conditions, investment trusts started recovering from this crisis. The price of their securities went regularly upward, companies improved their position and investors exhibited more confidence in them.[16] A number of new trusts were formed between 1905 and 1914. A new wave of formation of investment trusts took place during the mid 1920s; out of 103 trusts formed during the interwar period 82 were established between 1925 and 1929.[17] Investment trusts became more stable: there were about 84 trust companies in 1903, and out of 209 English and Scottish investment trusts operating in 1935, 90 were formed before 1914.[18]

### Objectives

The main objective of investment trusts was to act as a collective capitalist. They invested the capital of their shareholders and paid them a dividend based on the average yield of their diversified investments as well as the gains from a few other operations. However, their investments usually exceeded the amount of their share capital. In addition to issuing debentures,[19] investment trusts borrowed from the banks, using their capital as a security, in case their investments had to be sold at a loss.[20] In addition, investment trusts participated in underwriting syndicates and granted long- and medium-term loans to other companies.[21] Significantly, investment trusts did not seek to exert any form of control over the companies in which they had invested.

In that respect, investment trusts were financial institutions of a different kind from the German universal banks or the French 'banques d'affaires'.[22] The question remains, however, why investments trusts appeared in Britain in the 1870s and 1880s instead of investment banks. This question must be answered in the general context of the organization of the banking system in England. Investment trusts, and not investment banks, responded to a specific need at the time. The banking system in England, and even more so in Scotland, was already well developed in the late 1860s. Even before the amalgamation movement had concentrated in London a greater part of the resources of the country, the use of the inland bill of exchange had ensured that credit circulated throughout the country.[23] Industry was mainly self-financed and raised capital through the financial market rather than through banks.[24] At the same time, the superabundance of capital and a fall in the rate of return on home securities required new outlets for capital abroad. This could be done more easily through the organized structure of an investment trust than by an individual. Investment trusts were also the consequences of the extremely specialized character of the English banking system: the functions of deposit banks were limited to short-term credit, their investments being essentially a second line of reserve.[25] Long-term investments frowned on by the banks could therefore be made through the channel of investment trusts. As to merchant banks, they were not investment banks, their main function being the acceptance of bills of exchange and the issue of foreign loans.[26] Finally, it should be recalled that behind the various continental investment bank projects lay the willingness to promote industry in order to catch up on England. It has been argued that the existence of investment banks of the German type would have prevented the relative industrial decline which started in the 1880s.[27] This is a problem that cannot be discussed here. Some comparisons between the British and German banking systems can be found in Chapter 1. All that can be said is that the banking community was profoundly averse to any idea of investment bank and convinced of the superiority of the British financial system.[28]

Whereas investment trusts dealt with the interest and dividends from their investments and in principle never distributed profits realized through selling securities in the process of changing investments, it was precisely these speculative gains, together with those deriving from promoting and lending, that formed the essential part of the income of finance companies. In the 1890s, a significant proportion of these finance companies were connected with mining finance in South Africa, and included companies such as the South African Argonauts, the South African Gold Trust or the South African Trust and Finance Company. Similarly, investment trusts should be distinguished from the mortgage and land companies, such as the American Freehold-Land Mortgage Company of London, the Australian Mercantile Land and Finance Company or the New Zealand Trust and Loan Company, whose main business was to lend money on mortgage of real property. Unfortunately, both the *Stock Exchange Official Intelligence* (Burdett) and *The Stock Exchange Year Book* (Skinner) do not separately classify investment trusts, finance companies and land and mortgage companies. The 725 such companies recorded by the *Stock Exchange Year Book* in 1914 and the 854 recorded the same year by the *Stock Exchange Official Intelligence* by far exceed the number of pure investment trusts operating during this year, which can be estimated to be between 80 and 100. Since 1899, a fair proportion of the investment trusts is to be found under the new separate heading 'Financial Trusts' in the *Stock Exchange Official Intelligence*. This lack of clear distinction makes very difficult any attempt to evaluate the total assets in the hands of investment trusts, at the least until the appearance of a heading 'Investment Trusts' in the *Stock Exchange Official Yearbook* in 1930 and the foundation of the Association of Investment Trust Companies in 1932.[29]

## Estimated total assets

Before analysing the operations of investment trusts, it is essential to attempt to estimate their contribution as financial institutions, and their impact on the British economy. There are two ways to consider the relative importance of investment trusts as financial institutions. The first one is to compare their total assets with those

*Table 7.1    Assets of the financial institutions, 1903–33*

| | Investment trusts | Banks | Insurance companies | Post Office Saving banks | Trustee Saving Banks | Building societies |
|---|---|---|---|---|---|---|
| | £ millions | | | | | |
| 1903 | 70.0 | 934.0 | 352.6 | 146.1 | 57.2 | 65.0 |
| 1913 | 90.0 | 1,205.0 | 530.1 | 187.4 | 68.7 | 65.3 |
| 1920 | 112.0 | 2,604.1 | 712.1 | 267.1 | 91.3 | 87.0 |
| 1933 | 295.6 | 2,697.8 | 1,449.6 | 326.7 | 171.4 | 501.1 |

*Sources:*
Investment Trusts: Corner and Burton, *Investment Trusts*, pp. 49–50, 327; *The Economist*, December 1934. Other financial institutions: D. K. Sheppard, *The Growth and Role of UK Financial Institutions 1880–1962* (London, 1971).

of other financial institutions, the other is to compare their total assets with the aggregate value of securities traded on the London Stock Exchange.

Table 7.1 gives estimates of the total nominal capital including long- and short-term debentures of investment trusts for the years 1903, 1913, 1920 and 1932 which, as we have seen, is fractionally smaller than the investments held, and the total assets of banks, insurance companies, Post Office saving banks, trustee saving banks and building societies for the same years. It must be emphasized that the figures for investment trusts are only estimates, particularly for the years 1903, 1913 and 1920.[30] Throughout the period under review, investment trusts appear as dwarfs compared to clearing banks and even insurance companies. The funds at their disposal were only 7.5 per cent of those of the banks and 17 per cent of those of insurance companies on the eve of World War I and the gap even widened during the period up to 1921; however, their total assets were then larger than those of trustee saving banks and building societies. The second striking feature of the figures of Table 7.1 is the growth of the investment trust movement during the 1920s. They almost trebled their capital between 1920 and 1933, a higher rate of growth than any other financial institutions apart from building societies, which really took off during this period.[31]

Similarly, investment trusts did not hold in their portfolio more than a small fraction of the total stocks dealt in London. In 1913, their capital accounted for 0.3 per cent of the total nominal value of securities traded on the London Stock Exchange. Their total capital was minute compared with the values of two of their popular assets, foreign and colonial stocks and bonds and railway securities: the former had values of £3,746 millions, the latter of £4,148 millions in 1913.[32] In 1933, investment trusts held investments with a book value of £332,253,000, whereas the total of the 'Official List' securities, after deduction of 'British Funds' and 'American

Railways', which by that time were totally neglected by investment trusts, amounted to £10,530,896,389.[33]

But one should not conclude that investment trusts were therefore negligible. As far as their investments were concerned, they obviously did not carry the weight of banks and insurance companies. However, unlike them, they did not have to make provision to meet any sudden withdrawals of funds or excessive claims by their customers, and enjoyed therefore a much greater freedom in the choice of their investments. In the debate over the export of capital, their relative importance, even quantitatively, increases significantly as they invested about 90 per cent of their capital abroad before 1914. The importance of investment trusts also derived from their privileged position in the City of London, from their links, mainly through their directors, with the clearing banks, merchant banks, finance companies, insurance companies and stockbroking firms.

**Investments**

Investment trusts' investment profile can be analysed in three ways. First, the geographical distribution of investments, which raises the question of foreign investments; second, the industrial distribution of investments, which raises the question of the relationships between finance and industry; and third, the form of investments (debentures, preference, etc.) which raises the question of their entrepreneurial role. Also, the distribution of the trusts' investments suggests the way in which each company diversified its portfolio and spread its risks. The better managed trusts mixed a large amount of solid investment with a small degree of speculative activity. Most investment trusts spread their investments so that the average investment in any one security amounted at the most to a few thousand pounds.[34] Thus, in 1927 the Bankers' Investment Trust had invested £3 million in 500 different securities, while the Foreign American and General Investment Trust had £2,274,000 in around 450 securities.[35]

Unfortunately, the distribution of the trusts' investments is very difficult to assess because, at least until the 1950s, most companies did not publish the lists of their investments. For the pre-1914 period, there is almost a total lack of statistics of the amount and character of investment trusts' holdings. According to *The Economist*, some £14,657,000, at book value, controlled by ten companies in 1890, was geographically distributed as shown in Table 7.2.

Globally, *The Economist* estimated that trust companies owned about £50 million of overseas securities in 1890.[36] L. E. Robinson considered that in 1914, of the £75–£100 million of investment trusts' capital, 'fully 90 per cent were stuck in overseas holding, America being the single largest claimant'.[37] The investment policy of investment trusts, therefore, exemplifies the general trend towards investment overseas prevailing during the period 1870–1914. In 1914, about £3,500 million were invested abroad, representing one-third of the total capital held by British nationals both at home and abroad.[38] Investment trusts invested a much larger proportion of their funds in overseas securities than insurance companies, whose overseas

145

*Table 7.2    Geographical distribution of investment trusts' investments (book value) 1890)*

|  | United Kingdom | British Empire | USA | Latin America | Rest of the world | Total |
|---|---|---|---|---|---|---|
| £,000 | 1,878 | 840 | 5,288 | 3,990 | 3,263 | 14,657 |
| % | 12.8 | 5.7 | 36.1 | 23.1 | 22.3 | 100 |

Source:
The Economist, 1937, Vol. IV, p. 365

investments have been evaluated at about 40 per cent of their funds.[39] Their behaviour might be typical of that of the individual investor operating in the City of London.

With the war, a shift from American to home securities took place. Even though there are no global figures available, the general trend can be seen, in Table 7.3, from changes between 1914 and 1922 in the geographical distribution of two major investment trusts which followed different investment policies.

*Table 7.3    Changes in the geographical distribution of two investment trusts, 1914 and 1922*

|  | Merchants' Trust | | Industrial and General Trust | |
|---|---|---|---|---|
|  | 1914 % | 1922 % | 1914 % | 1922 % |
| Great Britain | 14.85 | 29.59 | 29.26 | 40.09 |
| British Empire | 10.73 | 9.22 | 13.57 | 13.06 |
| United States of America | 50.74 | 30.97 | 23.69 | 6.45 |
| South America | 9.28 | 12.47 | 25.67 | 34.19 |
| Europe | 2.14 | 3.55 | 3.22 | 3.40 |
| Others | 12.26 | 14.20 | 4.59 | 2.81 |
|  | 100.00 | 100.00 | 100.00 | 100.00 |

Source:
Robinson, Credit Facilities, pp. 189–90.

Investment trusts are known to have been very useful during World War I by making dollars available to the British government, through the disposal of their American investments or by depositing them with the Treasury. However, no estimate of their contribution to the dollar mobilization scheme, as compared to that of insurance companies or the general public, can be given.[40]

There are more statistics available for the inter-war period, calculated on the basis of a more significant number of companies. Table 7.4 shows the evolution of the geographical distribution of the trusts' investments between 1923 and 1939, and demonstrates the growing dominance of Home securities to the detriment of Central and South American as well as European securities; the former had markedly increased in the early 1920s, the latter in the mid- to late 1920s. American securities never regained the favour they enjoyed before World War I.

Table 7.4   Geographical distribution of investment trusts' investments (book value), 1923–39

|  | %  | | | |
|  | 1923 | 1928 | 1933 | 1939 |
|---|---|---|---|---|
| United Kingdom | 34.5 | 34.5 | 40.4 | 55.9 |
| Dominions and Canada | 10.5 | 10.6 | 13.2 | 10.7 |
| United States | 17.7 | 10.6 | 10.2 | 13.6 |
| Central and South America | 28.7 | 24.2 | 15.2 |  |
| Europe | 4.5 | 15.9 | 13.1 | 19.8 |
| Other countries | 4.1 | 4.2 | 7.9 |  |
| Total | 100.0 | 100.0 | 100.0 | 100.0 |

Source:
The Economist, 15 February 1930, 1 December 1934, 12 August 1939, quoted by Corner and Burton, *Investment and Unit Trusts*, p. 68. (The figures for 1923 and 1928 relate to 26 companies; those for 1933 to 56 companies, and those for 1939 to 61 companies.)

The industrial distribution of investment trusts' investments is more difficult to assess than the geographical one on the basis of the annual reports of the companies. In fact, Corner and Burton doubt 'whether any useful analysis could be made from the information available before the fifties'.[41] Table 7.5 gives some figures published by *The Economist* for the years 1929 and 1933, at book value, which suggest little change of distribution during these four years. However, this classification is very general because Industrials and Miscellaneous are grouped together.

For the year 1927–8, H. Linhardt offers a more detailed analysis of the industrial distribution of the investments of fourteen investment trusts based on the market value of the securities, in Table 7.6, which suggests a more significant proportion of industrial securities.

Table 7.5  *Industrial distribution of investment trusts' investments (book value), 1929–1933*

|  | % | |
|  | 1929 | 1933 |
| --- | --- | --- |
| Government and corporations | 14.2 | 12.8 |
| Railways | 13.6 | 12.9 |
| Public utilities | 6.4 | 8.1 |
| Industrial and miscellaneous | 65.8 | 66.2 |
| Total | 100.0 | 100.0 |

Source:
*The Economist*, 1 December 1934. The figures for 1929 relate to 23 companies and those for 1933 to 43 companies.

Table 7.6  *Industrial distribution of investment trusts' investments (market value of securities), 1927–8*

|  | % |
| --- | --- |
| Railways | 21.03 |
| Industry | 43.52 |
| Bank, finance | 12.62 |
| Government, municipalities | 13.20 |
| Public utilities | 8.63 |
| Miscellaneous | 0.95 |

Source:
Linhardt, *Britische Investment Trusts*, p. 222.

It would be interesting to know the industrial distribution of investments per geographical area, but there are no statistics which would enable us to make an estimate of the proportion of the trusts' funds invested in the British industry. Linhardt's figures for the year 1928, which should be interpreted with caution, reveal a certain order of magnitude. Linhardt based his estimate on the observation of the investment policy of about 40 trust companies, and built an index of industrial and geographical distribution, suggesting the distribution shown in Table 7.7.[42]

According to Linhardt's figures, investment trusts were investing only 16.2 per cent of their funds in the British industry in 1928 and there was no particular relationship between the investment trusts and the British industry, the latter being just another possibility of investment among many.[43] As far as the finance of small and medium-sized companies is concerned, the 'Macmillan Gap', the contribution of

Table 7.7  Index of industrial and geographical distribution of investment trusts'
investments, 1928

|  | 1<br>Britain and<br>Colonies | 2<br>Britain<br>alone | 3<br>Abroad | Total<br>1 & 3 |
|---|---|---|---|---|
| Industry | 20.0 | 16.20 | 25.0 | 45 |
| Railways and<br>    public utilities | 13.0 | 10.08 | ' 15.0 | 28 |
| Finance | 9.0 | 7.20 | 4.0 | 13 |
| Government and<br>    municipalities | 7.5 | 2.16 | 5.5 | 13 |
| Miscellaneous | 0.5 | 0.36 | 0.5 | 1 |
|  | 50.0 | 36.00 | 50.0 | 100 |

Source:
Linhardt, *Britische Investment Trusts* pp. 224–30.

investment trust does not even feature. According to the Report of the Macmillan
Committee, 'the investment trust companies do not look with any great favour on
small issues which could have no free market and would require close watching.'[44]

As far as the forms of investment are concerned, up to the early 1930s, the greater
part of their investments were in bonds and debentures, although during the thirties a
shift towards ordinary shares is evident (Table 7.8).

Table 7.8  Changes in investment trusts' investments, 1933–9

|  | Debentures/<br>Bonds<br>% | Preference<br>% | Ordinary<br>% | Total<br>% |
|---|---|---|---|---|
| 1933 | 38.9 | 27.1 | 34.0 | 100.0 |
| 1939 | 19.0 | 27.5 | 53.0 | 100.0 |

Source:
Corner and Burton, *Investment Trusts*, pp. 66–7.

The reason for this shift to ordinary shares was the need for investment trusts to
increase their profits, as these were adversely affected by the low long-term rate of
interest established in the early thirties and which was to last until 1952.[45]

## Directors and managers

The activity of an investment trust consists largely of buying and selling securities. Caution, right contacts and connections, knowledge of the market are the only skills required of the directors, manager or secretary. Table 7.9 shows the principal occupations of the directors of a selection of sixteen investment trusts for the years 1880, 1905, 1922 and 1935.[46] The permanent feature is the overwhelming presence of City men, whereas in Scotland, the boards of investment trusts included several representatives of the medium and small trade and industry.[47]

One of the principal changes over almost half a century concerns the declining

*Table 7.9*  *Principal occupation of the directors of sixteen English investment trusts, 1890–1935*

|  | 1890 % | 1905 % | 1922 % | 1935 % |
|---|---|---|---|---|
| Bankers, merchants | 27 (33.5) | 21 (30.0) | 16 (24.5) | 10 (18.0) |
| Financiers, company directors | 18 (22.0) | 13 (18.0) | 15 (23.0) | 21 (38.0) |
| Accountants | 1 (1.5) | 3 (4.0) | 3 (4.5) | 2 (3.5) |
| Stockbrokers | 5 (6.0) | 4 (6.0) | 5 (8.0) | 3 (5.5) |
| Solicitors, barristers | 6 (7.5) | 7 (20.0) | 6 (9.0) | 1 (2.0) |
| Aristocrats, politicians army officers | 10 (12.5) | 8 (11.0) | 7 (11.0) | 7 (13.0) |
| Investment trusts' managers | — — | 2 (3.0) | 6 (9.0) | 7 (13.0) |
| Others, unknown | 14 (17.0) | 13 (18.0) | 7 (11.0) | 4 (7.0) |
| Total | 81 100.0 | 71 100.0 | 65 100.0 | 55 100.0 |

*Source:*
The Directory of Directors.

proportion of bankers and merchants, and their replacement by financiers and company directors. Despite the disapproving position officially adopted by the City establishment towards investment trusts in their early stage, particularly during the boom of the late 1880s, prominent private bankers, merchants and merchant bankers were involved from the beginning in the new industry.[48]

Famous banking names such as Sir John Lubbock, later Lord Avebury, of Robarts, Lubbock and Co., Lord Hillingdon, of Glyn, Mills, Currie and Co., Lindsay Eric Smith, of Smith, Payne & Smiths, or Richard B. Martin, of Martin & Co., were chairmen or directors of the London Trust Company, the Bankers' Investment Trust, the Industrial and General Trust and the Debenture Corporation between 1888 and 1914. With the almost total disappearance of the London private bankers and the continuous decline of the traditional merchant firm, the dominant figure in the City became, besides the merchant banker, the company director, who had interests in various companies with a seat on the boards of several of them, but who was no more a partner in a private firm. For the years 1922 and even more 1935, the heading 'bankers, merchants' in Table 7.4 is made up of merchant bankers, who following the decline of their acceptance business, developed an interest in investment trusts. In the mid-1920s, merchant bankers, alone or in conjunction with other merchant banks, set up new investment trusts of which they held the whole capital and which they used to undertake their long-term finance business, particularly in Western and Central Europe. J. Henry Schroder & Co. were the pioneers in this field. In 1924, they founded the Continental and Industrial Trust, followed in 1928 by the Second Continental and Industrial Trust. In 1924, Hambros founded the Mid-European Corporation and in 1926, Erlangers took the initiative to establish the City and International Trust.[49]

Accountants and solicitors appear to have played a less prominent part in the investment trust movement than it is sometimes assumed: taken together, they never accounted for more than 15 per cent of the total of the directors between 1890 and 1935. In Scotland, however, accountants and Writers to the Signet formed, on the basis of the analysis of three Scottish investment trusts,[50] at any time, between 30 and 40 per cent of the directors. In addition, some of the leading figures of the investment trust movement in England came from the ranks of accountants. The most remarkable example is Sir George Alexander Touche (1861–1935): born in Edinburgh, son of a banker, he was indentured in 1878 to Alexander Thomas Niven, an original member of the Chartered Accountants of Scotland. Shortly after qualifying, he went to London and worked with Broads, Patterson & May, chartered accountants; one of the partners H. Evans Broad, was a director of several investment trusts, including the Debenture Corporation, which formed a group known as the Worcester House Group. In 1889, Touche was appointed secretary of the newly-formed Industrial and General Trust; he was appointed a director in 1888 and chairman in 1908. In 1901, he was appointed chairman of the Trustees, Executors and Securities Corporation, later renamed the Trustees Corporation. He quickly became prominent in the investment trust world and, as we shall see, became responsible for the biggest investment trust group in the City. In 1899, Touche founded his own accounting firm, George A. Touche & Co., with branches in Canada, the United States of America, and later in Paris, which provided management services for the investment trusts of his group.[51]

The same is true of lawyers, with another remarkable figure in the investment trust movement: John Wynford Philipps, later Viscount St Davids (1860–1938), eldest son of Canon Sir John Erasmus Philipps, twelfth Baronet, who qualified as a barrister in 1886 and became involved in the investment trust movement in 1890 through joining the board of the Government Stocks and Other Securities Investment Company. He was elected chairman a year later and was to lead one of the biggest investment groups, the St Davids Group or the '69 Old Broad Street Group' as it was also known.[52] Another major figure in the investment trust world, Sir Miles Mattinson

(1854–1944) also qualified as a barrister in 1877 and practised on the Northern circuit.

Stockbrokers were a small but important group of directors. As their investments were done through the Stock Exchange, stockbrokers obviously had a strategic importance to investment trusts. Before 1914, half of the investment trusts considered in the sample had one, sometimes two stockbrokers on their board, with the same broker usually sitting on the boards of the trusts of the same group. The most common name was James Capel & Co., one of the most prestigious firms on the Stock Exchange, with one of its partners on the boards of the Foreign and Colonial Investment Trust, the Foreign American and General Investment Trust, the Industrial and General Trust, the International Investment Trust and the Investment Trust Corporation.

Another important change between 1890 and 1935 was the growing professionalization of the investment trusts, reflected in the number of secretaries and managers sitting on the board of their trust, most of them also having several outside interests. Whereas in some cases the appointment on the board was a gratuity for services rendered, a few secretaries rose to the very top of the investment trust movement, such as George A. Touche, already mentioned, or William Sanford Poole, secretary of the Industrial and General Trust in 1905 and director of eleven companies in 1922 and sixteen in 1935.

The presence of aristocrats, politicians and army officers on the boards of investment trusts reflects, particularly for the period before 1914, the general trend of the aristocracy seeking new sources of income in the City[53] as well as the attempts by the promoters of investment trusts to gain the confidence of the public by having titled persons on their boards. In the absence of internal records of the firms, it is impossible to assess their role precisely.

An important characteristic of the directors of investment trusts, whichever category they belonged to, is the fact that they were almost invariably interested in several investment trusts. Alongside City men who mixed their directorships of investment trusts with a variety of other companies, some of the investment trusts' directors were above all what could be called 'investment trust men', in the sense that investment trusts constituted the greater part of their business interests. There were, of course, the men whose names were associated with an investment group, such as Lord St Davids, who was a director, or more often the chairman of, 22 companies in 1922, eleven of which were investment trusts, or Sir Miles Mattinson, chairman of thirteen companies in 1935, eleven of which were investment trusts. Some were merchant bankers involved in the investment trust movement, such as Guy H. Benson, chairman of Robert Benson & Co., whose eight out of nine directorships were in investment trusts. However, there were also some 'outsiders' whose main concern in the City was investment companies: in 1890, Lord Eustace Cecil was, besides being chairman of a railway company, chairman or director of five investment trusts, and Ernest Noel, nephew of the first Earl of Gainsborough, was director of seven of them.

These interlocking directorships relate to the wider issue of the investment 'groups'.

## Investment groups

The notion of a 'group' has often been used about investment trusts to designate companies which shared the whole or part of the same board or the manager and sometimes also the same premises. From the beginning of the investment trust movement, the directors of successful trusts preferred to form another trust rather than to enlarge the existing one, because the optimum capital size of an investment trust was then considered to be between £1 and £1.5 million. The fact that the directors would receive an extra fee by creating another company undoubtedly also played a role. This development can be noted in the growth of the Scottish American Investment Trust. Following its formation in 1873, the directors quickly founded a Second and a Third Scottish American Investment Trust. In the same way, the promoters of the Foreign and Colonial Government Trust founded the American Investment and General Trust in 1879, and the Foreign, American and General Investment Trust in 1883. These three trusts, together with the Alliance Investment Company, established in 1889, were known as the C. M. Rose group,[54] because from their inception their common secretary was Charles Marston Rose (1858–1924). The Rose group also shared the same chairman, Lord Eustace Cecil. By the late 1920s, together with five other companies, they were known as the Le Marchant group,[55] and in the 1930s, in a slightly different composition, as the 'Stockholders' group.[56] By 1936, this group was made up of ten companies with a total share and debenture capital of £20 million. In that year, the other major investment trust Groups were the St Davids Group, with sixteen companies and a capital of £21.1 million, the 'Touche', or 'Industrial and General' group, with ten companies and £25.7 million capital, and the 'Robert Benson' Group, with seven trusts and £20.3 million capital.[57] These four Groups controlled a capital of nearly £100 million out of a combined capital of some £300 million for the whole investment trust movement in that period.

The evolution of the Foreign and Colonial Government Trust, shows that the frontiers of investment trust groups were shifting, as they were based on interlocking directorships and not through cross-holding of capital, which was a most unusual feature of the movement. These groups should therefore in no way be seen as 'financial groups' in the sense of one company having a control, through a majority or even a minority shareholding, over a number of companies belonging to the group.

The significance of investment trust groups should be considered in the light of the business of investment trusts – diversified investment, no seeking of control over a company through an investment – which appears to be of a passive rather than of a dynamic nature. In that respect, investment trusts did not constitute an appropriate structure for the entrepreneurial activities of a group of capitalists, such as creating new companies, financing new undertakings or taking control over a company in order to orientate its policy. Since this entrepreneurial role was not assumed by joint-stock banks,[58] as for example in Germany, it was left to the company promoter, discussed by Armstrong in this volume, and only indirectly to the merchant banks, through their control over 'finance companies', such as the Rothschilds and the Exploration Company.[59] Apart from insurance companies, and later pension funds, which became their main shareholders after 1914, large investors in investment trust companies consisted of people with business or family links who shared the same view, or benefited from the same advice about their investment. There were for example several brewery magnates among the major shareholders of the London Trust Company in 1899: Combes, Watneys, Lord Iveagh, Henry C. Bonsor, Edgar Lubbock.[60] Several members and relatives of the Bevan family, of Barclays Bank, were large shareholders in the Merchant's Trust.[61]

However, the existence of strong investment trust groups means that the decision to invest sums of money much larger than the capital of a single investment trust was taken by the same small coterie of key managers and directors. This had no doubt an influence on the direction taken by investment trusts' investments. Besides, even though investment trusts did not themselves assume any entrepreneurial role, they could be of some assistance by occasionally giving their support to a new enterprise or to a financial operation. For example, the St Davids group was important in the financing, in the late 1890s, of Lord St Davids' brother, Owen Philipps, later Lord Kylsant (1863–1937), in his ventures into shipping.[62]

### Conclusion

To summarize, investment trusts appeared in Britain in the last quarter of the nineteenth century as a new financial institution apparently offering the small investor the same advantages as the large capitalist by spreading its investments over a great variety of securities. However, it is questionable whether they ever succeeded in attracting small investors for their shareholders belonged to the wealthy classes or, increasingly after 1914, became institutional investors, like insurance companies and, later, pension funds. Investment trusts invested their funds abroad to a larger extent than any other financial institution: nearly 90 per cent of their investments during the period up to 1914 and, despite a shift towards home investments, more than 50 per cent during the greater part of the interwar period. Consequently, their contribution towards the finance of the British industry cannot have been of any great significance. Nevertheless, even though they did not assume any entre-preneurial role, largely because of the very nature of their business, and their aggregate size was much smaller than that of the major financial institutions such as banks and insurance companies, investment trusts were not minor players in the British financial system. Not only was the capital that they controlled in no way negligible, but also, and perhaps of more importance, they can be seen as representing the pattern of the investment behaviour of the City establishment.

### Notes

I should like to thank Jean-Jacques Van Helten for his corrections on an earlier draft of this chapter.

1.  L. E. Robinson, *Credit Facilities in the United Kingdom* (New York, 1923), p. 109.
2.  The most significant are L. E. Robinson, *Credit Facilities* and *Investment Trust Organization and Management* (New York, 1926); T. J. Grayson, *Investment Trusts. Their Origin, Development and Operation* (New York, 1928); H. Linhardt, *Die Britischen Investment Trusts* (Berlin/Wien, 1935).
3.  D. L. Corner and H. Burton, *Investment Trusts and Unit Trusts in Britain and America* (London, 1963). See also H. Bullock, *The Story of Investment Companies* (New York, 1959).
4.  Among the anniversary histories, see D. Last, *The Foreign and Colonial Investment Trust Company. A Centenary Review 1868–1968*; R. B. Weir, *A History of the Scottish American Investment Company Limited 1873–1973* (Edinburgh, 1973); Sir A. C. Blair, *Edinburgh American Assets Trust Limited. A Centenary Review 1878–1978*; (Edinburgh); J. H. Busby, *London Trust Company Limited, 1889–1964* (London, 1964). See also W. S. Gammel, *The Association of Investment Trust Companies. The First 38 Years: 1932–1970* (London, 1973).
5.  R. C. Michie, 'Crisis and opportunity, the formation and operation of the British Assets Trust, 1897–1914', *Business History*, Vol. XXV, No. 2 (1983).
6.  In particular, E. T. Powell, *The Evolution of the Money Market* (London, 1915) and A. R. Hall, *The London Capital Market and Australia* (Canberra, 1963).
7.  Grayson, *Investment Trusts*, pp. 11–14, Bullock, *The Story of Investment Companies*, pp. 1–3.
8.  Quoted in A. Scratchley, *On Average Investment Trust* (London, 1875).
9.  On Robert Fleming, see W. T. Jackson, *The Enterprising Scot. Investors in the American West after 1873* (Edinburgh, 1969), pp. 21–2, 69–71.
10. Busby, *London Trust Company*, p. 1.
11. *Bankers' Magazine* (1893), Vol. 55, pp. 563–5.
12. Ibid., Vol. 56, pp. 165–73.
13. *The Economist*, 6 April 1889, pp. 433–4.
14. Ibid., 9 August 1890, p. 1017.
15. Corner and Burton, *Investment and Unit Trusts*, p. 42.
16. See *The Economist*, 23 May 1896, p. 653.
17. Ibid., Investment Trusts Supplement, 1 December 1934, p. 2.
18. Corner and Burton, *Investment and Unit Trusts*, p. 47.
19. The most popular capital structure of investment trusts was of equal value of debentures, preferred and deference shares. However, the ratio of fixed interest capital to ordinary capital could vary from 1:1 to 4:1 for a few companies; Corner and Burton, *Investment and Unit Trusts*, p. 45.
20. Michie, 'Crisis and opportunity', p. 132.
21. E. T. Powell, *The Mechanisms of the City* (London, 1910), pp. 29–31.
22. See J. Riesser, *The Great German Banks* (Washington, DC, 1911); J. Bouvier, *Un siècle de banque française* (Paris, 1973); K. E. Born, *International Banking in the 19th and 20th Centuries* (Leamington Spa, 1983).

23. See W. Bagehot, *Lombard Street: A Description of the Money Market* (London, 1878); W. T. C. King, *History of the London Discount Market* (London, 1936).

24. See P. C. Cottrell, *Industrial Finance 1830–1914. The Finance and Organization of English Manufacturing Industry* (London, 1980); F. Lavington, *The English Capital Market* (London, 1921); A. K. Cairncross, *Home and Foreign Investment 1870–1913* (Cambridge, 1953); L. Davis, 'The capital markets and industrial concentration: The US and UK, a corporation study', *Economic History Review*, 2nd series, Vol. 19, No. 2, (1966).

25. See C. A. E. Goodhart, *The Business of Banking 1891–1914* (London, 1972).

26. See S. D. Chapman, *The Rise of Merchant Banking* (London, 1984).

27. See for example H. S. Foxwell, 'The financing of industry and trade', *Economic Journal* (1917). W. P. Kennedy's analysis of the deficiencies of the London capital market point to the same direction: see 'Institutional response to economic growth: capital markets in Britain to 1914', in L. Hannah (ed.) *Management Strategy and Business Development* (London, 1976), and *Industrial Structure, Capital Markets and the Origins of British Economic Decline* (Cambridge, 1987); and Chapter 3 in this volume.

28. See Y. Cassis, *Les Banquiers de la City a l'époque édouardienne 1890–1914* (Geneva, 1984), pp. 212–15.

29. Although this distinction does not really apply during the period under review, investment trusts should also be differentiated from unit trusts, which were established during the 1930s, but did not become popular before the 1950s and really expanded during the 1960s. The main difference is that an investment trust is a limited liability company, with a body of shareholders, whereas the investors in unit trusts are not shareholders but hold units issued by the managers, which are not dealt in on the Stock Exchange and the price of which is fixed by the managers. A unit trust is governed by a trust deed and unit holders' rights are protected by a trustee. In the case of fixed unit trusts, which dominated at the beginning of the movement, managers are not permitted to vary the trust's investments.

30. Estimates vary according to the number of companies considered as pure investment trusts. L. E. Robinson, *Credit Facilities*, p. 218, estimates the total capital of investment trusts at £75 million in 1912 and at £100 million in 1920.

31. See E. J. Cleary, *The Building Society Movement* (London, 1965).

32. Corner and Burton, *Investment and Unit Trusts*, p. 46.

33. *The Economist*, 1 December 1934.

34. Robinson, *Credit Facilities*, pp. 123–4.

35. Linhardt, *Britische Investment Trusts*, p. 214.

36. Ibid., p. 364.

37. Robinson, *Credit Facilities*, p. 189.

38. M. Edelstein, *Overseas Investment in the Age of High Imperialism: the United Kingdom 1856–1914* (London, 1982), pp. 24–5. See also on overseas investment P. L. Cottrell, *British Overseas Investment in the Nineteenth Century* (London, 1975); and A. R. Hall (ed.), *The Export of Capital from Britain*

*1870–1914* (London, 1968). For a general evaluation of the consequences of the export of capital see S. Pollard, 'Capital exports, 1870–1914: harmful or beneficial?', *Economic History Review*, 2nd series, Vol. XXXVIII (4) (1985).

39. B. Supple, *The Royal Exchange Assurance. A History of British Insurance, 1720–1970* (Cambridge, 1970), p. 346.
40. See E. Victor Morgan, *Studies in British Financial Policy, 1914–1925* (London, 1953), pp. 326–31.
41. Corner and Burton, *Investment and Unit Trusts*, p. 66.
42. Ibid., pp. 224–30. Linhardt reaches the conclusion that there was less investment in industry, railways and public utilities, and more investment in bank and finance companies and Government and Municipal Bonds in the British Empire than in foreign countries. This seems to him consistent with the general economic conditions, the structure of the capital market, the type of capital requirements. Similarly, he considers that there was more investment in industry, railways and public utilities, and less in bank and finance companies and in Government and Municipal Bonds in Britain than in the colonies. *Britische Investment Trusts*, pp. 224–30.
43. Ibid., p. 340.
44. Quoted by W. A. Thomas, *The Finance of British Industry 1918–1976* (London, 1973), p. 118.
45. Corner and Burton, *Investment and Unit Trusts*, pp. 66–7.
46. The following companies have been studies: Alliance Investment Company, American Investment and General Trust Company, Bankers' Investment Trust, Charter Trust and Agency Asset, Consolidated Trust, Debenture Corporation, Foreign American and General Investment Company, Foreign and Colonial Investment Company, Industrial and General Trust, International Investment Trust, Investment Trust Corporation, London Trust Company, Mercantile Investment and General Trust, Merchants' Trust, Metropolitan Trust, Omnium Trust.
47. Linhardt, *Britische Investment Trusts*, pp. 48–50.
48. Cassis, *Les Banquiers de la City*, p. 186. Between 1890 and 1914, a third of the City bankers and bank directors had a seat on the board of at least one investment trust.
49. Linhardt, *Britische Investment Trusts*, pp. 332–3. Cf. R. Davenport-Hines, 'Pam, Albert Samuel (1875–1955), Merchant Banker' in D. J. Jeremy (ed.), *Dictionary of Business Biography*, Vol. IV (1985).
50. The three Scottish investment trusts considered are the Alliance Trust Company (Dundee), the British Investment Trust (Edinburgh) and the Scottish American Investment Company (Edinburgh).
51. See A. B. Richards, 'Touche, Sir George Alexander (1861–1935), Professional Accountant', in *DBB*, Vol. V (1986); and M. E. Murphy, 'Sir George A. Touche, CA, 1861–1935', *Business History Review*, Vol. XXXIV (1960).
52. See J. P. Scott, 'Philipps, John Wynford, 1st Viscount St Davids (1860–1939), financier', in *DBB*, Vol. IV.
53. See F. M. L. Thompson, *English Landed Society in the Nineteenth Century* (1963), pp. 305–6.

54. Robinson, *Credit Facilities*, p. 215.
55. Linhardt, *Britische Investment Trusts*, p. 96.
56. *The Economist*, 26 September 1936, p. 567.
57. Ibid.
58. See Y. Cassis 'Management and strategy in the English joint stock banks 1890–1914', *Business History*, Vol. XXVII, No. 3 (1985).
59. See R. Turrell and J.-J. Van Helten, 'The Rothschilds, the exploration company and mining finance', *Business History* Vol. XXVIII (1986).
60. Company File, 28, 255, London Trust Company, 1899.
61. Company File, 28, 276, Merchants' Trust (1901).
62. Scott, 'Philipps, John Wynford', p. 663.

# 8 Mining, share manias and speculation: British investment in overseas mining, 1880–1913

*Jean-Jacques van Helten**

## Introduction

The dramatic increase in British capital exports after 1870 can be counted, according to Edelstein, 'among the most important phenomena of British and world history in the late nineteenth and early twentieth centuries'.[1] It has been estimated that between 1870 and 1914 British net investment overseas increased from £1 billion to £4 billion. These estimates have recently been challenged by Platt, who suggests that by the end of 1913 the value of British stock held overseas was only £2.5 billion while data on the sectorial, political and geographical composition of UK overseas investments have been further refined by Davis and Huttenback. Their re-working of Matthew Simon's data on British portfolio foreign investment in which they also re-classify securities into private and public issues confirms that the bulk of private finance went into transportation between 1865 and 1914. Other industrial sectors that absorbed capital included agriculture and extractive industries, public utilities and manufacturing .

Around 8 per cent of total British overseas investment in the half-century before 1914 went into agriculture and extractive industries, with the majority of funds invested after 1880 in a series of mining share booms on the London Stock Exchange.[2] These frenzied booms and share manias were not aberrations of the otherwise smooth functioning of the Stock Exchange but were an integral feature of the operations of the Victorian securities market.

In fact, the secular increase in investment in overseas mining that lay at the heart of the booms reflected a number of trends in the late nineteenth century and international economies. In Britain, as this paper demonstrates, it marked a rising risk element and a shift among investors into more diversified types of securities as the number of domestic outlets for public savings was diminishing. Internationally, the second wave of industrialization led to a rising demand in non-ferrous metals like copper, tin, lead and zinc, that formed the chief raw materials of the new electrical engineering and metallurgical industries.[3] Along with Germany and the United

159

States, Britain was one of the world's major consumers of base metals and the London Metal Exchange, formed in 1882, was the centre of the international metals trade. As a result of these developments, London became the main source of capital and enterprise to exploit new sources of raw materials abroad.

After the 1870s, monetary reform and the progressive adoption of the Gold Standard by Germany, the United States and a large number of other countries also led to a rise in the demand for gold for financial purposes. Until the mid-1890s demand exceeded supply, despite the increased output of gold from Californian and Australian deposits, discovered in the 1840s and 1850s. This resulted in an increase in the value of gold and a dramatic decline in the value of silver and encouraged the world-wide search for, and exploitation of, new sources of gold-bearing mines in which British capital and companies figured prominently. The impact of British investment in mining in certain parts of the world was particularly significant. Nowhere was this more so than in Africa and in parts of Asia, where the lack of domestic capital formation and the absence of a skilled labour force led to external financing of mineral developments and the employment of foreign miners and managerial personnel.[4] By 1914 after a series of investment booms South Africa and Rhodesia had absorbed £369 million out of total British capital invested in Africa, in all sectors, of £441 million. Diamond and gold mines attracted 35 per cent of total British investment in southern Africa in 1910 with a further 21 per cent going into finance and land investments directly associated with mining. Colonial government stock, most of which supplied infrastructural facilities to service the mining industries of Kimberley and the Witwatersrand accounted for the bulk of other British investment in the region.[5]

Similarly, in 1910, in West Africa, 'where the rate of development has recently been rapid owing to the discovery of gold',[6] mines, finance and land investments accounted for nearly 60 per cent, while in the Straits Settlements and Malay States they attracted fifteen per cent of total British investments. In parts of the self-governing Empire like Canada and Western Australia, the discoveries of rich seams of gold and other minerals opened up the wild interior. Here, and in Africa and Asia, investment in mining quickened 'the pace of economic activity of which the growth of urbanisation and immigration were some of the major indicies'.[7] New towns like Kalgoorlie, Dawson City and Johannesburg grew virtually overnight and acted as magnets for capital and labour around the world.[8]

The flurry of gold and other discoveries, and the rising demand for base and precious metals, spurred investors to take a closer interest in overseas mining investments. Between 1880 and 1914 in a series of share booms on the London Stock Exchange, the majority of mining and mine exploration companies operating around the world were placed before the investing public with the result that as early as 1898, British-owned companies produced 60 per cent of the world's annual output of gold.[9] By 1914 some twenty of the world's largest copper mines, a quarter of the tin output of the Straits Settlements and Malay States and 60 per cent of the Chilean nitrate industry was owned and controlled by British-based firms. In this period, the volume of British investment in mining companies operating abroad increased from around £9 million a year in the 1880s to £20 million in the 1890s, after which investment declined to around £10–15 million between 1902 and 1914.[10] In the course of this surge in mining investments, the City of London developed a mining capital market with its own characteristics and discrete practices which, in the early 1900s, saw the emergence of new forms of corporate organization to finance and manage mineral extractive industries around the world.

In this chapter we shall consider the emergence of London as the premier mining capital market and the development of a new mining securities market paying particular attention to share speculation and company promotion associated with the 'kaffir' (South African) and Western Australian gold mining share booms of 1895–6. The argument is divided into three sections. The first surveys both British investment in overseas mining and the social composition of investors in mining companies. In the second part the operations of the mining capital and securities markets are considered while in the third section the post-1900 world of base-metal mining and the emergence of British-based international mining management and engineering firms is analysed.

### British investments in overseas mining

Table 8.1 gives the nominal capitalization of the 8,408 companies registered in Britain between 1880 and 1913 for mining and mine exploration abroad. Of course, these figures have to be treated with caution particularly as there is little or no relationship between nominal capitalization and the actual capital subscribed and invested abroad. While the market share values and data on the authorized capital of companies can easily be collected, 'this information', as Kubicek notes, 'does not reveal with any precision how much capital was put into mining shares and debentures or how much of this capital actually went into mining'.[11] In fact, there are considerable difficulties in assembling usable data on the actual capital formation of overseas mining companies and estimating the amount of British capital invested. Few of the 8,408 overseas mining companies, for example, were ever listed on the Official List of the London Stock Exchange, or issued prospectuses. Even fewer companies survived for any length of time with bankruptcies, fraud and over-optimistic engineers' reports on the value of the ore deposits taking a heavy toll, particularly in the early years of registration.[12] Of the 62 companies registered in Britain in 1890 for mining in North and Central America, including the United States, with a combined nominal capital of £9.2 million, 39 disappeared almost immediately, five were reconstructed, and eighteen were still working five years later. Of these eighteen mines, however, only two companies with properties in Montana and Colorado had even paid a dividend.[13] Similarly, of the 780 West Australian gold mining companies registered between 1894 and December 1896, 140 mines were still in existence five years later.[14] Few of these mines floated with a combined nominal capitalization of nearly £80 million paid a return on their capital. In 1897 just one company, Bayley's Reward, was responsible for 16 per cent of Western Australian dividends with more than half of the balance coming from two

161

Table 8.1  Nominal capitalization of limited liability companies registered in Britain for overseas mining, 1880–1913 (£ million)

| | (1) World | (2) Australia | (3) South Africa | (4) South Africa (other) | (5) United States | (6) North America (other) | (7) South America | (8) Europe | (9) Burma (India) | (10) Asia (other) |
|---|---|---|---|---|---|---|---|---|---|---|
| 1880 | 8.81 | 0.25 | 0.62 | 0.10 | 1.60 | 0.40 | 1.30 | 0.80 | 0.70 | — |
| 1881 | 13.10 | 0.45 | 2.10 | 0.30 | 3.18 | 0.23 | 2.16 | 1.72 | 2.70 | 0.12 |
| 1882 | 8.55 | 0.14 | 0.72 | 0.61 | 3.16 | 0.26 | 2.35 | 1.11 | 0.06 | 0.11 |
| 1883 | 11.28 | — | 1.12 | 0.02 | 3.74 | 0.73 | 4.24 | 1.29 | 0.02 | 0.10 |
| 1884 | 10.60 | 0.18 | 0.98 | — | 3.86 | 1.25 | 2.74 | 1.17 | 0.40 | — |
| 1885 | 10.57 | 0.13 | 3.07 | 0.16 | 2.54 | 1.75 | 1.76 | 0.82 | 0.13 | 0.19 |
| 1886 | 26.93 | 3.70 | 0.73 | 0.03 | 8.99 | 2.45 | 3.29 | 2.66 | 4.22 | 0.39 |
| 1887 | 30.52 | 7.86 | 4.40 | 0.32 | 9.89 | 2.40 | 2.60 | 1.73 | 0.03 | 1.53 |
| 1888 | 46.82 | 3.84 | 10.13 | 0.41 | 12.86 | 3.67 | 6.85 | 6.55 | 1.26 | 0.52 |
| 1889 | 37.91 | 2.36 | 14.47 | 2.17 | 5.54 | 3.84 | 4.65 | 2.25 | 0.31 | 1.60 |
| 1890 | 27.14 | 2.43 | 5.28 | 0.64 | 5.31 | 3.95 | 3.50 | 3.58 | 0.96 | 1.49 |
| 1891 | 15.00 | 1.56 | 2.22 | 1.54 | 3.21 | 2.57 | 1.34 | 1.35 | 0.65 | 0.31 |
| 1892 | 16.79 | 1.90 | 5.09 | 0.77 | 2.96 | 1.83 | 1.36 | 1.91 | 0.24 | 0.54 |
| 1893 | 11.96 | 0.84 | 2.80 | 1.59 | 2.71 | 0.91 | 1.13 | 0.85 | 0.66 | 0.05 |
| 1894 | 19.77 | 7.32 | 3.83 | 2.39 | 0.83 | 0.85 | 2.26 | 1.22 | 0.71 | 0.22 |
| 1895 | 103.85 | 40.87 | 27.59 | 18.49 | 3.90 | 1.56 | 4.25 | 1.69 | 0.92 | 0.75 |
| 1896 | 91.08 | 44.72 | 13.16 | 5.36 | 6.10 | 4.58 | 2.84 | 2.82 | 0.99 | 0.34 |
| 1897 | 58.04 | 25.03 | 4.34 | 3.46 | 5.20 | 11.64 | 1.84 | 1.53 | 0.24 | 0.91 |
| 1898 | 49.04 | 17.50 | 3.74 | 3.52 | 3.21 | 12.77 | 1.62 | 2.51 | 0.77 | 0.98 |
| 1899 | 61.08 | 20.30 | 1.72 | 10.30 | 6.17 | 8.88 | 1.70 | 5.02 | 0.86 | 1.75 |
| 1900 | 49.02 | 12.82 | 1.39 | 12.63 | 1.82 | 6.76 | 1.97 | 6.67 | 0.42 | 3.27 |
| 1901 | 42.53 | 7.16 | 1.41 | 22.10 | 0.92 | 1.93 | 2.85 | 3.04 | 0.68 | 2.19 |
| 1902 | 40.26 | 6.45 | 8.85 | 11.78 | 1.59 | 4.14 | 1.26 | 3.59 | 0.85 | 0.88 |
| 1903 | 37.32 | 7.81 | 6.42 | 10.35 | 0.44 | 3.91 | 2.51 | 4.44 | 0.31 | 0.65 |
| 1904 | 23.21 | 4.06 | 4.12 | 3.59 | 1.95 | 1.45 | 2.27 | 3.43 | 0.36 | 0.56 |
| 1905 | 27.94 | 1.84 | 10.04 | 5.54 | 0.42 | 2.85 | 2.48 | 1.47 | 0.38 | 2.75 |
| 1906 | 25.36 | 4.85 | 2.53 | 3.60 | 0.58 | 2.84 | 2.49 | 5.20 | 0.46 | 2.53 |
| 1907 | 17.40 | 4.03 | 0.64 | 2.36 | 0.63 | 1.54 | 1.09 | 3.78 | 1.25 | 1.70 |
| 1908 | 14.83 | 0.52 | 0.96 | 2.00 | 0.81 | 1.37 | 2.00 | 3.54 | 0.69 | 2.76 |
| 1909 | 26.42 | 1.78 | 4.78 | 10.62 | 1.61 | 2.54 | 2.27 | 1.18 | 0.25 | 1.39 |
| 1910 | 23.94 | 2.24 | 2.63 | 9.82 | 1.30 | 3.75 | 1.59 | 1.52 | 0.04 | 1.05 |
| 1911 | 27.64 | 2.47 | 1.69 | 5.42 | 2.25 | 7.93 | 3.47 | 2.75 | 0.34 | 1.32 |
| 1912 | 21.91 | 2.02 | 2.18 | 7.39 | 1.37 | 1.66 | 2.95 | 3.29 | 0.27 | 0.78 |
| 1913 | 14.59 | 3.34 | 1.42 | 1.77 | 1.75 | 3.49 | 0.89 | 1.12 | 0.36 | 0.45 |

Source:
These figures are taken from: the PRO BT31 Register of Companies; E. Ashmead, Twenty-five Years of Mining, 1880–1904 (London, 1909); E. Ashmead's annual returns of new mining companies in the January issues of the Mining Journal, 1905–9; McCarty, 'British investment in overseas mining', pp. 262–3; W. Skinner, Mining Manual (London, 1910–14). The total of columns 2–10 may, on occasion, be less than the nominal capitalization of companies registered in Britain in column 1 as marginal sums invested in regions like the Pacific, including New Zealand, have been deliberately omitted. Only British investments in the world's major mining regions, where data are more easily verifiable, have been enumerated in

other companies, Lake View Consols and Great Boulder Proprietary, both situated on Kalgoorlie's Golden Mile.[15]

The large nominal capitalizations which characterized these and other Western Australian mining companies bore little relationship to the intrinsic worth of their ore deposits. Instead, they reflected the marketing acumen of the parties promoting the new mine and the amount of capital the vendors wished to allocate to themselves.[16] A number of the Western Australian mines were also floated privately with equity allocated to the vendors and underwriters who later 'dribbled' their shares onto a bull market and made fortunes in the process. Recent research by McCarty suggests that vendors' capital as a proportion of fully subscribed capital in British overseas mining companies increased from 53 per cent in 1891 to 65 per cent in 1901 only to decline to 38 per cent in 1914.[17] The initial rise coincided with the share booms of the 1890s which were characterized by grossly inflated capitalizations while the subsequent decline reflected better information flows between promoters and potential buyers and the market's increasing efficiency at allocating funds to more soundly-based ventures.[18]

Estimates of British investment in overseas mining are further complicated by the fact that many companies which attracted large amounts of capital were registered abroad. The bulk of Witwatersrand gold mining companies were Johannesburg-based concerns and British investors were known to own substantial blocks of shares in other foreign registered mines such as the El Callao in Venezuela, the Anaconda Copper Mining Company in the United States and Broken Hill Proprietary in New South Wales.[19] Local investment in British-registered mines was also extensive at times, particularly in Australia where capital markets were well developed and in South Africa, where by 1914 domestic investors owned nearly 15 per cent of the capital in Rand gold mines. In London, the Stock Exchange also acted as a conduit for foreign investors anxious to participate in the increasingly active mining share market. A substantial proportion of the funds raised on the stock market by South African companies originated on the Continent; in 1906 French investors owned 30 per cent of shares worth £14 million in 27 premier Witwatersrand gold mines with an aggregate market value of £46 million.[20] Despite the above reservations attached to their use, the data on nominal capitalization at least illustrate the timing and geographical variations in the pattern of company registrations, and give some indication of the volume of British investment in overseas mining after 1880.

### Investors in mining companies

Many investors, who in the late nineteenth century began to place at least some of their savings in overseas mining companies, came from what Reader has characterized as the 'Forsyte level of society and upwards . . .'[21] Clergymen, spinsters, army and naval officers, shopkeepers and provincial merchants dabbled in gold mines and were encouraged to do so both by the expanding financial press and declining interest rates on older more established forms of investment like mortgages and Consols.[22] Samuel Cox and Abraham and Lewis Marks were typical of this group of small to middling investors: in 1898, Cox, a chemist of Dukes Street, Leicester owned a variety of stocks and shares valued at £1,357 including 70 Consolidated Gold Fields and 100 Exploration Company shares worth £1,156. Cox's commitment to mining shares was in sharp contrast to the Marks brothers who were fruit salesmen in Leicester and owned Robinson Deep, and Johannesburg Consolidated Investment Corporation shares worth £694 in a portfolio with a total value of £2,584.[23] The appeal of mining equities to investors like the Marks brothers depended largely on the marketability and low denomination of the shares, usually £1 or less, as well as the prospect of high rates of return. The Robinson Deep mine, for example, was registered in South Africa in 1894 and although it only paid its maiden dividend of 25 per cent in 1899, the Marks brothers would have received a total dividend of 75 per cent by 1904 if they had acquired their shares at par when they were first issued. Of course, only a limited number of mines were as successful as the Robinson Deep and the internal rate of return on capital on Transvaal gold mines with a nominal capital of £500,000 or more was, in fact, a modest 2.1 per cent for the period from 1887–1914.[24]

In Western Australia where gold was discovered in the 1890s, 'at best British investors recovered their investment, without interest, by 1915, an extremely unprofitable result.'[25] One company, Great Boulder Proprietary, paid a 40 per cent dividend in 1895, followed within twelve months by a further dividend of 100 per cent. By 1912 the mine had produced over £8 million in gold and paid more than £4 million in dividends, the equivalent of a 2,333 per cent return on nominal capital since 1895.[26] The Great Boulder Proprietary, the St John del Rey mine in Brazil and the Mysore GM Co. in India, which, after 1896, paid dividends of 100 per cent a year, were 'the occasional successes . . . that underlay the continued promotion of overseas mining companies, despite their exceedingly high mortality rate'.[27]

No one was more aware of the need to dazzle potential investors with stories about fabulously rich mines and the promise of high dividends than the company promoter and member for South Hackney, Horatio Bottomley. In the 1890s Bottomley's Western Australian Joint Stock and Finance Corporation and the Western Australian Market Trust epitomized the gross fraud and speculation that came to characterize so much of the London mining market. 'Give them [the shareholders] a good dividend', Bottomley observed, 'and they will not come near your meetings. Show them any rubbish in print and they will be disposed to believe it. Offer them a worthless share at a great premium and they will scramble for it – offer them a sound investment at a discount and they will throw it at you . . . All mining companies are gambles'.[28] Bottomley's contempt for his shareholders was not entirely unwarranted. The gullibility of investors in the mining market was legendary among City promoters. Yet, for even the most naive investor shares in dubious companies promoted by Bottomley and others possessed some worth in excess of their nominal value in that they were usually highly marketable. This ensured that investors could accumulate capital through judicious speculation in the market if genuine dividends were not forthcoming .

The marketability of overseas mining shares exceeded that of nearly all other securities. They tapped the gambling spirit of the investing public and while domestic industrials and the securities of small firms suffered from a variety of institutional restrictions on the London Stock Exchange, South African 'kaffirs' and Westralians were so popular that jobbers deserted the traditional American rails market in droves to trade in gold mining shares.[29] As a result, by the mid-1890s there were between 400 and 600 'kaffir' jobbers on the floor of the Exchange where 360 South African mines, 260 West Australian mines and 174 miscellaneous mining companies were traded daily. Such was the popularity and turnover in mining equities that the Committee of the Stock Exchange had been forced to introduce an extra fortnightly settling day for traders to record their 'bargains'.

The marketability of mining shares was also not solely dependent on dealings on the floor of the Exchange. Investors had a wide choice when buying or selling 'kaffirs' or other mining equities, the bulk of which were not even registered on the Exchange's official list. The London mining market had always incorporated a wide and informal constituency of brokers, jobbers and bucket-shop operators who traded extensively in shares in 'the jungle' or kerb-market of Throgmorton Street.[30] Small-time brokers like H. Hanbury and Co. of Broad Street who 'opened speculative accounts on the usual one per cent deposit or satisfactory references', or W. H. Bumpus of Cornhill, EC, who 'devotes special attention to S.A. and W.A. goldfields',[31] complemented securities trading on the official Stock Exchange and further enhanced the marketability of mining shares to potential investors.

Although after the 1870s the small to middling investors had progressed from local savings bank to Stock Exchange, wealthy shareholders continued to own the bulk of the capital. By 1913, only a little over 1 per cent of stocks, shares and funds traded on the Stock Exchange were owned by those whose property was worth less than £1,000 net while 27.5 per cent were owned by those whose property was valued between £1,000 and £20,000 net.[32] Even in the overseas mining market the small denomination of shares and their undoubted marketability had not led to a noticeable democratization of investment. It appears that apart from occasional and highly speculative forays into the market the bulk of investors followed the *Economist's* advice, 'those who have money they can afford to lose may speculate in them [kaffirs] as they would in a lottery . . . no prudent man who is dependent for his living upon the return of his capital would feel warranted in touching them.'[33]

The ownership of shares in overseas mining companies also appears not to have been geographically widespread. Well-known companies like Anaconda Copper, Consolidated Gold Fields, De Beers and Rio Tinto were dealt in Edinburgh, Glasgow, Halifax, Liverpool, Manchester and other provincial Exchanges, while the Glasgow Stock Exchange had been the focus of the Indian gold-mining mania of 1879–80 and Liverpool and Birmingham had their own 'kaffir circus' in 1895.[34] The bulk of overseas mining shares, however, were traded on the London market where companies could tap the speculative instincts and savings of the burgeoning middle classes of the south-east and draw on the extended 'social web of investment' that linked the City with traditional landed society.[35] Social and business connections played a particularly important role in the mining market where 'insider' information was at a premium and the key to short-term share speculation or long-term portfolio investment. As early as the 1860s Cornish investors had utilized their intimate knowledge of mining to invest in Mexican silver mines while in the 1890s the 4th Earl Grey called on relatives working in the City for advice on investments in the volatile 'kaffir' market.[36]

Share registers bear witness to the preponderance of southern, largely middle-class investors in mining ventures abroad. In 1891, for example, nearly half of the shares in Rhodes' Consolidated Gold Fields were held by people living or residing within a ten mile radius of Charing Cross. Approximately 24 per cent of shareholders resided elsewhere in England and 9.4 per cent of the mine's issued shares were owned by European investors.[37] An analysis of the share register of the London and West Australian Exploration Company, formed in 1895 with a nominal capital of £300,000 reveals a similar profile of investors. In April 1896 around 68 per cent of the company's issued capital of £270,000 was owned by investors who chose to describe themselves as 'gentlemen', a term which reflected Victorian upward social mobility . The remainder of the shares were owned by unmarried and married women, lawyers and JPs, bankers, merchants and industrialists, clergy, members of the French, German and British aristocracies, naval and military officers, physicians as well as one bank manager, two lace manufacturers and a ship-owner. Of the 'gentlemen' shareholders, 38 per cent resided in and around the City and were largely brokers, jobbers, rentiers or financiers; 19.5 per cent lived in the counties while 34 per cent of shareholders lived abroad, largely in France and Germany.[38]

This high proportion of 'gentlemen' and continental shareholders was not unusual in British-registered mining companies. The lax self-regulatory practices of the Stock Exchange whose own members regularly flaunted its rules were particularly attractive to domestic speculators and foreign investors anxious to avoid paying taxes. This absence of legal constraints and regulations, however, was not wholly beneficial to the investors. For example, while 'equity shares traded on capital markets are not just gambling counters but also represent a means to change the management and policies of companies',[39] if potential investors wanted to use shares to affect a company's affairs they needed information on assets and policies. Yet, Victorian legal requirements governing managerial behaviour and the public disclosure of company assets were so permissive as to place the directors and promoters in complete control of the company's assets. Ordinary investors lacking insider information were rarely able, on the basis of published accounts, to ascertain the net worth or long-term viability of the company whose shares they owned. Even after the passing of the 1900 Companies Act, shareholders remained largely ignorant of the internal affairs of a company with the proliferation of different accounting methods contributing to the widespread incomprehensibility of balance sheets and accounts.[40]

These problems were particularly acute in the mining industry. South African gold mining companies, for example, regularly submitted two different sets of accounts and few overseas mining companies could meet the London Stock Exchange's minimal requirements for a quotation on the Official List such as the public subscription of two-thirds of the issued capital.[41] Company promoters, vendors and underwriters were far better informed about the prospects of the ventures they were selling than the bulk of potential buyers. They used their privileged insider information to rig the market and speculate on the difference between the current and the expected future prices of the assets. Mining lent itself to such speculative activities as it generally entailed a higher degree of risk than more conventional industries for investors. For example, there was usually a long period of time between flotation and investment and the payment of a mine's first dividend during which dramatic changes in the world demand for the metal, political instability or shortages of labour could seriously affect the success or otherwise of the venture. Technological problems of ore recovery or geological uncertainties also affected mining operations and ore bodies, which showed great promise during exploratory operations, sometimes proved to be uneconomic at greater depth. Not surprisingly in view of these risk factors and the great, if rather infrequent, rewards attached to successful mining investments, overseas mining companies attracted the attention of 'an important group of professional speculators centered in London. Jobbers, stockbrokers, both "inside" and "outside", and other members of the financial community formed the core of this group'.[42]

## Speculators

This coterie of professional speculators accounted for a substantial proportion of the shareholders in overseas mining companies. On the basis of insider information and familiarity with the operations of the securities market they were able to minimize risks in investment decisions in sharp contrast to the ordinary investor who, more often than not, had to rely on the financial press or gossip when purchasing shares. City speculators came in 'on the ground floor' of a flotation through personal or professional contacts with promoters and vendors and became involved in 'market-making'. This 'making' of a market took many forms ranging from 'puffing' a new issue in a prospectus or in the pages of the new financial press by means of bribing journalists, to pre-allotment dealing and the creation of fictitious premiums. 'At present', the *Economist* noted in 1889,

> there are few new companies brought out whose shares were not, immediately after the appearance of a prospectus, quoted at substantial premiums – some of the most worthless mining investments often commanding a premium of from 50 to 100 per cent.[43]

In their attempts to 'make' a market, brokers and promoters were nothing if not imaginative. As Cecil Braithwaite of the City brokers, Foster and Braithwaite, recalled,

> The broker appointed by the promoting group went into the market and told his friends that he was bringing out a company to exploit, we will say, a gold mine. He – the broker – explained what the company was, and let his friends have some shares, with possibly a call of more. He then arranged to have the shares bid for in order to attract attention, his friends in the market having 'bated [sic] the swim, among their friends.[44]

167

At this stage with dealing prior to allotment, as Braithwaite observed, the company had not even been formed and 'if the shares stood at a premium, the public stood very little chance of obtaining any', though once the lists had been closed and shares allotted, the premium would quickly disappear as the brokers and their friends scrambled to sell their scrip and pull out of the market. In due course such pre-allotment subscriptions were found to be inadequate in the mining market where the public had slowly woken up to the questionable activities of the professional speculator. As a result, new methods were devised and 'Now' according to the *Statist* in 1897,

> underwriting has, with the more speculative concerns almost taken the place of the original subscriptions and especially has been so during the last two years – originated or rather carried to its present excess, by those who engineered the flotation on the English market of South African mining shares, and *perforce* adopted by the founders of the 'Westralia' boom – and collapse – . . .[45]

'Market making' also increased, and formed an integral part of the marketability of 'kaffir' and Westralian shares as well as the scrip of other mining companies. Throughout the 1890s and early 1900s mining shares of all descriptions could be bought and sold at close prices which further broadened the circle of potential investors to include continental *rentiers* and small-time speculators. These French and German investors grew in number in the 1890s and formed an increasingly large proportion of shareholders in overseas mining companies registered in Britain like the aforementioned London and West Australian Exploration Company.[46]

### Internationalization of the mining market

London was particularly attractive to foreign investors for a number of reasons.[47] First, more than 30 per cent of the world's negotiable securities were listed in London where potential investors had a greater choice and stocks and shares were sold quicker, at lower prices and at a faster rate than in any other financial centre. Secondly, investors could call on the services of market specialists, like 'kaffir' jobbers, or brokers, who dealt exclusively in West African gold shares, as well as on any number of other facilities offered by the City of London. Finally, the plethora of financial services provided by the City was in sharp contrast to the attempts by the German government to outlaw share speculation in 1896 or the restrictive practices of the *Agents de Change* on the official Paris Bourse, the *parquet*, which for many years refused to list South African gold mining shares.[48]

In the 1890s as more and more companies and foreign loans were floated in England, continental investors flocked to the British capital markets with French investors becoming particularly influential.[49] The close links between the London and Paris markets which had been forged since the opening of the telegraph link in 1851 were further strengthened in this period by the cross-channel arbitrage activities of brokers with offices in both cities. The internationalization of securities trading was beginning in earnest in the 1890s and was a reflection of 'strong trade and money market links between these countries'.[50]

Nowhere was this process of internationalization in securities trading more advanced than in the mining market. Almost from the outset the exploitation of mineral resources in Africa, Asia and Australasia had been international in terms of its technical and capital requirements. Skilled personnel for the development and management of mines had to be drawn from around the world with, for example, Cornish tin miners working as far afield as Mexico, Peru and south Australia.[51] The international dimension received an impetus in the 1890s when it became clear that the continued development of the South African gold mining industry and the long-term exploitation of the newly-discovered gold fields at Kalgoorlie would require ever increasing amounts of working capital. In South Africa, after some difficulties in the 1880s, the Witwatersrand mining industry had proved itself beyond all doubt and Johannesburg had grown from a temporary digger's camp into a sprawling urban settlement with all the signs of permanency. From 1893 onwards, deep-level mines were being placed before the British and European investing public in increasing numbers with the major mining finance houses vigorously competing among themselves for funds. A web of financial transactions and share deals tied the Witwatersrand to the capital markets of London and Paris and the economics of gold mining became the topic of detailed analyses in the pages of French and British papers.[52]

The internationalization and growing volume of gold mining share transactions also contrasted sharply with a general malaise which had overtaken the London capital market since the Baring crisis of 1890. Barely had this crisis passed when Australia witnessed a series of banking failures, thereby straining the nerves of British investors further, while, on the Continent, investors were abandoning their traditional support for American railways.[53] Increasingly, gold was seen as the only safe hedge in a period of falling prices and international depression. Not surprisingly, 'only foreign concerns such as the very speculative South African and West Australian mining companies were able to elicit any interest from the most adventurous of investors . . .'[54]

Of course, a nervous share market was not alone in steering British and Continental investors in the direction of gold mining companies. The demand for gold for financial purposes was increasing particularly following the adoption of the gold standard by Germany. By the 1890s, it was clear that the demand for gold exceeded supply and that this state of affairs would continue for some time as in the United States the political tide was also turning in favour of moving the dollar onto the gold standard in line with other major currencies.[55] Internationally, gold mines were rapidly becoming potentially profitable investments. It was against this background of lacklustre stock markets in Britain and Europe and a rising international demand for gold that, on 8 September 1894, the *Statist* confidently proclaimed:

there will be a boom by-and-by, and that some special industry or some special country will be peculiarly identified with it, [and later on 15 September] as far as we can see at present it is to South Africa that we must look for the occasion of the next boom. . . . If the production increases, as there seems reason to expect, then new gold mining companies will be created, there will be an active speculation in the shares of the successful companies and of those companies with distinct prospects. Furthermore, there will be a rush of immigrants from Europe, the country will be opened up, new towns will be founded, old towns will be enlarged, railway extension will be pushed forward, and the area under cultivation will be widened. . . . So it will be in South Africa'.[56]

## The operations of the mining market

In the event the *Statist's* prognostication was largely correct. 1895 saw the greatest boom in South African gold mining shares ever on the London Stock Exchange in which the nominal capitalization of British-registered Rand mining companies shot up from £3.8 million in 1894 to £27.5 million in 1895, only to decline to £13.1 million in the following year (see also Table 8.1). The actual amounts of capital invested in all South African gold mines, both Transvaal- and British-registered, was a more modest £10.5 million in 1895, but still reached £15.2 million in 1896. The market value of 'kaffirs' showed even more spectacular increases in this period; by September 1895 the Rand's seven biggest dividend-paying mines had a total market value of £17 million while Rand Mines Ltd and Consolidated Gold Fields had a market value of £26.6 million.[57] The upsurge in the price of 'kaffirs' and in the number of Witwatersrand mining companies registered in London and Johannesburg was dwarfed by the number of Westralian companies registered in the London market. In 1895, 401 mines with a nominal capital of £40.8 million were floated to exploit the fields in and around the Golden Mile. In 1896, a further 410 companies were placed before investors and frenzied trading in 'kaffirs' and Westralians all but dominated Stock Exchange business for eighteen months throughout 1895–7 in London as well as, in due course, Paris.

As share prices rocketed they bore increasingly less relation to production and asset values. 'Company promoters', as McCarty notes, 'bought up hundreds of shares and offered them to investors as tickets in a lottery.'[58] Terms like 'lottery' or 'kaffir circus', however, do little justice to the complexities of speculative securities trading. By the 1890s, arbitrageurs moved stocks and shares with great rapidity between London, Paris and Berlin and between each of these capital cities and Melbourne and Johannesburg. The gold mining share boom of 1895–6 demonstrated that global securities trading was possible and profitable, and provides an insight into the operations of the late Victorian capital market. Interestingly, in London and, to some extent, Paris, the flames of speculation were fuelled by English commercial or joint-stock banks through an extended network of credit and bills of exchange.

The involvement of the joint-stock banks was the off-shoot of structural changes in Victorian banking which had been in progress for some time and centred on the reduction in the number of banks as a result of mergers and amalgamations. This trend towards domination of this banking sector by a few 'high street' banks also led to a dramatic increase in joint-stock banks' deposits from £500 million in 1880 to £850 million in 1899. Much of this growth in deposits was due to the absorption of other banks rather than internal growth and coincided with a relative decline in the number of inland bills of exchange seeking discount.[59]

The decline in inland bills of exchange also meant that the joint-stock banks found it more difficult to employ their surplus funds in the purchase of bills on the open market and the making of call loans to bill brokers and in an effort to off-set these developments they turned to the Stock Exchange. Lending money to brokers, usually for a fortnight at fairly high rates of interest, was remunerative, and allowed the banks to have money at call and short notice with the result that within a very short period of time 'the financing of the Stock Exchange had occupied a greater part of the bankers' attention every year.'[60] By World War I the volume of Stock Exchange loans by banks was estimated at £80 million[61] and, according to Cole, 'Nearly the whole of the professional speculation on the Stock Exchange is carried on with bank money which can be borrowed on negotiable securities with ease and cheapness.'[62]

First class stocks and shares like railways and Consols were preferred but banks were, at first, willing to accommodate brokers who offered mining scrip as collateral. The collapse of the first rather modest boom in South African gold mining shares in 1889 in which a number of colonial banks in the Cape sustained losses or closed their doors as a result of advances against grossly inflated shares, altered Lombard Street's perception of mining companies.[63] Thereafter, joint-stock as well as some merchant banks looked askance at overseas mining securities. Mines joined a multitude of other industrial and speculative ventures like rubber companies which bankers were loath to accept as collateral except with a large margin of 30–40 per cent.[64] Such variable margins were not unreasonable from the banker's point of view. In fact, in the wake of the dramatic collapse in the market value of the 105 leading South African gold mining shares of around 35 per cent between October and November 1895, the *Statist* observed that

> It follows that if a bank had lent upon a large number of the securities included in the list [of South African mines] and insisted upon a margin of 35 per cent, it would have been safe: while if it had asked for a margin of fifty per cent, the margin would not have nearly run off.[65]

Apart from checking the quality of the securities pledged against the loans and to vary the margin according to the risk factors involved, the banks' lending policies in the London market also depended on the standing of the brokers' partnerships in the City. This was particularly important as partnerships were private firms with no limited liability provisions.[66] The uses to which these loans were put by brokers also varied considerably. Insider trading and the acquisition of particularly profitable investments, for example, enabled some brokers to derive a substantial income from market operations and the difference between the interest paid for the borrowed funds and the yield of the investment. R. H. Savory, one of the partners in the leading stockbrokers, Foster & Braithwaite 'did well enough out of the kaffir boom to set himself up very handsomely at Chertsey in Surrey and a little later he bought Kelling Hall estate, one of the best sporting properties in Norfolk.'[67] It was more common, however, for brokers to lend part or all of the capital borrowed from the joint-stock banks to dealers or jobbers at the Stock Exchange under 'Contango' or carrying-over arrangements. As part of the 'Contango' a dealer sold securities to a broker while reserving the right to buy back the equivalent in securities at a higher price in order to cover the broker's interest and expenses.[68] This practice was widespread in the City by the 1890s and 'it is the custom of bankers to lend to brokers for the very purpose of their lending to dealers'.[69] Apart from being customary it was also very lucrative, particularly in the crowded mining market where hundreds of jobbers scrambled to cover their fortnightly Contangos. In the 'kaffir', Westralian and miscellaneous mining markets, brokers deliberately set the Contango rate 'from seven to twelve per cent and often they are higher than even twenty per cent'.[70] The reasons for the extraordinarily high rates of interest were simple; 'mining shares are not looked upon by bankers as a desirable form of security. The investor in mining shares . . . has not good credit with the banks; and few capitalists, therefore, who are willing to lend to him are to exact onerous rates.'[71] The high interest rates also helped to create fevered speculation in the mining market among the many small-time jobbers who had come onto the floor of the Exchange after 1890 and who were determined to maximize their turnover of securities and strike the greatest possible number of bargains; under pressure to carry over stocks or meet their fortnightly obligations they had a vested interest in a bull market in mining scrip and participated eagerly in 'the boiling whirlpool of the Kaffir Circus'.[72]

The joint-stock banks and accepting houses did not only help to fuel speculation by lending to brokers who lent to dealers. In the 1890s, mining share speculation in Europe was also made possible indirectly through the drawing of bills on London. In 1895, for example, Paris bankers, who were heavily involved in promoting South African gold mining companies, advanced funds to their customers in the form of three-month bills on London to tempt them into the 'kaffir' market. These bills were then offered for discount in the City through the banks and discount houses. This procedure of manufacturing bills on London was known as 'pig on pork' and was widely commented on by contemporaries. In late 1895, the practice ran into disfavour in the City as bill brokers and discount houses discovered that the discount rate on foreign paper was rather low while the legality of paper, the drawer and acceptor of which resided abroad, was in doubt. Consequently, the City restricted its discounting operations of foreign bills. This forced the French banks to call in money from the market, thereby also compelling borrowers to sell their assets such as South African gold mining shares at any price. It also choked off supplies of credit to the French investor who, according to *Statist*, 'has been the mainstay of the South African boom'.[73]

This action of the part of the City's banking community had serious repercussions across the Channel as it coincided with a large-scale remittance of French capital to Russia as part of a recent loan and a run on the Constantinople-based Imperial Ottoman Bank which had speculated heavily in 'kaffirs' and sustained heavy losses.[74] It threatened to ruin both the bank's largely French shareholders and the Sublime Porte's shaky international credit.[75] The malaise on the Paris mining market quickly spread to London and later Johannesburg, where 'kaffir' prices plummeted and the share bubble burst in spectacular fashion. The *Statist* was clear about who was to blame for this state of affairs: the result of the City 'boycotting certain foreign bank acceptances was to create a scare upon the Stock Exchange and the Continental Bourses, to check investment in gold shares, and thereby to render it extremely difficult to place new gold mining companies.'[76]

The manner of the 'kaffir' boom's demise also demonstrated how, in the wake of technical advances, like the intercontinental telegraph and telephone, and the growth of international securities trading, the London, Paris and Johannesburg markets had become intimately interlinked. Similarly, the role of certain London banks in precipitating the collapse of the boom suggests that the City's policies had wide ramifications which extended beyond the national frontier and materially affected the operations of financial markets abroad.

### British-based international mining firms

The collapse of the 'kaffir' boom in the autumn of 1895 was followed in December 1895 by the Jameson raid in the Transvaal in which, among others, the mining magnates Cecil Rhodes and Alfred Beit were implicated. The Raid further shook investor confidence which was reflected both in a fall in share prices and a decline in the number of new South African mining company registrations in Britain from 138 in 1895 to thirty in 1897.[77] Speculation in Westralians continued for a while, but by the end of 1896, this share mania had also dissipated. In 1896, 352 new Western Australian companies with a nominal capital of £37.7 million had been registered in London. In the following year these fell to 119 (£19.2 million) only to decline to 18 (£2.2 million) by 1904.[78]

The downturn in the mining market after 1895–6 also threw a number of problems, which had emerged in the course of the share manias, into sharp relief. Jobbers, speculators, promotors and brokers had flooded onto the market in large numbers and this had seriously limited the ability of the major mining finance houses like Consolidated Gold Fields, Wernher, Beit and Company, the General Mining and Finance Corporation and Barnato's Johannesburg Consolidated Investment Company to influence market behaviour.[79] At the height of the boom, Julius Wernher of Wernher, Beit lamented that the market had become 'so big and so cosmopolitan that it becomes more hopeless than ever to prophesy'.[80] Wernher, Beit and other Rand houses had committed themselves to costly, long-term, deep-level operations and were determined to maintain a steady flow of working capital from Europe to the Transvaal. From the outset the mining houses had been involved in promoting companies and raising the original capital for development and their view of mining was therefore different from that of investors who simply bought shares, whether new or old, in the secondary market and whose main concerns were high dividends and marketability. While not averse to profit-taking in a bull market, the mining houses were none the less anxious to distance themselves from raucous speculation or the shady promoters who inhabited the 'kaffir' circus. With the aid of widespread press bribery and close links with a number of Paris *haute banques*,

Wernher, Beit was particularly successful in steadying the nerves of French investors after 1895–6.[81] So much so that when, in 1905, the firm re-organized its operations in South Africa and floated, the Central Mining and Investment Corporation with a nominal capital of £6 million, nearly 50 per cent of the capital was taken up in France.[82]

Meanwhile in London, Wernher, Beit joined Consolidated Gold Fields and a number of foreign banks and brokers' firms like the Disconto Gesellschaft, Comptoir d'Escompte and S. Japhet and Co. and Keyser and Co. in forming the so-called 'shop', which in a very short period between 1896 and 1904–5 came to exercise 'a controlling interest over the market in these [i.e. South African] shares'.[83] Determined to stamp out speculation and wild, unwarranted price movements and attract respectable investors, the outside houses that made up the 'shop' set out to destroy the ability of jobbers in the Stock Exchange to set share prices by ensuring that in future the bulk of mining shares were traded on the informal 'kerb market' outside the Stock Exchange building altogether. As the mining finance houses issued or traded extensively in scrip while the banks purchased shares on behalf of clients, often from abroad, the power of the members of the 'shop' to determine price and market behaviour, were considerable. This became clear very quickly from the late 1890s onwards. Increasingly, brokers with a buying or selling order bought or sold their shares from a member of the 'shop' and traded only a nominal number of equities with a jobber inside the house merely to establish the going rate and to get the price marked in order to satisfy their clients. The net result was that, as one jobber bitterly complained in 1906, 'Ten years ago a business price was always obtainable in the House in South African shares. The outside houses had destroyed the power of the markets to make such prices.'[84] The growing influence of the outside houses in the market probably contributed to the substantial lessening in share price volatility after 1900. It certainly also helped to reduce the marketability and speculative appeal of mining shares – their chief attributes – as investors were less willing to buy scrip at a price set by forces outside the Exchange.[85]

The relative price stability in the 'kaffir' market after 1900 (1902 saw a minor boom following the Peace of Vereeniging at the end of the Anglo-Boer War) reflected more than just the influence of the 'shop'. The era of mining share manias was passing though booms in other commodities like rubber continued to rock the Exchange. In the City, investors and promotors also looked more towards production than company mongering. The days of haphazard exploration by prospectors, equipped only with pick and shovel, were over. The Klondyke gold rushes of the late 1890s were in many respects the stirrings of a bygone era.[86] And as 'the prospector stands aside, the engineer steps forward' with mining becoming more scientific and technically complex.[87] The application of science and technology to mineral production was costly but could be offset, in part, by economies of scale in larger mining concerns; consolidation and rationalization became the hallmark of mining industries around the world in the early 1900s.

The process of rationalization had been in progress in South Africa for some time but it was not confined to the Transvaal gold mining industry. In Western Australia, for example, in the wake of the 1895–6 boom, the directors of a number of the state's major producing companies like Lake View Consols and the Ivanhoe Gold Corporation handed over the management of their mines to Bewick, Moreing and Company to cut working costs, rationalize production and assuage the fears of sceptical British investors. Bewick, Moreing was a London-based firm of consulting mining engineers and managers who, according to the senior partner Algernon Moreing, 'manage mines on behalf of their owners who are the British public'.[88] The firm's best-known employee was the engineer and future President of the United States, Herbert Hoover, who joined its Western Australian branch in 1897 and later became a partner in London. From the late 1890s onwards, Hoover and his colleagues were highly successful in reducing operating costs and increasing output of the mines which they managed. By 1904 Bewick, Moreing's mines were responsible for 40 per cent of the monthly output of gold of Western Australia and, according to the *Engineering and Mining Journal*, 'are to be thanked for the services they have done in eliminating speculative management from the Western Australian market'.[89] The growing influence of firms like Bewick, Moreing in Western Australia and, later in China, and John Taylor & Sons in the Southern Indian gold mining industry reflected a

> tendancy to place mines under the direction of firms of mining engineers, subordinating the control of directors to that of the engineering staff . . . the growth of the system will . . . assuredly depend upon the entire severence of share speculation from professional work.[90]

Speculation, of course, did not disappear altogether. It continued to be a prominent feature of the mining market; but as Hoover observed in the early 1900s, 'out of the chaos of mine promoters, finance and exploration companies there, has come to the front entirely another form of mining finance and management. There are certain firms composed of partners . . . who . . . are fast controlling the great bulk of mining enterprise.' These firms, Hoover wrote, dominated mining in specific regions around the world; Wernher, Beit & Company in southern Africa; J. Taylor & Sons in India; Tarbutt, Janson & Sons in West Africa; and Bewick, Moreing in Australia. As 'firms of this character have a name to maintain', Hoover concluded, they were also anxious to distance themselves from overt speculative activities.[91]

In London, the 'shop' curtailed speculation in the 'kaffir' market and when in 1900–2 a boomlet of Egyptian gold mines took place, it was deliberately 'ignored by the groups of big investors now interested in big base metal propositions . . . Egypt was the only area which old-style promoters could find and when it failed they disappeared for neither investors nor the world mining industry had any use for their services'.[92] Thereafter, what little speculation did take place on the London market 'owed its existence in too large a measure to the dealings of the financial companies and . . . little to the interest of the public'.[93]

The shift in the market from gold to base metal mining had its origins in the late nineteenth century and was the result of a rapid expansion in the consumption of copper, tin, zinc and lead in Europe and North America. Base metals were required in the new processes and technologies developed during the second industrial revolution particularly in the electrical and chemical industries, as hardening agents in alloys of other metals and the manufacture of armaments.[94] Following the collapse of the Secretan copper ring in the 1880s, copper prices were once more rising, while the demand for tin was regularly outstripping supply so that the average price rose from £80 per ton in 1891–5 to £155 in 1906–10.[95] These developments had an immediate impact on the London mining market where between 1898 and 1914 over 100 Australian copper mining companies were floated. Similarly, between 1890 and 1913, 83 British companies were formed, partly by Cornish tin interests and smelters, to develop tin deposits in various states in Malaya.[96]

Unlike the earlier gold and silver mines, base metal exploitation required from the outset highly-skilled technical personnel, applied scientific and metallurgical techniques and, importantly, 'far too much capital for mining development and metallurgical plant to suit the ordinary promoter'.[97] This meant that early on, 'big investors' played a vital role in base metal developments as was evident in Nigeria, where by 1910, Consolidated Gold Fields and Wernher, Beit were actively involved in tin mining promotions as well as in New South Wales, where in 1905, at Broken Hill, Hoover, Bewick, Moreing and other City interests, previously associated with the Lake View Consols mine in Western Australia, formed the Zinc Corporation.[96] Large amounts of capital, lengthy and costly experimentations and the skills of its metallurgists eventually enabled the Zinc Corporation to achieve a notable *coup* and develop a revolutionary flotation process able to separate the valuable zinc from the remaining lead and silver residues and waste.[99] By then the company had also acquired the Broken Hill South Block mine at the extremity of the local lead – silver – zinc deposits and was on its way to become eventually, after a series of mergers, one of the world's largest multinational mining concerns, the Rio Tinto-Zinc Corporation.[100]

**Conclusion**

In 1909 one observer contemplating 'a career of nearly twenty years in the City of London and an experience of a few mining booms', wistfully concluded that 'one cannot get rich by speculating in mines'.[101] Broadly speaking he was right. Yet it is evident that between 1880 and 1914 hundreds of millions of pounds were raised in London for investment in mining abroad. Along with public utilities and railways that have long been the more conventional subjects of studies of British investment abroad, overseas mining was clearly a very significant sector that attracted popular interest and capital in equal numbers. As this article has demonstrated, British capital and enterprise dominated the exploitation of new mineral resources around the world. London was the hub of international mining finance where company promotion and speculation were developed into a fine, if questionable, art.

In spite of financial losses sustained by the many, a number of British investors, notably in the City, received high returns on capital invested in overseas mining ventures. Yet, mining was widely regarded as risky. From the 1890s onwards rapid advances in geological intelligence and metallurgical techniques and the employment of skilled engineers and managerial personnel, made it possible to minimize some of the risks and achieve greater economies of scale. Changes in the nature of mineral production in this period, however, were far from protracted. They derived from an increasing number of pressures on profitability, capital formation and metallurgical techniques. Around the turn of the century, mining and mining finance werc in a state of flux.

In South Africa the finance houses were the organizational forms through which risk was spread, capital was raised, new technology was introduced and a low-cost structure imposed on the gold mining industry. Elsewhere, in Australia, West Africa and India, the structural transformation of mining enterprises centred on a small number of engineering and managerial firms. They were also the forerunners of the multinationals that rapidly came to dominate international mining after the first world war. By then, however, London had also ceased to be the hub of international mining finance and the financial centre of gravity had decisively shifted to New York.

## Notes

*I would like to thank the ESRC for a post-doctoral fellowship and financial support in writing this article (grant no. A/23/32/0015). I am especially grateful to Richard Davenport-Hines, Youssef Cassis, Ranald Michie, Adrian Graves, Forbes Munro and David Kynaston for comments on an earlier version of this article, which was read at the Economic History seminar, University of Edinburgh.

1. M. Edelstein, *Overseas Investment in the Age of High Imperialism* (London, 1982), p. 3.
2. C. Platt, 'Some drastic revisions in the stock and direction of British investment overseas, 31 December 1913', in R. Turrell and J. J. van Helten (eds), *The City and the Empire*, Institute of Commonwealth Studies (1985), pp. 11–25; M. Simon, 'The pattern of new British portfolio foreign investment 1865–1914', in A. R. Hall (ed.) *The Export of Capital from Britain 1870–1914* (London, 1968), pp. 33–59; L. Davis and R. Huttenback, 'The export of British finance, 1865-1914', in R. Holland and B. Porter (eds.), *Money, Finance and Empire, 1790–1960* (London, 1985), pp. 28–76.
3. E. Staley, *Raw Materials in Peace and War* (New York, 1937), Appendix A, 'Important raw materials of industrial society and their chief uses', pp. 247–8.
4. On the decline in the value of silver and the impact of the demand for gold upon international liquidity, see P. Vilar, *A History of Gold and Money, 1450–1920* (London, 1976), pp. 332–40; and A. G. Ford, *The Gold Standard 1840-1914: Britain and Argentina* (London, 1962), pp. 24–6.
5. A. J. H. Latham, *The International Economy and the Underdeveloped World 1865–1914* (London, 1978), pp. 59–60.
6. G. Paish, 'Great Britain's capital investments in individual colonial and foreign countries', *Journal of the Royal Statistical Society*, Vol. LXXIV, No. 2 (1911), p. 179.
7. P. Richardson, *Chinese Mine Labour in the Transvaal* (London, 1982), p. 2.

8. See K. Buckley, *Capital Formation in Canada 1896–1930* (Toronto, 1955), passim; C. van Onselen, *Studies in the Social and Economic History of the Witwatersrand, 1886–1914*, Vols 1 and 2 (London, 1982).

9. *Statist*, 4 August 1888, p. 140; Edward Ashmead wrote that 'It will thus be seen that the great stride made in mining enterprise taken its rapid rise in the last twenty-five years – that is from 1880' (*Twenty-five Years of Mining*, London, 1909, p. 2).

10. J. W. McCarty, 'British investment in overseas mining 1880–1914' (unpublished DPhil, Cambridge, 1960), pp. 4–7.

11. R. Kubicek, *Economic Imperialism in Theory and Practice* (Durham, N. C., 1979), p. 18; C. C. Spence, *British Investments and the American Mining Frontier 1860-1914* (Ithaca, N.Y., 1958), pp. 77–9.

12. Ashmead, *Twenty-five Years*, p. 173.

13. *Mining Journal*, 3 January 1891, p. 7; W. Skinner, *Mining Manual for the Year 1895* (London, 1896), pp. 136–7. The two mines that paid a dividend were American Belle Mines Ltd, and the Elkhorn Mining Co. Ltd.

14. J. W. McCarty, 'British investment in Western Australian gold mining, 1894–1914', *University Studies in History*, Vol. IV, No. 1 (1961–2), p. 13.

15. M. K. Quartermaine and E. McGowan, 'A historical account of the development of mining in Western Australia', in R. Prider (ed.), *Mining in Western Australia* (Nedlands, 1979), p. 12; C. Paton, 'Early days of Coolgardie', *Western Australian Historical Society*, Vol. 4, No. 2 (1950), pp. 63-73; J. Basin, 'Western Australian gold fields: 1892–1900. The investors and their grievances', *Historical Studies, Australia and New Zealand*, Vol. 6 (1954), pp. 252–89.

16. See the *Economist*, 28 March 1895, pp. 389-90 and 25 April 1896, pp. 518–19; also A. R. Hall, *The London Capital Market and Australia 1870–1914* (Canberra, 1963), p. 112, 'the leading characteristic of mining company promotion was the large proportion of capital going to the vendors as purchase price for the properties.'

17. McCarty, 'British investment', p. 270; see also J. B. Jeffreys, *Business Organisation in Great Britain 1856-1914* (New York, 1977), p. 451, Appendix A, 'Percentage of the paid up capital of new companies going to vendors in each of the years 1885–1914'.

18. See W. P. Kennedy, 'Notes on economic efficiency in historical perspective. The case of Britain, 1870–1914', *Research in Economic History*, Vol. 9 (1984), pp. 109–41.

19. See C. Harvey, *The Rio Tinto Company. An economic history of a leading international mining concern 1873-1954* (Penzance, 1981), pp. 15–46; R. Turrell with J.-J. van Helten, 'The Rothschilds, the exploration company and mining finance', *Business History*, Vol. XXVIII (1986); G. Blainey, *The Rush that Never Ended* (Melbourne, 1963), pp. 259–82.

20. On French and local investment in Witwatersrand gold mines, see J.-J. van Helten, 'La France et l'or des Boers: Some aspects of French investment in South Africa between 1890 and 1914', *African Affairs*, Vol. 84, pp. 247–64.

21. W. Reader, *A House in the City. A Study of the City . . . based on the records of Foster and Braithwaite. 1825–1975* (London, 1979), p. 110; also J. Vincent, *Pollbooks. How Victorians Voted* (Cambridge, 1967), p. 41, on 'wealth-holding . . . concentrated in the hands of widows, spinsters, rich farmers, clergymen, academics, squires and rentiers claiming gentility'.

22. R. C. Michie, 'Options, concessions, syndicates, and the provision of venture capital 1880–1913', *Business History*, Vol. XXIII, No. 2 (1981) pp. 149–50.

23. Midland Bank Archives, London. K56, Loans Against Stocks and Shares, Leicestershire Banking Co. Ltd, p. 4–9, 20 January 1898.

24. Ibid.; S. H. Frankel, *Gold and International Equity Investment* (London, 1969), p. 19; *Annual Report of the Transvaal Chamber of Mines for the Year 1914* (Johannesburg 1915), 'Dividend list, 1887–1914', pp. 279–81.

25. McCarty, 'Investment in West Australian gold mining', p. 22.

26. Ibid., p. 16.

27. R. C. Michie, *Money, Mania and Markets. Investment, Company Formation and the Stock Exchange in Nineteenth Century Scotland* (Edinburgh, 1981), p. 157; on gold mining in Mysore see H. M. White, 'The Champion Reef Mine', *Mining Magazine*, Vol. 47, No. 2 (1932), pp. 73–82; the history of the St John del Rey mine is discussed in B. Hollowood, *The Story of Moro Velho* (London, 1955).

28. H. Bottomley, *Bottomley's Book* (London, 1909), pp. 140–1. On Bottomley's financial and political career, see J. Symons, *Horatio Bottomley* (London, 1955), pp. 48, 50–7.

29. *Economist*, 4 February 1888, p. 146; *Rialto*, 1 December 1894, p. 3 on Nichalls and Paxton's desertion from the rails market and their re-emergence as 'Kaffir' jobbers. According to P. L. Cottrell, *Industrial Finance 1830–1914* (London, 1980) p. 149, 'Artificial premium creation and the inability of small issues . . . to obtain a London Stock Exchange quotation . . . were factors which . . . militated against domestic industrial issues succeeding in the London market.' Some indication of the marketability of mining shares can be obtained from the weekly stock market prices in the *Mining Journal*. Throughout 1895, for example, prices varied considerably as the following list suggests

|  |  | 12 Jan. | 18 May | 14 Sept. |
| --- | --- | --- | --- | --- |
| City and Suburban | (Transvaal) | 17 | 25 5/8 | 27 |
| Meyer and Charlton | (Transvaal) | 6 3/4 | 7 9/16 | 7 3/8 |
| Nundydroog | (India) | 2 | 2 | 8 1/2 |
| Broken Hill Prop. | (New South Wales) | 1 11/16 | 2 1/4 | 37/6 |

30. D. Kynaston, 'The London Stock Exchange, 1870–1914. An institutional history' (unpublished PhD, London 1983), p. 225; *Statist*, 7 September 1889, p. 274, 'Speculation in mines'; R. Burt, 'The London Mining Exchange 1850–1900, *Business History*, Vol. XIV, No. 2 (1972), p. 140; confusingly, the West African gold mining share market was also known as 'the jungle'.

31. Advertisements by H. Hanbury and Co. and W. H. Bumpus in Skinner, *Mining Manual* (1895).

32. A. K. Cairncross, *Home and Foreign Investment 1870–1913* (Cambridge, 1953), p. 86; Hall, *London Capital Market*, p. 39.
33. *Economist*, 25 September 1886, p. 1194.
34. See *Burdett's Official Intelligence, 1908*, p. 1613 on the markets where Rio Tinto preference and ordinary shares were traded; in 1908 of the 10,065 domestic and foreign mines (excluding domestic iron and coal mines) on the Official List of the London Stock Exchange, only 92 were listed on the provincial stock exchanges and included well-known mines like Anaconda (Glasgow, Halifax, Edinburgh, Liverpool and Manchester) and Consolidated Gold Fields (Glasgow) (*Burdett's Official Intelligence*, 1908, passim); W. A. Thomas, *The Provincial Stock Exchanges* (London, 1973), pp. 189, 190, 309–11; on the Indian gold mining boom of 1879–1881, see also Michie, *Money, Mania and Markets*, p. 215.
35. On the links between the City and landed society see Y. Cassis, *Les Banquiers de la City a l'époque édouardienne* (Geneva, 1984), pp. 113–38, 241–310; also J. Harris and P. Thane, 'British and European bankers 1880–1914: an aristocratic bourgeoisie?', in P. Thane, G. Crossick and R. Floud (eds), *The Power of the Past* (Cambridge, 1984), pp. 215–34; M. de Cecco, 'The last of the Romans' in R. Skidelsky (ed.), *The End of the Keynesian Era* (London, 1977); for a fascinating and imaginative analysis of the City of London in this period see Martin Daunton, 'The City of London and British society, 1850–1914. Some hypotheses', Urban Research Unit Seminar, Australian National University, October 1985.
36. Cf. PRO, BT31/483/1904, Memorandum and Articles of Association, Pachua Silver Mining Co.; R. Michie, 'The social web of investment in the nineteenth century', *Revue Internationale d'Histoire de la Banque*, Vol. 18 (1979), esp. 164–8.
37. Kubicek, *Economic Imperialism*, p. 93.
38. PRO, BT31/5948/41896 and BT31/6553/46119, London & West Australian Exploration Company Ltd, Share Register, 3 April 1896; on the formation and activities of the company see, *inter alia, Statist*, 9 November 1895, p. 571; 7 August 1897, p. 237; and 5 June 1909, p. 1301.
39. W. P. Kennedy, 'British portfolio behaviour and economic development in the late nineteenth century: hypotheses and speculation', in R. Turrell and J.-J. van Helten (eds), *The City and the Empire* (Institute of Commonwealth Studies, London 1985), p. 33.
40. On the 1900 Companies Act, see Cottrell, *Industrial Finance* pp. 72–5.
41. Cf. Kynaston, 'The London Stock Exchange', passim: *Economist*, 8 December 1888, p. 1541, on the rules governing a quotation on the Stock Exchange. Different sets of accounts used by many South African gold mining companies enabled them to 'massage' annual returns by omitting depreciation and redemption changes thereby artificially inflating net working costs. The plethora of accounting and book-keeping methods make it difficult to estimate returns in the Rand mining industry. See, for example, F. Pollak, *The Transvaal Mining Crisis: Its Causes and Solution* (London, 1908).

42. Hall, *London Capital Market*, p. 46; H. Withers, *Stocks and Shares* (London, 1910), pp. 255–82; on speculation, see A. Cutler, B. Hindness, P. Hirst and A. Hussain, *Marx's Capital and Capitalism Today*, Vol. 2 (London, 1978), pp. 96–7; F. Lavington, 'The social interest in speculation on the Stock Exchange', *Economic Journal* XXIII (1918) pp. 36–52.

43. *Economist*, 5 January 1889, p. 5.

44. Reader, *A House in the City*, p. 98.

45. *Statist*, 2 January 1897, p. 17.

46. See van Helten, 'La France et l'or des Boers',' for continental holdings in British-registered overseas mining companies.

47. See R. Michie, 'The London Stock Exchange and the British securities market, 1850–1914', *Economic History Review*, Vol. XXXVIII, No. 1 (1985) pp. 61–82 for an analysis of the relationship between the London and provincial stock exchanges; see also R. Michie's 'The London Stock Exchange and the international securities market, 1830–1914', in Turrell and van Helten (eds), *City and Empire*, pp. 37–42.

48. Van Helten, 'La France et l'or des Boers', p. 253; a jobber was one of two distinct classes of member of the Stock Exchange (a distinction that disappeared in the autumn of 1986), and could only deal with brokers and not the general public. Jobbers actually set the prices on the Exchange. A broker who wished to buy or sell a particular share asked the jobber to quote a dealing price and like any other dealer a jobber made his profit out of the difference between the buying price and the selling price.

49. Many loans were floated simultaneously on the London market and in Paris or Berlin; see C. K. Hobson, *The Export of Capital* (New York, 1914), p. 219. On French investment in South African mines via London, see Foreign Ministry Archives, Paris, Affaires Diverses Commerciales, Carton 288, A 81$^{A4}$, Consulat General de Londres à Affaires Etrangères, 26 February 1907; also NS 32 ff. 73–9, P. Cambon, Ambassade à Londres à Affaires Etrangères, 8 August 1902.

50. A. G. Ford, 'The trade cycle in Britain 1860–1914', in R. Floud and D. McCloskey (eds), *The Economic History of Britain since 1700*, Vol. 2 (Cambridge 1981), p. 38.

51. See, for example, J. Rowe, *The Hard Rock Men: Cornish Immigrants and the North American Mining Frontier* (Liverpool, 1974); T. Noer, *Briton, Boer and Yankee. The United States and South Africa 1870–1914* (Kent, Ohio, 1978), pp. 21–43 on the role of American technology and engineers in the Rand mining industry.

52. See, for example, a series of articles published every week in the *Economist* by the celebrated mining engineer and journalist, J. H. Curle, between December 1902 and March 1903; also R. Charleton, *Useful Information for Gold Mining Investors* (London, 1899) and K. Robinson, *The Mining Market* (London, 1907). Robinson was the financial editor of *The Globe* and wrote extensively on overseas mining.

53. *Statist*, 26 March 1893, pp. 352–3; on the Baring crisis see M. de Cecco,

*Money and Empire. The International Gold Standard 1890–1914* (Oxford, 1974).

54. Cottrell, *Industrial Finance*, p. 168.
55. See R. Triffin, *The Evolution of the International Monetary System: Historical Reappraisal and Future Perspectives*, (Princeton, NJ, 1964).
56. *Statist*, 8 September 1894, p. 286 and 15 September, pp. 314–15.
57. G. Blainey, 'Lost causes of the Jameson Raid', *Economic History Review*, Vol. XVIII (1965), p. 361.
58. McCarty, 'British investment in Western Australian gold mining', p. 11.
59. On the amalgamation movement in English joint-stock banking see F. Capie and G. Rodrick-Bali, 'Concentration in British banking 1870–1920', *Business History*, Vol. XXIV, No. 3 (1982), pp. 280–92.
60. J. Clapham, *An Economic History of Modern Britain* (Cambridge, 1938), p. 295; on inland bills, see S. Nishimura, *The Decline of Inland Bills of Exchange in the London Money Market 1885–1913* (Cambridge, 1971).
61. F. Lavington, *The English Capital Market* (London, 1921), p. 142. Political uncertainty throughout 1914 had considerably discouraged lending and borrowing so that Lavington's figure is probably an underestimation of the normal level of bank lending to the Stock Exchange.
62. W. A. Cole, 'The relations between banks and stock exchanges', *The Journal of the Institute of Bankers*, Vol. XX, No. 7 (1899), p. 409; also G. Rae, *The Country Banker* (London, 1885), ch. XV.
63. *Statist*, 7 December 1895, p. 685; C. H. Webb, 'Witwatersrand genesis: a comparative study of some early gold mining companies 1886–1914' (unpublished PhD thesis, Rhodes University, 1981), pp. 1–23.
64. Rothschilds and some other merchant bankers, however, were involved in mining ventures around the world; see Turrell with van Helten, 'The Rothschilds, the exploration company'; also C. A. E. Goodhart, *The Business of Banking 1891–1914* (London, 1972), p. 125; *Statist*, 12 October 1895, p. 429, refers to large margins 'of 30 or even 40 per cent'. If, for example, a banker lent £1,000 with a margin of 40 per cent to a broker offering mining scrip as collateral then the broker had to deposit £1,400 worth of shares, at a time when margins of 10–15 per cent were rather more common in the City. I am grateful to Dr Kynaston for this information.
65. *Statist*, 23 November 1895, p. 624.
66. Goodhart, *Business of Banking*, pp. 121–2.
67. Reader, *A House in the City*, p. 114.
68. *Economist*, 6 November 1909, p. 913–14, 'The employment of money by Contango'; Withers, *Stocks and Shares*, pp. 273–6.
69. *Statist*, 31 January 1891, p. 128.
70. *Statist*, 19 October 1895, p. 468.
71. Ibid.
72. Withers, *Stocks and Shares*, p. 268; on the speculative activities of jobbers, see Lavington, *English Capital Market*, pp. 259–61.
73. *Statist*, 19 October 1895, p. 460; the discounting of bills is discussed in W. M.

Scammell, *The London Discount Market* (London, 1968), esp. pp. 159–91; the 'pig on pork' procedure and the 1895 share boom are analysed in some detail in the *Statist*, 8 December 1894, pp. 688–9; 12 January 1895, p. 47; 8 June 1895, p. 713; 5 October 1895, p. 409; 12 October 1895, pp. 428–9, 436, 447.

74. Kubicek, *Economic Imperialism*, p. 119.

75. R. Davenport-Hines and J.-J. van Helten, 'Edgar Vincent, Viscount d'Abernon, and the Eastern Investment Company in London, Constantinople and Johannesburg', in R. Davenport-Hines (ed.), *Speculators and Patriots* (London, 1986), pp. 35–61.

76. *Statist*, 26 October 1895, p. 500; the links between the London Stock Exchange and overseas markets extended as far afield as Melbourne, see A. R. Hall, *The Stock Exchange and the Victorian Economy 1852–1900* (Canberra, 1968), p. 233.

77. *Mining Journal*, 11 January 1896, pp. 38–9; 8 January 1898, pp. 35–6; Blainey, 'Lost causes', passim.

78. Ibid., 9 January 1897, pp. 44–5; 21 January 1905, pp. 57–8.

79. The origins and activities of the major South African mining finance houses or groups are discussed in D. Innes, *Anglo-American and the Rise of Modern South Africa* (London, 1984), pp. 45–74.

80. J. Wernher to Eckstein and Co., 15 June 1895 quoted in Kubicek, *Economic Imperialism*, p. 67.

81. In 1895 Wernher, Beit and Co., were involved in the formation of the Banque Française de l'Afrique du Sud to tap the French financial markets and allay the fears of French investors. Consolidated Gold Fields established the Trust Français in 1896 with the same objective: see J.-J. van Helten, 'British and European economic investment in the Transvaal with specific reference to the Witwatersrand district and gold fields 1886–1910' (unpublished PhD, London, 1981).

82. Barlow Rand Archives, Sandton, South Africa (hereafter BRA), HE 167 Wernher, Beit, 17 June 1901; AN 65 A Q A 151[1-2] 'Banque française pour le commerce et l'industrie' (1909); R. Poidevin, *Les Relations Economiques et Financières entre la France et l'Allemagne de 1898 à 1914* (Paris, 1969), p. 206 on the merger of the Banque Française de l'Afrique du Sud with the Banque Internationale; BRA HE 72f. 188, Wernher Beit to Hirsh and Co., 5 April 1905; also Kubicek, *Economic Imperialism*, pp. 188–9.

83. Guildhall Library, London, Stock Exchange Archive (SEA), Ms 14.600 Vol. 73, 1902–3 Cttee of General Purposes, evidence by D. E. Higham, jobber, 7 January 1903; see also evidence by H. C. Blyth to the Committee on the same issue; S. Japhet, *Recollections of My Business Life* (London, 1931).

84. Guildhall Library, SEA, Ms 14.600, Vol. 79, Committee of General Purposes, evidence on 'outside houses' by various jobbers including Higham and Blyth, 6, 8 and 13 November 1906.

85. *Financial Times*, 23 March 1905, p. 4 on 'the public will not purchase mining shares unless . . . the price will always be made to dealers' instead of outside houses.

86. P. Richardson and J.-J. van Helten, 'The development of the South African gold-mining industry, 1895–1918', *Economic History Review*, Vol. XXXVII, No. 3 (1984), p. 319 for a brief outline of the gold discoveries and the last of the classic gold rushes of the nineteenth century.

87. T. A. Richard, *The Utah Copper Enterprise* (San Francisco, 1919), p. 9; see also C. Goodrich, *The Miner's Freedom* (Boston, 1925), pp. 108–10; and E. T. Layton's, *The Revolt of the Engineers* (Cleveland, 1971), pp. 3–55, on the disappearance of the prospector and the application of science and technology in the mineral production process.

88. *West Australian Mining, Building and Engineering Journal*, 18 June 1904, pp. 4–5, 'Interview with Mr Moreing'; for Bewick, Moreing and Co.'s activities in Western Australia, see G. Nash, *The life of Herbert Hoover. The Engineer 1874–1914* (New York, 1983), pp. 52–95.

89. *Engineering and Mining Journal*, 14 April 1904, p. 616.

90. Ibid., 28 April 1904, p. 670 'Editorial'.

91. Ibid., 28 April 1904, pp. 675–6. 'Another aspect of mining finance'; on the early history of J. Taylor and Sons see R. Burt, *John Taylor: Mining Entrepreneurs and Engineer, 1779–1863* (Buxton, 1977): PRO BT 31 3690/ 22945, Memorandum and Articles of Association, Gold Fields of Mysore Ltd, 1886–91 gives an example of the power and influence of Taylor and Sons as the engineers of one of India's major gold producing companies.

92. McCarty, 'British investment', p. 181; on Egyptian gold mining, see *Engineering and Mining Journal*, 17 November 1904, p. 784 and 5 November 1910, p. 925.

93. *Mining Journal*, 7 January 1911, p. 2.

94. David Landes, *The Unbound Prometheus. Technological Change and Industrial Development in Western Europe from 1750 to the Present* (Cambridge, 1969), pp. 281–90; Staley, *Raw Materials*, pp. 247–8.

95. Yip Hoong, *The Development of the Tin Mining Industry of Malaya* (Singapore, 1969), p. 149; O. Herfindahl, *Copper Costs and Prices 1870–1957*, (Baltimore, 1959), pp. 80–91.

96. Wong Lin Ken, *The Malayan Tin Industry to 1914* (Tucson, 1965), p. 214.

97. *Engineering and Mining Journal*, 21 January 1899, quoted in McCarty, 'British investment', p. 170–1; on the Secretan copper ring of 1889, see M. Wirth, 'The crisis of 1890', *Journal of Political Economy*, March 1893, pp. 214–35; also C. Kindleberger, *Keynesianism vs. Monetarism and Other Essays in Financial History* (London, 1985), pp. 233–5.

98. On base and precious metal mining in West Africa see Bill Freund, *Capital and Labour in the Nigerian Tin Mines* (Harlow, 1981); the involvement of the major Rand mining finance houses in company promotion in Nigeria and the Gold Coast can be gleaned from A. N. Jackmen and W. Morgan (eds), *West African Mining Handbook* (London, 1909); Nash, *Herbert Hoover*, pp. 348–70 considers the involvement of Berwick, Moreing in the Zinc Corporation.

99. G. Blainey, *The Rise of Broken Hill* (Melbourne, 1968), pp. 68–9.

100. Nash, *Herbert Hoover*, p. 370; for a critical assessment of RTZ, see R. West,

*River of Tears*, (London, 1972) and *The Rio Tinto-Zinc Corporation Ltd – Anti-report* (CIS, London, 1971).

101. H. S. Wheatley, formerly of the *Investor's Chronicle*, writing in *The Mining Investor*, October 1909, p. 3.

# 9 Capital, nation and commodities: the case of Forestal Land, Timber and Railway Company in Argentina and Africa, 1900–45

*Michael Cowen*

## Introduction

When banking capital is reckoned to be distinct and estranged from industrial capital in Britain, the argument is about an apparent peculiarity of British capitalism which makes supposedly British capital incapable of fulfilling industrial need in Britain:

> Paradoxically, the capital of world finance never witnessed the world of finance capital, in the Marxist sense of the term. Hilferding himself, noted in his classical work on the subject, how far London departed from the German or Austrian, French or American phenomenon of a fusion of financial and industrial capital, under the control of powerful investment banks.[1]

Hilferding's argument of 1910 was that 'the organisationally backward English banking system, with its division between deposit and merchant banks' held back industrial development in Britain. Banks did not act, around the turn of the century, to further the concentration and centralization of industrial capital in the face of competitive pressure from larger-scale and technically more efficient industry on the continent, and particularly in Germany. Because banks held off, at arm's length, from quite a large number of small firms, relative to the scale of production on the Continent or in the United States, 'the tendency of both bank and industrial capital to eliminate competition' in the common pursuit of profitability did not occur in Britain.[2]

In extensive retrospective studies of British economic decline and de-industrialization, this point has become commonplace without being closely bound within Hilferding's Marxist framework. Thus, 75 years after Hilferding, a recent influential work states: 'In contrast to the experience of the emerging corporate economies, British bankers lacked direct involvement in industry and had little ability or incentive to use financial leverage to re-organize industrial structures or enterprise management.'[3] But, then, the state is introduced to become a part of the banking problem: given their filial ties to the *ancien régime* of the old landed aristocracy, and cohesively concentrated in London, bankers exercised 'a much more concerted and coherent influence over national policy than industrial capitalists, who were divided along enterprise, industry and regional lines'. With this sleight of hand, Hilferding's original distinctive point is obliterated because his focus was on the institutional division between deposit or commercial and merchant banks, a division which was reinforced by the 'legislative compulsion' of national policy. In short, banks were no less divided than industrial firms. The coherence of banking capital is assumed from the banking imprint upon state policy which acted to protect the value of sterling internationally, in the cause of supporting the real value of unearned incomes of *rentiers* and speculators, rather than protecting work for productive workers. However, the contrast between the chronically abnormal and industrially disabling character of the British form of state and the ideal state form which makes banks work for industry in the national interest can be traced back to Hilferding. Finance capital, supposedly absent from Britain, 'detests the anarchy of competition and wants organisation'.[4] When finance capital, the integration of banking with industrial capital, is dominant, the strong state eliminates industrial division in the national interest, protects domestic markets, facilitates the conquest of international markets and ensures 'respect for the interests of finance capital abroad'. In Britain, *laissez-faire* liberalism made the state shy off from state regulation of industry and confine itself 'to the maintenance of public order and the establishment of civil equality'.[5] Merchant banks were held off from industry to prevent the organization of capital. Abroad, sea power was exercised to support the distinct interest of bank capital which was oriented towards lending on international markets. The British problem was about the absence of finance capital which did not make a national interest congeal around capital.

The question here is why a specific company, Forestal, which ran against the grain of the British peculiarity, and practised 'continental banking notions in financial London'[6] and so expressed the character of finance capital, was forced to acquire a national stamp of identity. When finance capital, in this case, came to London, it expressed an alien character for the British state whose officials were concerned to make the company fulfil British need. But equally, when the company appeared in Argentina, the United States, South Africa and Kenya, a distinct national or colonial interest, distinct from that of Britain and any other national entity, was imposed upon Forestal. Furthermore, a series of national actions, concerned with 'liberation', 'freedom', 'production for national need', made the company relocate from one national area to another, to become international.

This kind of question has been raised more generally, as in the Warren–Murray debate over the territorial non-coincidence of nation-state and capital. Warren stated that: 'The point about British imperialism is, of course, that no one ever doubted that however "internationally" imperialist firms operated, they were *British* and their fortunes were in a sense the fortunes of the British economy.'[7] But, as this paper will show, everybody doubted whether Forestal was British, including British state officials. To be British, Warren suggested in a footnote, a company had to be 'owned by British capitalists and their profits contributed to British national income and foreign exchange'. This is precisely the assumption which, for instance, Joseph Chamberlain had employed to make the claim for a centralized British imperial economic entity:

> We are the landlords of a great estate; it is the duty of the landlord to develop the estate. . . . In my opinion it would be the wisest course for the government of this country to use British capital and British credit in order to create an instrument of trade in all . . . new important countries.[8]

Chamberlain failed to re-organize industrial capital from the vantage-point of a politically inspired industrialist. Here, capital becomes exclusively British because it is regarded as an instrument to fulfil a British national object of imperial development. Likewise, when the Kenya government officials regarded the company as aberrant towards Kenya and as such to be South African or Dominion, they implied that it should be an instrument to develop commodity production in Kenya. When Americans, during World War II, objected to the company as Argentine, it was because it was thought that Forestal was withholding a strategic supply for the national war effort. Whatever the problem of ownership, the practices of the company did not meet the stated national need, in specific cases for specific periods, of the state in question.

Andrew Porter captures this point when he states that:

> In the late nineteenth century, certain types of capitalist activity increasingly involved alliances across national boundaries quite as much as competition between national units. Inevitably they had their difficulties with governments necessarily responsive to a wide range of more parochial or stridently nationalist options.[9]

State officials, when they wrote of 'our practical interest' to distinguish it from the general profitability interest of the company, were making the same point. For the state to dictate to a company or, equally, to refrain from acting for a company was precisely to acknowledge that the practical or pragmatic or specific national interest was separate from the interest of profitability for capital, whose expression is universal. In the specific case of Forestal, this was not simply a matter of strategic alliances between firms whose national origins were different. As a capitalist company, Forestal was an institution which integrated different relations of capital. When attempts were made to make the practical or parochial interest dominate the general interest of profitability and thus stamp the company with the badge of nationality, the upshot would be to disintegrate and reintegrate, without the immediate national stamp, the different relations of capital within the institution of the company.

The different relations of capital were those of banking and productive or industrial capital. Ingham, for instance, contests those who explain the separation of banking from industrial capital in Britain because of the City's 'overseas orientation'. He states that 'City organizations have acted almost exclusively as *intermediaries* between investors and borrowers, and have been traditionally characterized by a marked organisational separation from any form of productive enterprise.'[10] But it was precisely in overseas financial involvement that some merchant bankers did involve themselves directly, in product enterprise and not merely, as Ingham would have it, through acting as an entrepot for international money, deposited in London and then advanced, via its portfolio, to mainly non-British-controlled firms in South America and elsewhere. Thane points to the case of Cassel, who 'like most City men cannot be described as "finance capitalist" in the sense meant by Hilferding in relation to British industry', but who 'surely can as regards his overseas interests'.[11] Cassel took a strategic interest in the management of companies, operating overseas, in which he had shareholdings. This was a minimal case of finance capital – the integration of banking with productive capital – in the British context of overseas investment. Forestal is a maximal case because it was founded upon the marriage between productive enterprise and banking capital: a German-owned company in Argentina went to the City of London for money and Emile D'Erlanger, as merchant banker, met the demand by incorporating the quebracho enterprise under his management control.

Ingham overstates the distinction between portfolio and direct involvement when claiming that commercial practice should be distinguished from the financial practice, presumably, of speculation.[12] A conventional economic historian like Kennedy, for instance, sees that equity shares 'are not just gambling counters but also represent a means to change the management and policies of companies'.[13] Ideas about pecuniary capitalism put a premium upon financial practice as determining overseas investment practice.[14] If there is a problem, as Ingham would have it, about the instrumentalist conception of the state, there is equally one about an instrumentalist idea of capital. The argument about the divorce between money and production supposes that City of London institutions can be used for British industrial development at the behest of the subjective will of state agency. This view, as I have mentioned, has a marked pedigree. Equally, the argument that finance can be marked off as a self-enclosed arena of organization to be counterposed to production, pure and simple, with a different kind of organization and will, can be reckoned to take a subjectivist view of capital.

When Sir Robert Kindersley of Lazards, another City of London merchant bank, gave evidence to the 1931 Macmillan Committee on finance and industry, the first question that he was asked was why merchant banks had been created by 'foreigners'. His reply, was that the 'foreigner had a different type of mind to the Englishman'.[15] D'Erlangers, like most merchant banks in London, originated in Germany. From Frankfurt, a Paris branch was established in 1859 and in 1866 Emile and his brother, Baron F. A. D'Erlanger came to London to open another branch which then became the centre of their operations.[16] Initially, the company specialized in raising loans for governments, such as a loan of £3 million to the Confederate states during the American Civil War. Secured mainly by cotton, the issue gave a £405,000 profit for D'Erlangers. Other important clients were central and local authorities in Hungary, Greece, South America and South Africa.[17] C. K.

Priolean, the Liverpool partner of Frazer, Trenholm and Company, the Confederate bankers in Europe, made the meaning of foreign more precise.

> This man Erlanger is a dangerous one; he has the quickest intelligence I have ever been thrown in contact with . . . but I judge him to be ambitious, selfish, daring and unscrupulous, and he is a Jew with an enormous connexion and entanglement with others of his persuasion all over the world.[18]

If this was the view of a northern English banker, it is hardly surprising that industrial capitalists in the English regions would be suspicious, by inclination, towards raising finance from merchant banks, however much they may have, in Kindersley's words, 'merged their personalities in the country'.

Indeed, as Cottrell has insisted, the separation between City banks and industrial firms, even after the 1870s when industrial capital profitability started to decline, owed much to 'the lack of growing demand for external finance by industrial firms'.[19] The relatively small industrial firms used internal profits, short-term commercial bank loans and commercial credit to finance their investment and recurrent activity: 'There was strong resistance to raising capital externally, particularly equity, for this could dilute the family's control over its concern.'[20] This picture fitted even the ship-building industry, well into the inter-war period, where the large integrated firm was exceptional: 'The majority of shipyard enterprises remained small and independent. Frequently, under family ownership or control, they tended to a jealous guarding of independent action.'[21] From the vantage-point of merchant banks, Kindersley initially argued in 1930 that 'the industrialist as a rule does not come to us'; as an issuing house, the merchant bank issues debentures but cannot make an advance of cash or lock up money to assume a liability for a company: 'It cannot father a company; in my opinion it should not.'[22] A day later, Kindersley proclaimed that he 'would like to adjust somewhat my statement' or that he was being economical with the truth. Now he said that industrial companies were being bled to death by an overburden of debentures which made them pay interest out of capital. Lazards had made 'a new departure', to 'reconstruct' an electrical enterprise through funding its equity, 'by putting the new money behind and not new debentures which I believe to be fatal'.[23] This involved taking risk and control over the management of the enterprise. Moreover, since 1918, Lazards had started to place issues for British industry; £15 million of £24 million raised for domestic issues went to Lever Brothers alone.[24] But what Kindersley did not say was that D'Erlanger, the competing merchant bank, had long been engaged in fathering or reconstructing companies, by issuing shares, funding equity and taking control over management. It did so, however, by tying rentiers in Britain to industrial companies in South America.

From the vantage-point of *rentiers*, investment of savings in Forestal as a holding company was portfolio investment, made attractive in the mid-1900s because of rising raw material prices in Argentina. *Rentiers* wanted dividend payments in sterling derived from a prudent use of assets. But, from the viewpoint of D'Erlanger's management, investment in productive capacity in a particular raw material, tanning agents, had to be protected through widening the sources of the material. The company, against the expressed interest of a significant proportion of its share-holders, used profits to acquire competing companies during periods (1912–14, 1919–21) when raw material prices fell. The use of a pool, to force competing companies which had not been acquired, was likewise dictated by competition to protect vegetable tanning agents against substitute commodities. The company was committed to tanning agents as a commodity, which, after World War I, was set in a secular state of decline because its use value was concerned with that of leather, itself facing substitution from oil-based substitutes. Forestal, initially a holding company for portfolio investment, became a form of direct investment in the face of competitive pressure. The appearance of a monopoly, capturing monopoly profit as the company moved capital from Argentina to South Africa and then to Kenya, was so because the company became the international arena for regulating the world supply of a particular commodity. Competitive pressure was universal and not contingent[25]; the company incorporated universal criteria of global profitability to equilibriate supplies from different national areas in the face of given demand. It subsumed the nationality of rentier interest and the partial interest of nation state. Forestal, as a capitalist firm, maintained a partial interest because, like all capitalist enterprises, it could not regulate and determine demand for leather or derived demand for tanning agents. Furthermore, unlike other forms of enterprise, the company could not successfully diversify away from tanning materials. Born in 1906, the year in which Chamberlain's imperial plan failed to materialise, it was entirely fitting that Forestal should die in 1968, a victim of Slater Walker, who took over and stripped the tanning assets of the company, divesting them in Lonhro, the 'unacceptable face of capitalism'.

Tanning agents were produced from the bark stripped from trees. Quebracho trees, like oak or chestnut, were indigenous and a non-cultivated source of bark with a gestation period of about 100 years. Wattle trees were not indigenous to Africa and were cultivated with a gestation period of about 10 years. Given that quebracho was in finite supply while wattle, as a perfect substitute for quebracho in terms per unit of bark, was relatively elastic in supply, the unconstrained planting of wattle in South Africa, from the 1900s, and in Kenya, from the 1920s, threatened Forestal's control over the supply side of the market for quebracho. Potentially, therefore, the company would be forced to move capital from Argentina to South Africa, and from South Africa to Kenya to constrain the rate at which wattle output increased to threaten Forestal's investment in quebracho production. Competition between wattle and quebracho appeared to be national competition from the vantage-point of state agencies in different national areas. Forestal could attempt to override national interest, whether the interest was concerned with supply, as for Argentina, South Africa and Kenya, or with demand, as for Britain and the US. But the actual, as opposed to potential movement of capital, was determined by political and ideological forces at play within any one national arena. To be secure of supply within Argentina, the company amassed land on a scale which made it appear as an agent of foreign rule in one or two remote provinces. The political struggle which Forestal's mere presence provoked culminated in the events of 1919–20 and induced the company to start disinvesting in Argentina and investing in South Africa. In both

South Africa and Kenya, the supply of bark from independent producers was regulated through the administrative and political action of the state. To counter unregulated and independent supply in South Africa before 1934, Forestal started to invest in Kenya. Post-war difficulties over regulating supply from Central Province middle-peasant producers induced the company to buy up settler-owned estates in Western Kenya to create its own large-scale basis for direct production, as in Argentina. The survival of collusion and combination between Forestal and independent manufactureres in Argentina depended upon state regulation. It was because Forestal operated in international space that it could command state regulation over supply, but, equally, because it was a form of international capital, it could not act for any one nation state. It was precisely during periods of war that the company came under severest national attack, not least in Britain, and it is during war that capital was most Anglo-Argentine, amply exemplifies these points of conflict.

From the outset, Forestal was not a typically British merchant company engaged in the procuring and extraction of raw materials. The formation of the company owes as much to German industrial technology as it did to City of London banking capital. Quebracho extract production in Argentina was established by German productive capital, in the name of Dr Schmidt, in 1894.[26] If Forestal was atypical, it was only because German industrial investment was relatively sparse, apart from electricity and power supply, in Argentina before World War I. But the formation of Forestal was entirely typical in so far as German firms in South America used English rather than German banks to raise large-scale issues of money capital.[27] Extract was directed primarily towards the United States of America, where the price of hemlock – the indigenous tanning agent – rose above the price of quebracho after 1892.[28] Logs were directed to extract factories in continental Europe – Germany, Austria, France, Russia – where import duties on manufactured extract from the 1890s made the import of extract prohibitive.[29] Only in Britain was extract imported duty free, and at the turn of the century there was no factory manufacturing extract in Britain.[30] The manufacture of quebracho extract was therefore established and reproduced by German technology, personnel and finance.

One company, Hartneck and Renner of Hamburg, owned or controlled the majority of extract companies in continental Europe. Together with a Franco-German company, Portalis and Company of Paris, Hartneck and Renner formed an Argentine company, the Compania Forestal del Chaco (CF d Chaco), during 1902.[31] CF d Chaco incorporated the extract factories which had been acquired after 1894 by Hartneck and Renner and Portalis in the Corrientes and Chaco provinces of northern Argentina.[32] It was this company which was to be the foundation upon which Forestal was formed.

The growth of quebracho production during the 1890s and 1900s was rapid but little different from the character of other raw material production in Argentina during the period. The production of raw materials was primarily set in motion by issues of capital raised in London; between 1880 and 1913 the value of all exports increased sevenfold.[33] By 1905, CF d Chaco's two extract factories produced nearly 28,000 tons of extract, a level of output which was not reached by factories in Kenya until the late 1940s.[34] Planning to expand productive capacity during 1905, CF d Chaco approached D'Erlangers to raise the finance capital for the expansion of extract production. D'Erlangers in London responded by acquiring the formal control over CF d Chaco in forming a new company, the Forestal Land, Timber and Railway Company, on 1 January 1906.[35]

## Formation and growth of the Forestal Company

Forestal was formed from the purchase of CF d Chaco for just over £1 million, of which £0.8 million was paid in cash, with the rest in debentures and shares. To raise the finance to cover the purchase, Forestal, at its inception, issued one million £1 shares. It declared that a fixed cumulative dividend would be paid and that 25 per cent of gross profits earned each year would be available for distribution to shareholders.[36] Personnel, resident in Argentina but of German origin and who were recruited by the Hartneck and Renner and Portalis companies, were to continue to manage the extract factories. Representatives of the companies remained as directors of Forestal along with Baron F. A. d'Erlanger and G. E. Gunter (also Director of the Bank of Tarapaca, which was linked to saltpetre with the same history as Forestal, and Argentine Chairman of Liebigs Meat Extract Company). Nor was marketing to be in the hands of Forestal: sales of extract to continental Europe were executed by the Renner Company. Within Britain, Humphreys, Percival and Ellis held Forestal's sales agency; the Vendors Company, by buying the output of logs five years in advance of production, likewise acted as a general sales agent. For exports to the United States, an agreement was concluded with the Central Leather Company of New York, who acted as extract sales agents for Forestal.[37] Forestal was not uniquely British, and did appear to conform to the classic embodiment of the contemporary form of finance capital. Money capital from the City of London banking institutions came to dominate the production processes which had been established by German firms as industrial capital. As Forestal's historian declared: 'There was no Forestal as such.'[38]

Kindleberger has pointed out that for the typical British company at the turn of the century, finance reigned supreme over marketing, which was separated from production. Marketing was regarded as a 'fishy' activity, best left to merchant companies operating in 'semi-protected imperial markets'.[39] D'Erlangers, like most City merchant banks, was both an issuing house and an acceptance house. As an acceptance house, it financed trade, for imports into Britain and British exports and, most importantly, trade between companies in third countries. Acceptance business earned a commission when the merchant bank lent its name to the buyer of commodities and the buyer paid for the loan of the bank's authority and security. A merchant bank, such as D'Erlangers, had more secure credit than that of a merchant company, trading on commodities, because it was regarded as having more information across a spread of markets and thus was better able to discount against the future risk of trade.[40] D'Erlangers went into acceptances in 1910, after Forestal had been formed, but Forestal gained from the marketing expertise which the acceptance business generated. Through acquiring both manufacturers and companies engaged in the trading of tanning materials, Forestal integrated marketing with the advanced technology of the production process. In 1912, six years after Forestal was formed, D'Erlanger put equity into an Argentine-registered company, South American Stores; a decade later the new company was acquired by Harrods (South America) Ltd to become the largest retail company in Latin America.[41] More generally, re-organization altered the relations between commercial and industrial capital within the shell of the old company. Marketing and commercial practices were used to protect the productive core of the company, to relocate capital from one national area to another and to ensure that the command over technology could be maintained to ward off competition. This was unlike the experience of industrial companies in Britain, who separated commercial and industrial practices and responded to the later nineteenth century decline in average profitability, partly the result of technological innovation elsewhere, by switching to safe imperial markets.

From 1906 to 1912, Forestal was eminently successful as a holding company. Whereas British-controlled railway companies in Argentina paid a 6–7 per cent dividend on ordinary shares, Forestal's average dividend during the period was 15 per cent.[42] Net profits tripled between 1906 and 1910. New share and debenture issues provided for the acquisition of land, lighterage and railways to expand productive capacity. The new issues also provided for the purchase of, or the acquisition of, an interest in extract factories controlled by Argentine domestic capital (see Appendix, p. 216). But, more significantly, it was the advantage of German productive technology which gave Forestal a competitive advantage in the production of extract. Forestal's costs of production were such as to permit it to realize operating profits during periods of falling market prices for extract. During such periods, competing companies were forced to close down plants and liquidate stocks of extract at prevailing market prices. It was during periods of recession and depression, governed by the amplified effect of the industrial trade cycle upon tanneries' purchases of extract, that Forestal acquired and amalgamated competing companies. The centralizaion of capital in the hands of Forestal was closely interwoven with the combinations of producers of extract through the operation of the quebracho pools.

Crises struck extract production in 1908, 1912–14, 1919–21, 1925–6, 1929–34. During 1908, Forestal maintained a dividend, came through the recession with 'flying colours', and acquired Tannino Elaboracion de Extracto de Quebracho Sociedad Anomina, an Argentine extract manufacturer. At the beginning of the 1912–14 depression, Forestal's total assets were valued at £5 million; it owned 2.5 million acres of land and controlled the production from eight extract factories. By 1914, the value of total assets had doubled and it now owned 4.25 million acres of land and controlled production from ten factories.[43] During the 1912–14 depression Forestal bought into the Renner Company, amalgamated with the Santa Fe Land Company, and acquired the New York Tanning Company, a subsidiary of Argentina Quebracho Company.[44] Between 1919 and 1921, the Renner Company (with four factories in Germany), Fontana Limited (with a factory in Argentina and a factory in

Barcelona, Spain), Calder and Mersey Extract Company (with the largest liquid extract factory in Britain at Liverpool) and the Natal Tanning Extract Company were all fully acquired through the purchase by finance accumulated during the boom periods of extract production.

Some of the acquired companies, such as the Santa Fe and Renners, were as large as Forestal. Santa Fe owned nearly 3 million acres of land, 80,000 head of cattle, and as much employed capital as Forestal.[45] Yet all, unlike Forestal, were unable to employ undistributed profits to expand productive capacity at costs of production which permitted the supply of extract at an average price of production equal to or less than the falling market price for extract during periods of depression. By 1922, Forestal could claim that 'We have thus established in the commercial world a chain of outposts, so that we can penetrate into all the more important tanning markets of the world, and be in a position to take full advantage of any trade revival.'[46] The claim, as the state personnel in Kenya and elsewhere were ruefully to recognize, was not exaggerated. During the depressions of 1925–6 and 1929–34, there was little else for Forestal to acquire. Over 1925–6 it acquired the controlling interest in the remaining competitor in Germany, Rheinische Gerbstaffe Extrakt, and took full control over its selling agency in Britain, Humphreys, Percival and Ellis. In the US, Forestal felt constrained by anti-trust laws in contemplating the takeover of sales agencies, a fear that proved, as we shall see, to be well founded.[47]

In 1932, it mopped up the tiny Kenya producer BEA Wattle Estates and Extract Company. Even so, in the same year, in Argentina and Paraguay 24 extract manufacturers – virtually all owned by indigenous forms of capital – lay off the path of Forestal's onslaught. The operation of the quebracho pool ensured that they remained within Forestal's orbit of control. The operation of the pool, during periods of rising market prices for extract, made it unneccessary for Forestal to take over competing companies. It could eliminate competition during periods of falling market prices for extract by directly absorbing competitors through take overs.

Quebracho pools operated before the formation of Forestal and survived only during periods of rising market prices for extract. Before 1906, it was stated that 'an agreement existed between the various manufacturers of quebracho extract to ensure reasonable prices for their products and to avoid cut throat competition'.[48] CF d Chaco, the lowest cost producer, also accounting for the largest share of total extract output, fixed the production price for extract. Forestal, by taking over CF d Chaco, took over the position of price leader within the pool and, therefore, from its inception, Forestal controlled both the price and the market shares of quebracho producers. Throughout its life, Forestal attempted to maintain the pool. Any other producer that attempted to break up the pool by seeking to garner a larger market share through unilaterally reducing the production price for extract was subject to the ultimate sanction which the company could exercise – the threat of takeover by Forestal.

Periods of rising market prices for extract, governed by sharp increases in the demand for leather, occurred over 1906–12, 1915–18, 1924, 1927–8. During each period, the pool operated. Take the first period, up to 1912, when Forestal was to comment that:

In years of a big demand there was room for disposing of the produce of both manufacturers [Forestal and its major competitor, the Renner Company] but in years when the consumption was smaller both Renner and [Forestal] were forced to approach the same clients and enter into competition with each other so that a very small surplus of extract affected prices considerably.[49]

The surplus of extract was that quantity of extract which was produced, but not sold, at the Forestal-controlled accounting price, which was fixed below the market price during periods of rising demand for extract but above the market price during periods of a falling demand for extract. Renner attempted to liquidate unsold stocks of extract in Europe at the prevailing market price. Renner produced liquid extract in Europe from Forestal, supplied quebracho logs in competition with Forestal, and supplied solid extract to Europe. Forestal responded by guaranteeing Renner an average annual level of profits to support the holding of unsold stock at Forestal's accounting price of extract. It was an unwilling move, for Forestal could not purchase Renner as a 'very serious increase of capital' would be required to do so.[50] Renner, the fount of Forestal, did not take heed of Forestal's warning.

In 1918, Forestal was 'successful in entering into a very important and satisfactory agreement with other manufacturers for the control and dispatch of extract from factories to Europe and elsewhere'.[51] Renner accompanied the agreement but in 1921, during the post-war depression, again attempted to breach the terms of the pool. This time round, Forestal responded by purchasing 98 per cent of Renner's shares 'at a low price'.[52] The pool broke up in 1923 and was resuscitated by Forestal in 1926[53], but when the pool broke up again during the 1925–6 recession it was resuscitated by non-Forestal producers in 1928 to operate for a short period over 1929–30.[54] This pool was breached by the major Argentine competitor of Forestal, Quebrachales Fusionadas. When the pool was again reconstituted by non-Forestal producers in 1934, Forestal joined the pool only after it had acquired the competitor 'to ensure that the 1934 agreement will not be wrecked'.[55] Take over, be it noted, was the ultimate sanction which Forestal possessed. Against the vagaries of competition emerging from the companies which were controlled by indigenous capital and supported by the Radical Party, ruling in Argentina from 1916 to 1930, Forestal acted to discipline the twenty to thirty smaller producers of extract. It did not employ the threat of predatory pricing, a course of action which would have followed if Forestal had been a merchant company embodying the practices of commercial capital.

We should only note here that, while the express commitment of the Radical Party was towards *laissez-faire*, the thrust of radical action was to support the formation of indigenous capital against the preponderant presence of international capital in raw material extraction. When the 1926 pool collapsed, Forestal reckoned that the state 'frowned upon any understanding which aimed at limiting production or preventing free competition'.[56] Again, in 1931, only the Argentine producers of extract were in a position to obtain the support of the state apparatus to permit collusion and combination to be resuscitated. We shall soon see why Forestal took *laissez-faire* to be an aspect of nationalism.

196

Yet , there was an equivocal response towards the threat of nationalism. In 1947, during the Peronist period, Gerard D'Erlanger (as Chairman of Forestal) claimed that Emile, his father, had always recognized that 'though Argentina would initially welcome foreign capital they would develop a legitimate ambition to participate in increasing measure in such industries as their wealth grew' [57] However, Emile D'Erlanger had declared in 1936: 'The world problem is a problem of nationalism.' [58] He was referring to the disruption of multilateral trading posed by the emergence of the clearing agreements which gave effect to bilateral trade and so reduced the degree to which Forestal was free to dispose of extract internationally. Equally, he could have been referring to the political intervention of *rentiers* in Britian who, during the 1914–18 war, sought to dislodge German personnel, and thereby productive technology, from Forestal in Argentina. He may even have been referring to the 1919–21 period of workers' struggle against Forestal in Argentina which, uninhibited by the absence of any significant state-sponsored repression, soon acquired the character of nationalism. To counter nationalism in both Argentina and Britain, Forestal was to localize itself in Argentina as it expanded in Africa. It would reduce and withdraw profits which were remitted to Britain and shift productive capacity away from Argentina. In this way, nationalism as a global, rather than singular local, force could be resisted. And, to deal with the twenty or so indigenous competitors in Argentina, Forestal responded in a classic manner – it acted as finance capital in Britain to override state intervention in Britian and to counter competition from capital in Argentina.

Forestal, after the collapse of the 1926 and 1929 pools, was in a position to employ the power of predatory pricing. In 1931, operating at full capacity,Forestal could have supplied 80 per cent of current international demand for extract. Even when operating at 50 per cent of capacity to produce extract at the current Hamburg cif market price during 1933, Forestal's accounting price covered average costs of production, including costs of amortisation. [59] By offloading extract stocks at lower than prevailing market prices, Forestal could have reduced unit costs of production by eradicating under-utilized capacity. By expanding its market share dramatically, Forestal would have driven the Argentine producers out of production. In the outcome, Forestal would then have restricted output at a higher accounting price for extract.

This course was not pursued. On the contrary, Forestal raised a £1 million debenture issue to hold stocks of extract during 1929 to prevent a further fall in the market price of extract and to counteract the offloading of stocks by Forestal's competitors. At the prevailing export price for extract, the competitors could not replace stocks at an average cost of production which provided for any profitability. [60] Nor were they in a position, like Forestal, to cover the exhaustion of short-term liabilities by raising long-term note issues – a necessary condition for the holding of stocks. Rather, the Argentine manufacturers were forced to close factories and appeal to state agency to regulate the export price of extract.

In a memorandum to the state, the Argentine manufacturers alleged that the relatively low market prices for extract were not the result of the growth of wattle bark production in South Africa and Kenya, but were 'exclusively due to lack of organisation amongst manufacturers'.[61] Price regulation should not thwart the 'laws of the Argentine either by the formation of a trust or "pool" . . . which would result in an increase in the cost of living in Argentina.' Only 1 per cent of full capacity output from extract plants, it should be noted, was marketed for internal consumption. The aim was to bring 'benefits to workmen, employees, and the national capitalists alike' while increasing national revenue by an increase in export duties. After 1921, the Radical Party government sought to protect real wages through price controls; from the mid-1920s the Party's base shifted from syndicalist-controlled unions to state functionaries whose rapidly growing wage bill was financed from export duties.[62] The memorandum stressed that the majority of factories 'were national or run by national capital'. The state responded by regulating the export price during 1929, the very result which Forestal wanted. Again, in 1934, Forestal insisted that before any pool be re-established, all other competitors should combine and, in conjunction with the state, present Forestal with a common agreement to regulate the export price of extract.[63] Now, and unlike 1929, the Conservative Party governed the Argentine state, which, in the new regime of protectionism, was not averse to urging manufacturers to agree to adjust offers of export sales to 'their real requirements'.[64] Between 1929 and 1934, Forestal reconstructed its capital by selling its Argentine assets to a subsidiary formed in Argentina.

The formation of the subsidiary, La Forestal, in January 1931, was prompted by the recognition that:

> [The] desirable ideal of the rationalisation of the quebracho industry by amalgamation would certainly remain beyond the realm of practical politics if this company were not formed.
>
> Owing to its preponderant position in the industry Forestal must be the keystone of any such scheme and no Argentinian or Paraguayan company would accept incorporation into an English company at the cost of having to pay heavy British income tax on dividends, depreciation and reserves . . .[65]

The formation of La Forestal turned Forestal into a holding company whose source of revenue was now dependent upon the dividend paid by subsidiaries rather than the profit obtained from the direct control over quebracho production. As it started in 1906, so it was concluded in 1931: 'Forestal is not now a manufacturing company but it purchases and resells produce of subsidiaries.'[66] But one of the subsidiaries was to be the Natal Tanning and Extract Company, the agency through which Forestal made its incursion into Kenya to balance the purchase and resale of quebracho and wattle.

Two currents marked the formation of La Forestal. The first was that Forestal dominated quebracho production through the combination of producers in Argentina, where combination was subject to state regulation. As long as combination was subject to state regulation and the perpetuation of production conditioned by combination, accumulation on the simple basis of industrial capital was stifled by the current of nationalism in Argentina. The second current was that of state intervention in Britain. It dated, in the case of Forestal, from the period of the 1914–18 war, and was wider than the instance of the increasing burden of company taxation which realigned the distribution of profits between capital and state. Nor was it a simple instance of the antagonism towards an embodiment of finance capital emanating from the City of London and so 'selling Britain short' of the finance for investment in industrial capital within Britain. The current state of intervention was part of a wider mood of antagonism towards the intertwining of relations of banking and industrial capital on an international basis of accumulation. The effects of different nationalisms were to disorganize and then re-organize the form in which money capital was combined with industrial production within the firm. We need to consider one wave of national antagonism, in the case of Britain. Later we consider waves of nationalism in Argentina. The upshot of nationalism was only to accelerate the internationalization of Forestal's organization of capital.

### The British attack on Forestal as a German company

During 1915, a group of Forestal's shareholders set up a campaign to rid Forestal of German productive technology and establish Forestal as a 'distinctive British Company'. The thrust behind the compaign was expressed by the most militant language, appropriate to the spirit of the ultimate in national wars: 'Let us turn out the cursed Huns: that is our duty as Englishmen.'[67] Referred to as 'agitators' who turned the OGM into a 'beer garden', the shareholders accused German staff of sabotaging the company 'from within' through intrigue, including transfer pricing.[68] Argentina was neutral during the war, and, for the majority of British-controlled companies, personnel of German origin were replaced as a matter of routine.[69] No such routine was possible for Forestal. To rid Forestal of German personnel, Forestal was forced to close down factories, replace directors, institute training schemes for newly recruited workers and staff, including 80 per cent of 'administrative' officers and four of the six local directors.[70] And all of this was accomplished after the Foreign Office, the War Office, the Admiralty and the Foreign Trade Department had undertaken a series of enquiries into the organization of Forestal.[71] Sir Arthur Lawley (formerly Administrator of Matabeland, Governor of Western Australia, Governor of Madras) replaced Mr Gunter as a director and explained why Forestal could not fit simply into the role of a British adjunct for the effort of national war:

> Forestal consistently forged ahead and left their competitors in the lurch; and it is impossible to resist the conviction that German brains and German activity in the matter of scientific research and experiments over many years . . . carried the Forestal to the front, and enabled that company to outstrip all rivals in the race for industrial success. It is, I know, for an Englishman, a somewhat humiliating confession, but it is true.[72]

Earlier, Emile D'Erlanger had insisted: 'I am a loyal Englishman. I have heard stories about "capturing the German trade". If there was any example of German industry captured for England, it is Forestal.'[73]

Thus, Forestal was no 'Anglo-Argentine' company which 'regarded war conditions as a perfect opportunity to secure the collaboration of the British Government in the elimintion of a major commercial competitor since British war strategy coincided with this aspiration'.[74] During 1915, less than 50 per cent of Forestal's total shareholding of three million shares was held by British nationals; nearly one-third of the total shareholding was held by German nationals since the Renner Company had yet to be taken over; while another quarter of the shareholdings were held by American and French nationals. Moreover, a sizeable but undisclosed proportion of Forestal's debentures had been placed on continental, particularly Swiss, financial markets.[75] Forestal refused to dismiss two directors, one French and the other naturalized British of Swiss origin. D'Erlanger remarked:

> How can I get rid of Baron Portalis . . . we are fighting alongside the French and Portalis has his brother and I do not know how many relations in the higher staff of the French army . . . If [Rueff] goes so does his bank's [Swiss Bankverein] securities.[76]

The status of Forestal as a 'British company' certainly did not derive from the national origin of productive technology applied to manufacture in Argentina. Now it was being admitted that the status derived from the national origin of finance capital invested in Forestal was most dubious.

To attempt to secure an unambiguous British status for Forestal would have meant the dismemberment of Forestal as a form of productive capital. The military demand for leather during the mainly horse and harness war of 1914–18 was such that only Forestal could meet the supply of extract to the allies.[77] But war, which had restricted the scale of Forestal's control over international markets by eliminating markets now occupied by Germany and its allies, only served to provide a quantitative leap in extract production and Forestal's profits. Between 1915 and 1918 Forestal realized the highest ever annual average level of net profits (£1 million) and paid the highest ever average dividend (20 per cent). Never again, not even during the Korean War commodities boom, would these peaks be reached (see Table 9.1). The undistributed net profits of the period, accumulated in reserves, were to provide the finance capital for Forestal's intervention in extract production in South Africa and Kenya.

National war provided the terms of the language expressing the antagonism towards the ambiguous nationality of Forestal. But the language of nationalism enlightened (even if it was supposed to obscure) the more profound tension within Forestal's organization of capital, that between the relations of finance and industrial capital. The campaign to secure Forestal as a 'British company' was founded upon the attempt to restrain the company from an expanded movement of capital into production and so maintain the status of Forestal as a form of banking capital. The terms of this wider antagonism were primarily set by disputation over the proportion of profits to be distributed as dividends. It is clear that the dispute arose out of the merger between the Santa Fe Land Company and Forestal; indeed, the campaign was mounted by ex-shareholders and directors of the Santa Fe Company. Santa Fe approximated more closely to the model of portfolio investment which secured the means of subsistence for a rapidly declining *rentier* class in Britain.

*Table 9.1    Forestal's ordinary dividend and accumulated reserves, three-year moving average, 1906–68*

|  | Final ordinary dividend (%) | Accumulated reserve and depreciation funds (£) |
|---|---|---|
| 1906–8 | 9 | 73,000 |
| 1909–11 | 18 | n.a. |
| 1912–14 | 15 | 878,000[a] |
| 1915–17 | 21 | 1,760,000 |
| 1918–20 | 16 | 3,100,000 |
| 1921–23 | 2 | 3,000,000 |
| 1924–26 | 8 | 2,670,000 |
| 1927–29 | 8 | 3,300,000 |
| 1930–32 | 2 | n.a. |
| 1933–35 | 2 | n.a. |
| 1936–38 | 11 | 3,100,000 |
| 1939–41 | 9 | 3,600,000 |
| 1942–44 | 9 | 4,300,000 |
| 1945–47 | 12 | 4,120,000[a] |
| 1948–50 | 12 | 5,550,000 |
| 1951–53 | 12 | 6,400,000 |
| 1954–56 | 10 | 7,530,000 |
| 1957–59 | 9 | 7,400,000 |
| 1960–62 | 4 | 6,820,000[a] |
| 1963–65 | 9 | n.a. |
| 1966–68 | 6[a] | n.a. |

a.   Averaged on basis of two years
n.a.   Not available.
*Source:*
Forestal Annual Reports and Ordinary General Meetings as reported in *Times* (London) and *Economist*.

*Table 9.2    Forestal's accounting rate of profit (rate of return) on net assets, 1915–61*

|  | 1915 | 1921 | 1929 | 1939 | 1953 | 1959 | 1961 |
|---|---|---|---|---|---|---|---|
| Post-tax profit rate | 14.0 | 1.6 | 4.0 | 5.3 | 2.9 | 6.4 | 2.3 |

The accounting rate of profit is the ratio between net profits and net assets. As measured here, net profits are not 'genuine' in that depreciation allowances and contributions to the reserve account are excluded from reported net profits:

Net profits = (trading profits + interest from investment) − (depreciation allowances + reserve contributions).

Net assets   = fixed assets + net liquid assets.

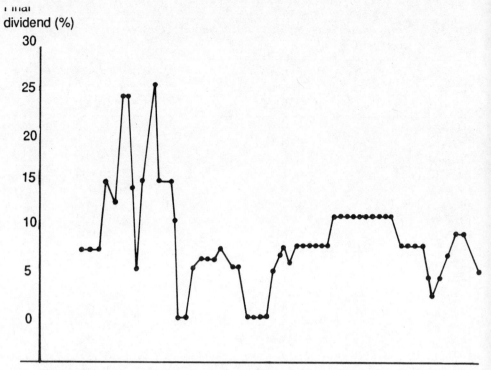

Figure 9.1   Forestal dividend on ordinary share capital, 1906–68

Accusations were made that Forestal's dividend was lower than the pre-merger Santa Fe dividend, that Forestal's series of acquisitions were reckless, that Forestal engaged in land speculation and dubious marketing practices, and much else. Now, accusations of this order should not be particularly surprising, except that they were little different from the order of accusations made by state personnel in Kenya during the 1930s. More fundamentally, the accusations, whether grounded in reality or not, expressed the form of Forestal's organization of capital. It is quite possible to see that the cause for accusation arose precisely from what Forestal was not – a mesh of banking and commercial capital.

Take the major point of accusation, that Forestal restrained the immediate distribution of profits to expand the retention of profits for growth in future profits and dividends. For example, in 1916 a 20 rather than a 10 per cent dividend was desired, and in 1920 the 18 per cent dividend was reckoned to be worth only 8 per cent in 1913 prices.[78] Forestal's management was acutely aware that the source of Forestal's material, quebracho forests, were wasting assets. Once destroyed for transformation into extract, the forests, taking 100 years to regenerate, were irreplaceable as a source of material for extract production. To maintain and expand capital, the forests would have to be reconstituted in a different form, as the non-quebracho commodity form of wattle. And, to provide the money capital for the reconstitution of the forest as capital in a different commodity form, Forestal withheld dividends and directed fixed proportions of net profits towards depreciation and reserve accounts. In 1908 the reserves (including depreciation) accounted for 17 per cent of net profits. In 1918, the reserves (excluding depreciation) accounted for nearly 50 per cent of issued capital. These reserves (including depreciation) reached £3.4 million, or nearly 70 per cent of the value of issued capital during 1921. Issued share capital rose slightly from £4.9 to £5.2 million between 1916 and 1926, and then remained constant at £5.75 million until 1953. Accumulated profits and not new share capital provided for Forestal's entry into wattle production – the new form of the commodity production which was reconstituted for the expanded reproduction of capital.

Forestal employed the quebracho pool to maintain the accounting price of extract. It fixed the accounting price at a level which provided for the maximisation of reserves: 'To sell at a price which will not leave a profit after amortising the value of self-owned forests or stripping rights is to live off capital and die without it.'[79] Forestal fought tooth and nail to maintain the combination of quebracho producers, thereby ensuring that the rate of cutting of forests would be minimized during periods of falling market prices for extract and maximized during periods of rising market prices. Unlike its competitors who compensated for falling market prices by increasing the quantity of output, Forestal attempted to maintain reserve capacity during periods of depression.[80] And, to maintain reserve capacity at a fixed cost of land per acre, Forestal not merely maintained but increased the proportion of net profits which were directed towards depreciation.[81] Against the desire of the *rentier* and antagonistic class of shareholders, Forestal's management forsook its promise to maintain the dividend rate in favour of its intention to maintain the rate at which profits were capitalized in the form of reserves.[82]

The company policy of promoting the capitalization of profits in Argentina, rather than the distribution of revenue in Britain, did not merely prove irksome to a minority of shareholders whose assets were bound to a relatively small international company. Under post-war company reform, not only the dividends but also the depreciation accounts of British-registered companies operating overseas, as well as dividends, were subject to taxation in Britain.[83]

It was the desire to prevent the payment out of capitalized profits, accumulated in Argentina, for state revenue in Britain as much as the necessity to secure combination in Argentina which prompted the formation of La Forestal. Forestal was fully aware that the move represented

> a loss of direct control and intervention in the management of the Argentine Company, for such control and intervention would stultify the whole process from the point of view of British taxation . . . Without this step, [Forestal] would pass into foreign hands.[84]

Once La Forestal was formed, profit accumulated in Argentina was subject only to tax as profit transmitted to London as dividends. Thus, Forestal was permitted to ensure that, while the capitalization of profits could proceed unencumbered in

Argentina, the future payment of revenue as dividends would be realized for Forestal in Britain.

The formation of La Forestal was the *denouement* to a series of reforms which Forestal had executed in the face of pressure from the state in Britain and, as we are about to see, in Argentina. The pressure to reform the organization of capital from the vantage-point of the nation state regenerated the movement towards the internationalization of capital. That movement had suffered a sustained hiccup during the hiatus of the 1914–18 war and it was released only by the action of labour in the aftermath of the war. In the case of Forestal in Argentina, the Radical government's campaign against 'foreign capital' (first British, then American) spurned and then provided a supreme vindication for the only course which that capital was bound to follow – to move elsewhere to expand commodity-production.

### The Argentine Attack on Forestal as a Foreign Company

It should not be supposed that the movement of finance from Argentina to South Africa to reconstitute the form of commodity production was some automatic mechanism which adjusted the secular decline of irreplaceable quebracho to the growth of cultivated wattle. The movement of accumulated reserves of profits out of Argentina was accelerated, if not activated, by a series of events between 1919 and 1923 which were sparked off by the 1916 election of Yrigoyen's Radical Party to power as a government which attempted to win working-class support by establishing close ties with the Trade Union movement.[85] As Rock has convincingly shown, the thrust of the Radical Party's first period of power was to act against non-Argentina capital. Forestal was no exception.

Between 1916 and 1917, Forestal (as far as we can ascertain) remained immune from the waves of workers' action striking heavily against British companies left unprotected by 'the Radical Government's labour policy [which] can be reduced to this simple specific decision – whether to use the police [or troops] for or against the strikers'.[86] But in early 1920 the British Ambassador sent a report to the Foreign Office. The report enclosed a covert investigation by an agent of Yrigoyen who had been sent, disguised as a Public Works Department official, to observe the insurrection in Santa Fe province: 'The investigation portrays a condition of affairs tantamount to anarchist rule. . . . However, it is the general belief that the Government will delay drastic methods to restore order until after the election.'[87] The Presidential agent, in reporting on the course of a Christmas 1919 strike at Villa Guillermina, noted that 'the police favours all acts of the workmen, either good or bad', and, he continued:

the abuses and outrages of the workmen are protected by the Police and the Chiefs of Police . . . I have been able to prove that the Santa Fé [provincial] Government tolerates and still allows [the] said abuses to be tolerated, for politcal reasons, because the Chiefs and officials of the troops quartered in these regions on strike, have stated to me they have no other orders than to guard in the future the interests of the Company . . . the native strikers told me they would win the strike because the Government required their votes in the elections in . . . February [1920].[88]

Although the Federal government assured the Ambassador that it would ensure law and order, it was only in May 1920, following the assassination of the Guillermina manager, that troops were sent to protect company property.[89] In August and December 1920, more unrest and insurrection were reported and Forestal was authorized to organize its own police force, probably in collaboration with *Liga Patriotica Argentina*.[90] During 1921 Forestal used its private mounted police force to protect property and staff in Chaco Province.[91]

Company and British ambassadorial officials were bemused by the organization behind the insurrection. Company officials claimed that there were no formal demands for improved wages, and that money wages had been 'systematically improved' during the war. It was 'a frankly anarchist organization', Federacion Obrera Argentina del Quinto Congreso, which was earmarked as the source for insurrection.[92] The fifth Congress, held in Buenos Aires in July 1920, was alleged to have been responsible for distributing firearms, on the grounds that 'leaders of the labour agitation in Buenos Aires favour the Province of Santa Fé and the factory districts of the Forestal Company in particular as most suitable for an attempt at a social revolution'.[93] The company, when it found references to a 'Soviet' at its Vila Ana factory, confused anarchists with 'Bolsheviks', and it was the British Minister in Buenos Aires who pointed out that the Argentine Socialist Party, with parliamentary representation, had not responded to the call of the 'Third International', meeting in Moscow during July 1919, to extend revolution to South America. Indeed, the British Embassy held that labour unrest in Chaco and Santa Fe 'is in reality mere South American disorder, and the work of wandering brigands feeding upon the cupidity of ignorant and drunken Indian half-castes or degenerate Spaniards'. The complaint was that labour action was not disciplined by socialist organization.[94]

Forestal, with its four million acres of land and dominant presence in the more distant provinces, was a sitting target for agitation, whether organized or not. The company, now stamped as British enterprise, could not depend upon the un-equivocal support of the Argentine state apparatus as a whole to protect its property. Labour action during 1919 and 1920 was universal but Forestal was particularly exposed to the wave of nationalism in Argentina. In 1921, the company increased money wages, reduced the length of the working week, and cut the prices of consumer goods in its stores; the cost of the strike wave further compounded the reduction in profits which had been induced by international depression.[95] Thus, labour action did maintain real wages after the war period, when a sharp increase in Forestal's profits had been registered. But the action also ensured that the growth in future expanded production capacity was to be shifted out of Argentina. This was Forestal's ultimate form of resistance to labour and governments in Argentina.

But this was not the case in 1918. In the Chaco and Santa Fé provinces, workers took strike action against Forestal during August, demanding higher wages and shorter working hours.[96] It is estimated that real wages in Argentina had fallen by 30 per cent between 1915 and 1918; in late 1915 Forestal was serving out 800 free meals per day to women and children in Chaco Province. This was despite the fact that 10,000 head of cattle were slaughtered annually to provide wages in kind for the 20,000 strong labour force.[97] Forestal responded by increasing money wages between 15 and 30 per cent and increasing its expenditure on company-provided housing, education and health services.[98] But there was no respite for Forestal. By December 1919, all factories were closed down as a result of further action. At one factory, 'Conditions assumed a revolutionary aspect.' At Tartagel, the factory was fired and totally destroyed[99], stocks of extract were burned. From La Forestal (where the largest lumber mill in Argentina was situated) it was reported that logs to the value of £200,000 (equivalent of 15 per cent of Forestal's gross profits during 1917) were destroyed.[100] More action occurred during 1920 and 1921. Among others, the manager of the Guillermina factory was assassinated; members of Forestal management and supervisory staff were reported to have 'their lives in their hands'. In 1921 and 1923, thousands of head of cattle were rifled by workers.[101] Only in 1923 did the action peter out. Between 1919 and 1923, Forestal stood determined to reinvest accumulated reserves in South African wattle extract production.

Towards the end of 1920, the British Minister in Argentina claimed that the Radical government's position was one of 'benevolent neutrality . . . holding out promises for the improved conditions for the poorer and working classes'.[102] However much the Radical Party was forced to denounce general strike action as 'revolutionary', it attempted to isolate British capital by restraining the state apparatus from militarily intervening to repress workers' action which struck against British companies. During the events of December 1919, the Government of Santa Fé province ordered troops to support police engaged in the protection of Forestal's property.[103]

The Radical government, from the moment it had taken hold of state power, attempted to 'reform the status of British companies in Argentina'.[104] Again, Forestal was no exception. Over 1919–20, at the peak of the strike action, Forestal brought former ministers (of the former Conservative government) on to the Argentine board, organized land colonization schemes and sold half of its stock of cattle and half of its land acreage of 2.3 million acres to an indigenous company.[105] The vast area of land, 4.4 million acres, held by Forestal, 'has given ground for criticism in London and Argentina and the Forestal has long wanted to sell off some of its land'.[106] The company reckoned that the finance realized from the land sale (£2.5 million upon a book valuation of £1.7 milion in 1920, providing an accounting profit of £0.8 million) would be employed 'profitably' within extract manufacture.[107] *The Times* thought otherwise, referring to the great estancia sale (as it came to be called) as 'an act of political expediency'. True to form, the dissident shareholders wanted the revenue from the estancia sale to be distributed amongst all shareholders rather than be used to expand production in South Africa. Finance from the estancia sale provided for the acquisition of the Natal Tanning Extract Company. Accumulated reserves of profits from extract manufacture in Argentina prevented the Natal company from collapsing during the 1920s and provided for the entry of the Natal company into Kenya.

The sale of land which held quebracho forest made Forestal turn to purchase rights

206

to cut state-controlled forests and purchase logs on the open market. First, the state apparatus during a period of rising extract prices, prevented Forestal from opening virgin forest and increased the price of stumping rights on existing forests. State officials favoured the leasing of forests, at a lower rent than Forestal, to companies of Argentine origin. D'Erlanger bemoaned that the destruction of forests 'with no profit to Government is an economic absurdity', and expostulated: 'I will not pry publicly into private affairs of our competitors.'[108] Secondly, the forcing of Forestal into open market purchases pushed up the market price of logs at a faster rate than the market price of extract.[109] The Renner subsidiary in Germany and the New York Tanning Corporation produced liquid extract from Forestal-supplied logs. Over 1925–6, Renner plants closed down when Forestal refused to contribute to Renner's debt of gold payments to the German government. The New York factory was sold when the reduction of log exports was compounded by an imposition of an *ad valorem* export tax upon the export of solid extract.[110] Forestal was forced to confine itself to the production of liquid extract from a severely restricted supply of quebracho logs.

The future longevity of Forestal-owned forests was estimated to be twenty years (to 1946) in 1926 and fifteen years (to 1943) in 1928.[111] From 1929, a fixed depreciation allowance was charged proportionate to the consumption of quebracho logs, but irrespective of the current level of profitability, to reconstitute Forestal's capital within fifteen to twenty years (1945–50).[112] Only the re-organization of productive capacity permitted Forestal to extend the estimate of extract production, albeit at a diminishing rate of increase, beyond the late 1940s. The refurbishing of factories and the perfection of the mechanical uprooting of tree stumps during the early 1920s provided for an increase in the extraction of tannins from any given quantity of logs and an increase in the yield of tannins per unit of land.[113] A smaller acreage of quebracho could now provide the same or larger yield of extract. In 1939, the longevity of forests was estimated to be twenty years (1959)[114], a more prescient forecast for the demise of Forestal-produced extract in Argentina.

As early as 1939, the Secretary of the quebracho pool openly acknowledged that wattle would replace quebracho as the predominant vegetable tanning material consumed in international markets.[115] However much Forestal might re-organize productive capacity for the extraction of tannin, it could not transcend the limits of rising costs of production which were imposed by dwindling supplies of quebracho logs. The material limits of expanded production, imposed by the 100 years gestation period of the quebracho tree and the increasing length of distance from forests to extract plants, were reinforced by the political constraints which operated upon Forestal as an embodiment of international capital.

In 1943, as Forestal battened down to face the onslaught of Peronism, it openly declared that 'reafforestation is not practical politics in Argentina'.[116] But by then the production of wattle had long begun to outstrip the growth of quebracho production. Peronism further concentrated expanded production in Africa. In the interim, between the post-war wave of nationalism and the Peron period, it was expanded wattle production which provided Forestal with the means to resist the state apparatus in Argentina – to maintain its control over quebracho production through operating the quebracho pool. The British Foreign Office knew that the

Argentine government was, on economic grounds, fearful of taking any action which would encourage extensive wattle planting.[117]

**Forestal in Africa**

Long before the rise of Peronism in Argentina, however, Forestal had moved into Africa to capture the increased output of wattle bark in South Africa and, in due course, Kenya. This was more than just a geographical shift in operations as far as Forestal was concerned. Wattle production, unlike quebracho production in Argentina, was a form of estate agriculture. Forestal's supply of wattle bark, unlike quebracho logs, were obtained from the cultivated acreages of wattle planted by private estate owners. The regulation of the quantity and the quality of bark supplied by estates to Forestal's extract plants foreshadowed the forms of regulation which were executed to control supplies of bark from household producers in Kenya.

From the early 1890s, the production of bark in South Africa had grown rapidly. In 1904, 30,000 acres of land were under wattle: by 1921, the area of wattle plantations increased to 288,000 acres.[118] Forestal entered production by two avenues. The first plant was established by the Natal Tanning Extract Company during 1916. The Federation of Tanners of Great Britain had encouraged the establishment of the plant, presumably to counteract the hold which Forestal held over markets for extract. The War Council in Britain authorized the shipment of extract in preference to the shipment of food commodities from South Africa.[119] In the pre-war period, Germany had provided the major market for South African-produced bark. Now, with the rapid switch in the extract/bark price ratio in favour of extract, British tanners induced an increase in the supply of extract from South African-produced wattle. The desire to increase the supply of extract to reduce market prices for extract could be realized only by way of an increase in productive capacity to manufacture extract. To obtain finance capital to expand productive capacity during 1919, the Natal Company approached its sales agents for extract, Humphrey, Percival and Ellis. Humphrey and Company were a sales agency for Forestal. So, to whom did Humphrey and Company turn on behalf of the Natal Company? It turned, just as CF d Chaco had approached D'Erlanger, to Forestal.

Forestal responded positively to the request by the Natal Company for finance, and then purchased the Natal Company for just over £550,000, of which £200,000 was paid in cash, the rest in debentures and shares. Wilson Fox, MP, who had defended Forestal in Parliament against the German company charge, had suggested to Forestal, in 1918, that the development of Empire resources would increase sterling assets to redeem the British war debt.[120] The second avenue to enter extract production was through the Calder and Mersey Extract Company. Calder and Mersey founded the South African Tanning Extract Company in November 1919 to compete with the Natal Company. Forestal had acquired a substantial but not controlling interest in Calder and Mersey in June 1919, so that Forestal held 35 per cent of the South African Tanning Extract Company's issued share capital.[121] When Forestal purchased the Natal Company during 1920, it acquired not only the full share capital of the SATE company but also two smaller companies, Alfred Wattle and Inanda. In 1921, the full share capital of Calder and Mersey was acquired. The desire to enter South Africa had been provided by both the competitive pressure of expanded bark production in South Africa and the Radical action of 1919–21 in Argentina. The financial capacity to intervene in South Africa to expand the production of wattle extract had been provided not so much from the great estancia sale of 1920 in Argentina as from the reserve of profits accumulated from quebracho production between 1906 and 1919.

Only the internationalization of the organization of Forestal's capital permitted extract production to survive in South Africa. In so far as Forestal advanced finance to the Natal Company it might be supposed that Forestal, as a holding company for a subsidiary, was simply fulfilling the speculative relation of banking capital. But Forestal advanced finance during the period of depression to re-organize productive capacity when expecting an upturn in the industrial trade cycle. Forestal's advance of finance came directly from the expanded extraction of surplus value in Argentina to expand the means of extracting surplus value in South Africa. In changing the form of expanded commodity production through replacing quebracho in South America by wattle in Africa, Forestal was fulfilling the relation of industrial capital.

The formation of this wattle pool involved Forestal in some conflict with local estate promoters who called upon the South African government to assist them against the activities of 'monopolies' which attempted 'to reduce bark output'.[122] Forestal remained unimpressed, however, for unlike in Argentina, there were no state-inspired moves to reduce Forestal's price-fixing as only a limited (even if growing) quantity of bark could be absorbed by extract manufacturing plants in South Africa. Any quantity of bark, accumulated from annual strippings, could be absorbed by international markets but at a lower market price than the Forestal-determined producer price for bark, Producers counted on the support of the state apparatus to raise the export price of bark without restraining the growth of bark output. During the war and post-war periods, the international demand for wattle extract surged upwards. It was only with the collapse of the international demand for vegetable-derived extracts, in the mid 1950s, that producers' quotas were applied, in 1956, to regulate the annual output of bark.

Forestal took its South African name, the Natal Company, into Kenya, and, in the same way that it had been stamped as an Argentine company in Britain, Kenya state officials treated Forestal as if it were South African. It was competition from 'South African' wattle which was at the forefront of the official mind when policy was applied to encouraging the planting and export of wattle, the bulk of which was produced, in the mid-1930s, by peasant producers. When the supply of Central Province-produced bark threatened markets for both wattle extract from South Africa and quebracho, Forestal used its South African name to impose controls over the quantity and quality of peasant production. The South African system of marketing controls had evolved in response to the demands of estate producers, who formed one of the co-ordinates for the political base of successive regimes of state power which paid unrelenting attention to estate agriculture. In Kenya, however, there was no such political basis for the application of controls over peasant production. Forestal's international presence was enough to force the colonial government to apply controls according to the South African model. However, the colonial government acceded to Forestal's demands only after much heart searching.

In 1936, the Kenya colonial government's Director of Agriculture declared the following: 'Government will make every effort to prevent the important wattle bark industry from falling into the clutches of a monopoly who will endeavour to manipulate it in favour of its South African interests.'[123] After he had failed to prevent the 'monopoly', Forestal, from controlling the supply from indigenous Asian enterprise which competed in buying bark from middle-peasant producers, the Deputy Director of Agriculture declared in 1939:

Liberation [from Forestal] may become possible after increased planting in Central Province and Nyanza and erection of new extract plants but even if Kenya were free, increased production would aggravate unsold world status unless Kenya produced bark undercut prices of Natal produced bark . . .

It is a point of consideration, however, whether the Imperial Government would care to see an important Dominion industry eliminated by a competing native industry in the colonies.[124]

It should now be clear why an apparently British company should incur the wrath of British colonial officials and why supposedly British capital should be incapable of fulfilling the Kenya government's intention to develop wattle production as the major form of commodity production to meet the demands for revenue, by state and peasantry, in Kenya. Furthermore, when the company relocated capital from Argentina to South Africa and then to Kenya, the source of relocation was as much to be found in reactions against the national actions of 'liberation' and 'freedom' as in relative prices and technical conditions of production.

As far as Kenya is concerned, the history of wattle has been shown elsewhere.[125] Colonial state officials in Kenya abhorred control because it provided a further constraint, over and above that compelled by the local presence of white estate agriculture, upon the expansion of commodity production to meet the revenue needs of both peasant households and the state. Officials, resisting and complaining all the way, were dragged into a position where the state apparatus intervened, without the political basis for mediation, between big capital and small-scale household production. Forestal formed a local pool by forcing an independent, competing manufacturer to buy jointly a lower total volume of bark from indigenous traders who were regulated, to contain bark sales by tens of thousands of producers. Middle-peasant producers resisted controls by producing too much rather than too little for Forestal's carefully planned capacity in Argentina, South Africa and Kenya. The response of the Department of Agriculture, at the behest of Forestal, was to tighten control and thereby provoke increasing political resistance in the prelude to the Mau Mau revolt of the early 1950s.

Forestal, as an expression of commercial capital in Kenya, may have appeared to be little different from other cases, say of Unilever or Cadbury in Nigeria and Ghana.[126] If there is a difference it is that Forestal brought commercial capital to expand industrial capacity and then took a single-minded approach to commanding and planning the world supply of a singular commodity. To enclose banks as City of London 'money capital' and manufacturing firms as 'industrial capital' makes an unwarranted empirical distinction out of theoretically determined categories of capital which refer to relations between different practices of capital rather than to phenomenal differences between firms or nations. Such an empirical approach does not reveal the limits of either financial or industrial organization which are based on capital. All that is said about bad financial practice for the industrial firm or nation can equally be construed to be bad industrial practice.

## Conclusion

Forestal was a relatively efficient international industrial enterprise but the low cost production processes were contained within an inflexible industrial shell. The company was committed to one commodity, tanning agents, and could not adapt to the secular decline in the demand for leather and the derived demand for chemical agents which were substituted for vegetable tanning agents. Substitution between commodities was promoted precisely by the international strategy of the company, attempting to maintain control over supply as the lowest-cost and swing supplier of the cartel.

Forestal could switch the basis of its national allegiance from country to country because of its singular commitment to a commodity. During World War II, the company was attacked by Congress and the Justice Department of the United States for pursuing an anti-American policy as an Argentine company but in the same period it was regarded as a British Company by the Ministry of Supply in London. In South Africa, the company could maintain autonomy from national control and regulation to the extent that it could maintain international control over a single commodity.[127] Likewise, because the company wanted to free itself from *rentiers* in Britian, it expanded through the constraint of internally generated profits; little of a problem when it gained the Argentina windfall in World War I but a big problem in inter-war South Africa and Britain in the 1960s when Forestal belatedly attempted to diversify into real estate and building materials. This preference for internal finance was precisely the subjective constraint which was exercised by the small, British industrial company well into the twentieth century. Forestal revealed the limits of a form of capital but indicated why the same form could expand internationally. There was little that was singularly British about a strategy for capital and little that makes British overseas investment peculiarly pecuniary or financial or commercial. The moral of the story is well known. Action by any single national force, whether official or not, drives international capital to another national arena, and differences in the sources of state action determine conditions whereby capital makes itself international.

## Notes

1. P. Anderson, 'The figures of descent', *New Left Review*, Vol. 161 (1987), p. 44.
2. R. Hilferding, *Finance Capital: a study of the latest phase of capitalist development*, ed. T. Bottomore (London, 1981), pp. 191–2, 293.
3. B. Elbaum and W. Lazonick (eds), *The Decline of the British Economy* (Oxford, 1986), p. 5.
4. Hilferding, *Finance Capital*, p. 334.
5. Ibid., p. 333.
6. R. Gravil, *The Anglo-Argentine Connection, 1900–1939*, (Boulder, Colorado, 1985), p. 93.
7. B. Warren, 'How international is capital?', *New Left Review*, Vol. 68 (1971).
8. *The Times*, 1 April 1985; quoted in L. Davies and R. A. Huttenback 'The export of British finance, 1865–1914', in A. N. Porter and R. F. Holland (eds) *Money, Finance and Empire, 1790–1960* (London, 1985).
9. A. N. Porter, 'Which city, what empire? Shipping, government and the limits of co-operation, 1870–1914', in R. Turrell and J.-J. Van-Helten (eds) *The City and the Empire*, Vol. 1 (Institute of Commonwealth Studies, 1985).
10. G. Ingham, *Capitalism Divided?: The City and Industry in British Social Development* (Basingstoke, 1984), p. 35.
11. P. Thane, 'Financiers and the British state, 1880–1914: the case of Sir Ernest Cassel', in Turrell and Van-Helten (eds), *City and Empire*.
12. Ingham, *Capitalism*, p. 35.
13. W. Kennedy, 'British portfolio behaviour and economic development in the late nineteenth century: hypotheses and speculation', in Turrell and Van-Helten (eds), *City and Empire*.
14. See, for instance, P. Cain, 'J. A. Hobson, financial capitalism and imperialism in late Victorian and Edwardian England', in Porter and Holland (eds), *Money*.
15. *Committee on Finance and Industry* (Macmillan Report, Cmd 3897, 1931), Minutes of Evidence, Vol. 1, 8th day, 1130–1.
16. R. J. Truptil, *British Banks and the London Money Market* (London, 1936), p. 149.
17. S. Chapman, *The Rise of Merchant Banking* (London, 1984), p. 86.
18. Ibid., p. 85.
19. P. L. Cottrell, *Industrial Finance 1830–1914: the finance and organisation of English manufacturing industry*, (London, 1979), p. 270.
20. P. L. Cottrell, *British Overseas Investment in the Nineteenth Century* (London, 1975), pp. 54–5.
21. E. Lorenz and F. Wilkinson, 'The shipbuilding industry 1880–1965', in Elbaum and Lazonick (eds), *Decline*, p. 111.
22. Committee on Finance and Industry, 8th day, 1308.
23. Committee on Finance and Industry, 9th day, 1489–500.
24. Committee on Finance and Industry, 9th day, 1484–5.

25.  See, for instance, R. Bryan, 'Monopoly in Marxist method', *Capital and Class*, Vol. 26 (1985).
26.  A. Hicks, *The Story of Forestal. Forestal Land Company* (London, 1956), pp. 2–3.
27.  I. L. D. Forbes, 'German informal imperialism in South America before 1914', *Economic History Review* Vol. XXXI (1978), p. 393.
28.  Hicks, *Forestal*.
29.  Forestal 9 OGM, *The Times*, 19 June 1915.
30.  Hicks, *Forestal*, pp. 2–3; Forestal 9 OGM, *The Times*, 19 June 1915.
31.  Forestal 9 OGM, *The Times*, 19 June 1915.
32.  Hicks, *Forestal*, pp. 2–3.
33.  A. G. Ford, *The Gold Standard 1880–1914*, (Oxford, 1962), p. 82; D. Rock, *Politics in Argentina 1890–1930* (Cambridge, 1975), p. 1.
34.  Forestal 1 OGM, 27 April 1906.
35.  Ibid.; Hicks, *Forestal*, p. 3.
36.  Ibid.
37.  Forestal 36 OGM, *The Times*, 5 October 1909, 18 June 1912.
38.  Hicks, *Forestal*, p. 10.
39.  C. Kindleberger, *Economic Growth in Britain and France 1851–1950* (Cambridge, Mass., 1964), pp. 126, 148.
40.  Committee on Finance and Industry, 8th day, 1136–39; also see Truptil, *British Banks* pp. 149, 131–2, 253; Chapman, *Rise*, ch. 7.
41.  Gravil, *Anglo-Argentine*, pp. 93–4.
42.  See Rock, *Politics*, p. 136.
43.  Forestal 8 OGM, *The Times*, 30 June 1914.
44.  Forestal 10 OGM, *The Times*, 17 June 1916.
45.  Forestal 8 OGM, *The Times*, 30 June 1914.
46.  Forestal 16 OGM, *The Times*, 23 June 1922.
47.  Forestal 8 & 10, *The Times*, 30 June 1914, 17 June 1916.
48.  Hicks, *Forestal*, p. 7.
49.  Comments on Forestal, *The Times*, 29 October 1912.
50.  Comments on Forestal, *The Times*, 29 October and 14 November 1912.
51.  Forestal 13 OGM, *The Times*, 13 June 1919.
52.  Forestal 16 OGM, *The Times*, 23 June 1922.
53.  Hicks, *Forestal*, p. 12; Forestal 19 OGM, *The Times*, 12 June 1925.
54.  Hicks, *Forestal*, p. 12.
55.  Comment on Forestal, *The Times*, 11 May 1935.
56.  Hicks, *Forestal*, p. 12.
57.  Forestal 41 OGM, *The Times*, 1 September 1947.
58.  Forestal 30 OGM, *The Times*, 9 May 1936.
59.  Forestal 25, 26 and 27 OGM, *The Times*, 22 May 1931, 28 May 1932, 27 May 1933; Hicks, *Forestal*, pp. 46–7.
60.  Comment on Forestal, *The Times*, 11 May 1929.
61.  Hicks, *Forestal*, p. 46.
62.  Rock, *Politics*, pp. 203, 225, 236.

63. Hicks, *Forestal*, p. 48.
64. Forestal 29 OGM, *The Times*, 11 May 1935.
65. Forestal 24 OGM, *The Times*, 27 May 1932.
66. Forestal 27 OGM, *The Times*, 27 May 1933.
67. Forestal 10 OGM, *The Times*, 17 June 1916.
68. Comment on Forestal, *The Times*, 8 June 1915; Forestal 10 OGM, *The Times*, 17 June 1916.
69. R. Gravil, 'The Anglo-Argentine connection and the war of 1914–18', *Journal of Latin American Studies*, 9 January 1977; Rock, *Politics*, p. 133.
70. Forestal 11 & 12 OGM, *The Times*, 16 June 1917 and 22 June 1918.
71. Forestal 10 OGM, *The Times*, 17 June 1916.
72. Ibid.
73. Forestal 9 OGM, *The Times*, 19 June 1915.
74. Gravil, 1977, 'Anglo-Argentine', p. 84.
75. Forestal 9 OGM, *The Times*, 19 June 1915.
76. Ibid.
77. Reports on Forestal and Forestal 11 & 12 OGM, *The Times*, 21 January 1916, 16 June 1917, 22 June and 10 July 1918.
78. Forestal 10 & 14 OGM, *The Times*, 17 June 1916 and 18 June 1920.
79. Forestal 19 OGM, *The Times*, 12 June 1925.
80. Forestal 17 OGM, *The Times*, 15 June 1923.
81. Forestal 8 & 18 OGM, *The Times*, 30 June 1914, and 20 June 1924.
82. Forestal Extraordinary Meeting and 8 OGM, *The Times*, 1 January and 30 June 1914.
83. Hicks, *Forestal*, pp. 43–4.
84. Forestal 13 OGM, *The Times*, 13 June 1919.
85. Rock, *Politics*, p. 123.
86. Ibid., p. 127.
87. Sir C. Mallett (Ambassador) Buenos Aires to FO, 26 January 1920, PRO: FO 371/4408.
88. Presidential agent to 'Dr A. M. Unsain, Acting President, National Works Department', 9 January 1920, enclosure in Mallett to FO, 26 January 1920, op.cit.
89. J. W. Macleay (Minister) Buenos Aires, to FO, 8 May 1920, FO 371/4408.
90. Mallett to FO, 26 January 1920, op.cit.
91. Forestal 16 OGM, *The Times*, 23 June 1922; D. V. Kelly, Buenos Aires, to FO, 11 August 1922; D. V. Kelly, Buenos Aires, to FO, 11 August 1920, FO 371/4408.
92. Kelly to FO, 12 August 1920, FO 371/4408.
93. V. Lindop (Local Managing Director, Forestal) to Macleay, Buenos Aires, in Kelly to FO, 12 August 1920, op.cit.
94. Macleay to FO, 20 October 1920, FO 371/4408.
95. Forestal 16 OGM, *The Times*, 23 June 1922.
96. Forestal 13 OGM, *The Times*, 13 June 1919.
97. Hicks, *Forestal*, p. 6.

98. Forestal 14 OGM, *The Times*, 13 June 1919.
99. Forestal 14 OGM, *The Times*, 18 June, 1920.
100. Reports on Argentina, *The Times*, 18, 23 and 24 December 1919, Forestal 14 OGM, *The Times*, 18 June 1920.
101. Forestal 15 OGM, *The Times*, 1 July 1921.
102. Rock, *Politics*, pp. 209–10.
103. Report on Argentina, *The Times*, 23 December 1919.
104. Rock, *Politics*, p. 149.
105. Forestal 13 OGM, *The Times*, 13 June 1919.
106. Comment on Forestal, *The Times*, 19 May 1920.
107. Forestal 14 OGM, *The Times*, 12 June 1925 and 24 June 1926.
108. Forestal 19 & 20 OGM, *The Times*, 12 June 1925 and 24 June 1926.
109. Forestal 20 OGM, *The Times*, 24 June 1926.
110. Hicks, *Forestal*, p. 20; Forestal 19 & 20 OGM, *The Times*, 12 June 1925 and 24 June 1926.
111. Forestal 20 & 22 OGM, *The Times*, 15 June 1923 and 28 May 1927.
112. Forestal 24 OGM, *The Times*, 27 May 1930.
113. Forestal 17 & 21 OGM, *The Times*, 15 June 1923 and 28 May 1927.
114. Forestal 33 OGM, *The Times*, 12 May 1939.
115. Director, Imperial Institute, London to Colonial Office, 13 August 1937, KNA: ARC (MAWR) 32 AGRI.
116. Forestal 37 OGM, *The Times*, 12 May 1939.
117. Sir E. Matheson-Jackson, Minute, 30 December 1943, PRO: FO 371/33557.
118. Hicks, *Forestal*, p. 25.
119. W. E. D. Knight, report to Limuru Farmers Association, Kenya, 2 August 1917, Ministry of Agriculture Library, Nairobi.
120. Hicks, *Forestal*, p. 27.
121. Ibid., p. 26.
122. South Africa, Department of Agriculture, Committee Appointed on Grading and Marketing of Wattle Bark, Pretoria, Government Printer, 1936.
123. Director of Agriculture to Chief Secretary, 8 May 1936, KNA: ARC (MAWR) 3 AGRI.
124. Deputy Director of Agriculture to Chief Secretary, 14 March 1939, KNA: ARC (MAWR) 3 AGRI.
125. M. Cowen, *Capital and Household Production: the Case of Wattle in Kenya's Central Province, 1903–1964*, (PhD thesis, Cambridge, 1979).
126. See R. J. Shenton, *The Development of Capitalism in Northern Nigeria* (London, 1985); R. J. Southall, *Cadbury on the Gold Coast, 1907–38: the Dilemma of the 'model firm' in a Colonial Economy* (PhD thesis, Birmingham, 1975).
127. See an earlier, fuller version of this paper, with the same title, given as a paper to the Institute of Commonwealth Studies, City and Empire Seminar, December 1985, for more detail on the United States and South Africa.

**Appendix:** *Selected acquisitions made by Forestal, 1907–26*

| | Assets purchased and form of purchase | Company acquired/Vendor |
|---|---|---|
| 1907 | 100,000 acres land (£61,500 from capital expenditure) | Provincial Bank of Santa Fé |
| 1908 | Extract factory (£7,450 from acquisition of 149 £50 shares) | Tannino Elaboracion del Extracto de Quebracho Sociedad Anomina |
| 1908 | Lighterage (£310,000 from share issue and two debenture issues) | La Compania Argentina de Lanchos |
| 1908 | Railways (controlling interest acquired) | Ocampo Railway Company |
| 1909 | 3 Extract factories in Paraguay; 343,000 acres of land (debenture issues with full control achieved in 1931) | Quebraciales Fusionades |
| 1909 | 270,000 acres of land; 25 miles of railway; rolling stock (issue of 500,000 £1 shares whose market value was £640,000) | n.a. |
| 1912 | £2.5 million net worth of land; cattle; 60 miles of railway; extract factory (issue of 1,000,000 shares to exchange 1 ordinary and 1 preference share for every 2 Santa Fé shares) | Santa Fé Land Company |
| 1914 | 2 Extract factories; 480,000 acres land (£1.4 million in cash (£1 million) and assumption of mortgages) | New York Tanning Company (subsidiary of Argentina Quebracho Company) |
| 1919 | Extract factories in Britain and South Africa (£420,000 with full control acquired in 1921) | Calder and Mersey Extract Company |
| 1920 | Extract factories; land (£550,000 in cash (£440,000) and shares) | Natal Tanning Extract Company |
| 1921 | Extract factories in Argentina and Spain (controlling interest acquired in 1923) | Fontana Limited |
| 1921 | 4 Extract factories in Germany (98 per cent of shares purchased) | Renner Company |
| 1924 | Land in Paraguay | n.a. |
| 1925 | Extract factory in Germany | Rheinische Gerbstaffe |
| 1926 | Tanning materials sales agency | Humphreys Percival and Company |

n.a. = Not available.
*Sources:*
Hicks (1954) pp. 6, 19, 20, 27; Forestal 2–21 OGM, *The Times*; *Investors Guardian* (London), 1 February 1926.

# Select bibliography

This bibliography is intended as a short guide to the most relevant literature on the history of British finance during the period 1870–1939. Further reference can be found in the footnotes of the individual essays.

Anderson, P., 'The figures of descent', *New Left Review*, Vol. 161 (1987).

Armstrong, J., 'Hooley and the Bovril Company', *Business History*, Vol. XXVII (1986).

Bamberg, J. H., 'The government, the banks and the Lancashire cotton industries, 1919–1939', (Unpublished PhD thesis, University of Cambridge, 1984).

Best, M. H., and Humphries, J., 'The City and industrial decline', in B. Elbaum and W. Lazonick, *The Decline of the British Economy* (Oxford, 1986).

Born, K. E., *International Banking in the Nineteenth and Twentieth Centuries* (Leamington Spa, 1983).

Cairncross, A. K., *Home and Foreign Investment, 1870–1913* (Cambridge, 1953).

Capie, F., and Webber, A., *A Monetary History of the United Kingdom, 1870–1982* (London, 1983).

Cassis, Y., 'Bankers in English society in the late nineteenth century', *Economic History Review*, 2nd series, Vol. XXXVIII (1985).

———, 'Management and strategy in the English joint-stock banks, 1890–1914', *Business History*, Vol. XXVII (1985).

———, *La City de Londres, 1870–1914* (Paris, 1987).

de Cecco, M., *Money and Empire* (Oxford, 1974).

Chapman, S., *The Rise of Merchant Banking* (London, 1984).

———, 'British-based investment groups before 1914', *Economic History Review*, 2nd series, Vol. XXXVIII (1985).

Checkland, S., 'The mind of the City, 1870–1914', *Oxford Economic Papers*, new series, Vol. 9, (1957).

Collins, M., *Money and Banking in the U.K.: A History*, (London, 1988).

Committee on Finance and Industry (Macmillan Committee): Report and Minutes of Evidence, 1931 (cmd 3897).

Corner, D. L., and Burton, H., *Investment Trusts and Unit Trusts in Britain and America* (London, 1963).

Cottrell, P. L., *British Overseas Investment in the Nineteenth Century* (London, 1975).

217

————, *Industrial Finance 1830–1914* (London, 1980)

Daunton, M., '"Gentlemanly Capitalism" and British Industry 1820–1914', *Past and Present*, Vol. 122 (1989).

Davis, L., 'The capital market and industrial concentration in the U.S. and the U.K.: a comparative study', *Economic History Review*, 2nd series, Vol. XIX (1966).

————, and Huttenback, R. A., *Mammon and the Pursuit of Empire* (Cambridge, 1986).

Diaper, S., 'Merchant banking in the inter-war period: the case of Kleinwort, Sons & Co.', *Business History*, Vol. XXVIII (1986).

Edelstein, M., *Overseas Investment in the Age of High Imperialism: the United Kingdom, 1850–1914* (London, 1982).

Goodhart, C. A. E., *The Business of Banking 1891–1914* (London, 1972).

Hall, A. R., *The London Capital Market and Australia 1870–1914* (Canberra, 1963).

Ingham, G., *Capitalism Divided? The City and Industry in British Social Development* (London, 1984).

James, H., *The German Slump. Politics and Economics 1924–1936* (Oxford, 1986).

Kennedy, W. P., 'Institutional response to economic growth: capital markets in Britain to 1914', in L. Hannah (ed.), *Management Strategy and Business Development* (London, 1976).

————, *Industrial Structure, Capital Markets and the Origins of British Economic Decline* (Cambridge, 1987).

Kynaston, D., 'The London Stock Exchange, 1870–1914: an institutional history', (Unpublished PhD thesis, London University, 1983).

Lavington, F., *The English Capital Market* (London, 1921).

Longstreth, F., 'The City, industry and the state', in C. Crouch (ed.), *State and Economy in Contemporary Capitalism* (London, 1979).

Michie, R. C., 'The social web of investment in the nineteenth century', *Revue Internationale d'Histoire de la Banque*, Vol. XVIII (1979).

————, 'The London Stock Exchange and the British securities market, 1850–1914', *Economic History Review*, 2nd series, Vol. XXXVIII (1985).

————, *The London and New York Stock Exchanges* (London 1987).

Moggridge, D. E., *British Monetary Policy 1924–1931* (Cambridge, 1972).

Morgan, E. V., and Thomas, W. A., *The Stock Exchange. Its History and Functions* (London, 1962).

O'Hagan, H. O., *Leaves from my Life*, 2 vols (London, 1929).

Platt, D. C. M., *Britain's Investment Overseas on the Eve of the First World War* (London, 1986).

Pollard, S., 'Capital exports, 1870–1914: harmful or beneficial?' *Economic History Review*, 2nd series, Vol. XXXVIII (1985).

————, (ed.), *The Gold Standard and Employment Policies between the Wars* (London, 1970).

Porter, A. N., and Holland, R. F., (eds), *Money, Finance and Empire 1790–1960* (London, 1985).

Reader, W. J., *A House in the City* (London, 1979).

Riesser, J., *The German Great Banks and their Concentration* (Washington, 1911).

218

Rubinstein, W. D., 'Wealth, elites and the class structure of modern Britain', *Past and Present*, Vol. 76 (1977).

———, *Men of Property* (London, 1981).

Sayers, R. S., *The Bank of England, 1891–1944*, 3 vols (Cambridge, 1976).

Scammell, W. M., *The London Discount Market* (New York, 1968).

Sheppard, D. K., *The Growth and Role of U.K. Financial Institutions, 1880–1962* (London, 1971).

Strange, S., *Sterling and British Policy* (London, 1971).

Thane, P., 'Financiers and the British State: the case of Sir Ernest Cassel', *Business History*, Vol. XXVIII (1986).

Thomas, W. A., *The Provincial Stock Exchanges* (London, 1973).

———, *The Finance of British Industry, 1918–1976* (London, 1978).

Tolliday, S., *Business, Banking and Politics. The Case of British Steel, 1918–1939* (Cambridge, Mass., 1987).

Turrell, R., and Van Helten, J.-J., 'The Rothschilds, the Exploration Company and mining finance', *Business History*, Vol. XXVIII (1986).

———, (eds), *The City and the Empire* (Institute of Commonwealth Studies, London, Collected Seminar Papers nos 35 and 36, 1985–7).

Wilkins, M., 'The free standing company, 1870–1914: an important type of British foreign direct investment', *Economic History Review*, 2nd series, Vol. XLI (1988).

# Index

accumulation 44
advertising 123
AEG 9, 31–2
agriculture 98, 102, 121–2
Aitken, Max 76, 77
Akerlof, George A. 28, 32
Amalgamated Industrials 80
Anchor Line 88
Andreae, Edward 77–8, 86, 87, 88, 89
Andreae, Herman 77
Argentina 191–9, 203–8
Armstrong, John 6, 42
Ashworth, W. 121
Austin 102
Australia 160–69 *passim*, 173–5

Baldwins (steel manufacturers) 80, 83
Balfour Committee 56
Balogh, T. 56
Bamberg, J. H. 56, 58
Bank of England
  and control of banking system 2, 56
  and industry 5, 52, 73, 76, 83, 87–8, 132
Bank of Scotland 53, 87
Bankers' Industrial Development Company
  (BIDC) 5, 54
Bankers' Investment Trust 145, 150
*Bankers' Magazine* 13, 141
Banks *see* Bank of England; clearing banks;
  merchant banks
Banque de Paris et des Pays-Bas 12
Barclays Bank 53, 54, 55
Baring Brothers 5, 73, 76, 116, 132
Baxter, Edward 141
Beall, Edward 125, 127
Beaumont-Pease, J. W. 55, 106
Beaverbrook, Lord (Max Aitken) 76, 77
Beit, Alfred 173
Belgium 14, 140
Benn, Ian Hamilton 77

Benson, Guy H. 152
Benson, Robert, & Co. 152, 153
Bergens Private Bank 85
Bewick Moreing & Co. 175, 176
Blythswood Shipbuilding Co. 79, 84
Bolton Committee 64
Boots the Chemist 124
Bottomley, Horatio 115, 123–7 *passim*, 131,
  164
Bovril 123, 124, 126
Braithwaite, Cecil 167–8
brewing industry 116
British Assets Trust 140
British Controlled Oilfields 85
British Linen Bank 53
*British Mining* (newspaper) 125
British Shareholders Trust 133
Broad, H. Evans 151
Brown Shipley & Co. 76
Brunner Mond & Co. 9, 32–3
Bumpus, W. H. 165
Burton, H. 147

Cairncross, A. K. 131
Cameron, R. 65
Canada 75–6, 77, 160
Canadian and General Trust Ltd 78, 79
Capel, James, & Co. 152
capital markets 4–5, 9, 11
  and competition 26–34
  and diversification 34–41
  *see also* Stock Exchange
Cassel, Sir Ernest 14, 115, 122, 127, 189
Cassis, Y. 12
Cecil, Lord Eustace 152, 153
CF d Chaco *see* Forestal Land Timber and
  Railway Co.
Chadwick, David 7, 130, 131
Chamberlain, Joseph 13–14, 188
Chapman, Stanley 12, 131

221